Certification Study Companion Series

The Apress Certification Study Companion Series offers guidance and hands-on practice to support technical and business professionals who are studying for an exam in the pursuit of an industry certification. Professionals worldwide seek to achieve certifications in order to advance in a career role, reinforce knowledge in a specific discipline, or to apply for or change jobs. This series focuses on the most widely taken certification exams in a given field. It is designed to be user friendly, tracking to topics as they appear in a given exam and work alongside other certification material as professionals prepare for their exam.

More information about this series at https://link.springer.com/bookseries/17100.

CompTIA Security+ (SY0-701) Certification Companion

Hands-on Preparation and Practice Guide

Kodi A. Cochran
Kyle Reis

Apress®

CompTIA Security+ (SY0-701) Certification Companion: Hands-on Preparation and Practice Guide

Kodi A. Cochran
Management Information Services
West Virginia Office of Shared Administration
Morgantown, WV, USA

Kyle Reis
Marshall Health Network
Huntington, WV, USA

ISBN-13 (pbk): 979-8-8688-1497-6
https://doi.org/10.1007/979-8-8688-1498-3

ISBN-13 (electronic): 979-8-8688-1498-3

Copyright © 2025 by Kodi A. Cochran, Kyle Reis

This work is subject to copyright. All rights are reserved by the Publisher, whether the whole or part of the material is concerned, specifically the rights of translation, reprinting, reuse of illustrations, recitation, broadcasting, reproduction on microfilms or in any other physical way, and transmission or information storage and retrieval, electronic adaptation, computer software, or by similar or dissimilar methodology now known or hereafter developed.

Trademarked names, logos, and images may appear in this book. Rather than use a trademark symbol with every occurrence of a trademarked name, logo, or image we use the names, logos, and images only in an editorial fashion and to the benefit of the trademark owner, with no intention of infringement of the trademark.

The use in this publication of trade names, trademarks, service marks, and similar terms, even if they are not identified as such, is not to be taken as an expression of opinion as to whether or not they are subject to proprietary rights.

While the advice and information in this book are believed to be true and accurate at the date of publication, neither the authors nor the editors nor the publisher can accept any legal responsibility for any errors or omissions that may be made. The publisher makes no warranty, express or implied, with respect to the material contained herein.

Managing Director, Apress Media LLC: Welmoed Spahr
Acquisitions Editor: Susan McDermott
Development Editor: Laura Berendson
Editorial Assistant: Jessica Vakili

Cover designed by eStudioCalamar

Distributed to the book trade worldwide by Springer Science+Business Media New York, 1 New York Plaza, New York, NY 10004. Phone 1-800-SPRINGER, fax (201) 348-4505, e-mail orders-ny@springer-sbm.com, or visit www.springeronline.com. Apress Media, LLC is a Delaware LLC and the sole member (owner) is Springer Science + Business Media Finance Inc (SSBM Finance Inc). SSBM Finance Inc is a **Delaware** corporation.

For information on translations, please e-mail booktranslations@springernature.com; for reprint, paperback, or audio rights, please e-mail bookpermissions@springernature.com.

Apress titles may be purchased in bulk for academic, corporate, or promotional use. eBook versions and licenses are also available for most titles. For more information, reference our Print and eBook Bulk Sales web page at http://www.apress.com/bulk-sales.

Any source code or other supplementary material referenced by the author in this book is available to readers on GitHub. For more detailed information, please visit https://www.apress.com/gp/services/source-code.

If disposing of this product, please recycle the paper

Table of Contents

About the Authors .... **xxiii**

Chapter 1: An Introduction to Cybersecurity and CompTIA **1**
   The Importance of Cybersecurity 1
   Introduction to CompTIA and Security+ Certification 2
   Overview of Cybersecurity and Its Importance 3
   The Role of Cybersecurity Professionals 4
   Impact of Cybersecurity on Organizations and Individuals 4
   Emerging Trends in Cybersecurity 5
   Understanding CompTIA and Its Certifications 6
   Why Choose CompTIA 7
   The Role and Significance of Security+ Certification 7
   Industry Recognition 8
   Career Benefits 8
   Overview of the Exam Structure and Objectives 9
   Retake Policy 10
   Updates and Changes to the Exam 11

Chapter 2: Core Concepts in Cybersecurity **13**
   The CIA Triad: Confidentiality, Integrity, and Availability 14
   Confidentiality 14
   Integrity 15
   Availability 16

TABLE OF CONTENTS

    Interconnectedness of the CIA Triad 17
    Conclusion 17
Real-World Applications of the CIA Triad 17
Healthcare Industry 18
    Confidentiality 18
    Integrity 19
    Availability 20
Financial Services Sector 20
    Confidentiality 21
    Integrity 21
    Availability 22
    Conclusion 23
Security Models and Frameworks 23
    1. Bell-LaPadula Model 23
    2. Biba Integrity Model 24
    3. Clark-Wilson Model 25
    4. Brewer-Nash Model (Chinese Wall) 26
    5. Lattice-Based Model 26
Practical Applications of Security Models 27
    1. Government Agencies 27
    2. Financial Institutions 28
    3. Healthcare Providers 29
    4. Consulting and Legal Firms 29
    5. Military and Defense Contractors 30
    Conclusion 31
Types of Security Controls 31
    Categorizing Security Controls 31

TABLE OF CONTENTS

Importance of Layered Security 41
Change Management in Cybersecurity 44
    The Importance of Change Management in Cybersecurity 44
    Components of an Effective Change Management Process 45
    Best Practices for Change Management in Cybersecurity 46
    Benefits of Change Management in Cybersecurity 47
Risk Management 47
Components of Risk Management 48
    1. Risk Assessment 48
    Outcome 49
    2. Risk Mitigation 49
    Outcome 50
    3. Risk Monitoring 51
    Outcome 52
Threat Identification 52
    1. External Threats 53
    2. Internal Threats 54
    3. Environmental Threats 56
Threat Intelligence 57
    Outcome 58
Defense in Depth 59
    1. Layered Security 59
    2. Redundancy 61
    Implementing Defense in Depth 61
Defining Security Architecture 66
Key Components of Security Architecture 66
    1. Security Policies 66
    2. Security Controls 67

TABLE OF CONTENTS

    3. Security Models 68
    4. Network Architecture 69
    5. System Architecture 70
    6. Security Frameworks 71
    Conclusion 72

Chapter 3: Attacks, Threats, and Vulnerabilities 73
    Insider Threats 75
        Types of Insider Threats 75
        Mitigating Insider Threats 78
        Strategies for Detection 78
        Strategies for Prevention 80
    Cloud-Based Threats 82
        Common Cloud-Based Threats 82
        Cloud Security Best Practices 87
    Phishing, Spear Phishing, and Whaling: Differences and Detection 88
    Key Differences Between Phishing, Spear Phishing, and Whaling 93
    Detecting Phishing, Spear Phishing, and Whaling 94
    Types of Cyberattacks 95
    Malware 95
    Denial of Service (DoS) and Distributed Denial of Service (DDoS) 97
    Man-in-the-Middle (MITM) 98
    Rogue Access Points 99
    Cross-Site Scripting (XSS) 99
    Cross-Site Request Forgery (CSRF/XSRF) 100
    Rootkits 101
    Service Chain Attacks 101
    Social Engineering 102

TABLE OF CONTENTS

Supply Chain Attacks 103
Zero-Day Attacks 104
Types of Threat Intelligence 105
How to Apply Threat Intelligence in a Security Strategy 109
Indicators of Compromise (IOCs) 113
Types of Indicators of Compromise 113
How to Use Indicators of Compromise 116
Understanding Vulnerabilities and Their Impacts 118
Types of Vulnerabilities 118
    Why Addressing Vulnerabilities Matters 122
    Reducing the Attack Surface 123
Assessing the Severity of Vulnerabilities 124
    Mitigating Vulnerabilities 125
    Common Vulnerability Scoring System (CVSS): How Vulnerabilities Are Rated 125
    Components of CVSS 126
    Effective Vulnerability Management Strategies 127
Using CVSS in Vulnerability Management 128
    Prioritization 128
    Risk Assessment 129
    Patch Management 130
    Communication 131
Overview of Security Assessment Tools 132
Vulnerability Scanners 132
    Types of Vulnerability Scanners 132
    Real-Time Detection and Reporting 133
    Limitations and Considerations 133

TABLE OF CONTENTS

Penetration Testing Tools 133
    Common Penetration Testing Tools.. 134
    Assessing Exploitability and Real-World Risks............................. 134
    Customized Testing... 134
    Reporting and Documentation 135
Configuration and Compliance Management Tools......................... 135
    Common Configuration and Compliance Tools 135
    Risk Management and Compliance... 136
    Real-Time Monitoring and Reporting.. 136
Security Information and Event Management (SIEM) Tools 136
    Popular SIEM Solutions 136
    Enhanced Threat Detection 137
    Compliance and Forensics 137
    Reporting and Alerting.. 137
    Additional Security Assessment Frameworks 138
Integrating Security Tools into a Cohesive Assessment Strategy 139
Manual Penetration Testing: Importance and Limitations 139
    Importance of Manual Penetration Testing 140
    Limitations of Manual Penetration Testing 142
The Hybrid Approach: Combining Automated and Manual Testing ... 143
    Advantages of the Hybrid Approach 144

Chapter 4: Network Security 145

Secure Network Architecture and Design 145
Network Segmentation and Segregation 146
Microsegmentation 147
Demilitarized Zones (DMZ)... 147
Network Security Devices.. 148
Firewalls... 148

TABLE OF CONTENTS

Intrusion Detection and Prevention Systems (IDS/IPS) 149
Proxies 150
Secure Protocols and VPNs 151
    Importance of Secure Communication Protocols 152
    Implementation Considerations 152
VPN Types 152
Advanced Network Security Protocols 153
RADIUS and TACACS+ 154
802.1X 154
Network Address Translation (NAT) and Port Address Translation (PAT) 155
    Differences and Use Cases 155
Zero Trust Networks 156
Zero Trust Architecture 156
Securing Wireless Networks: WPA3 and Wireless Security Settings 157
    WPA3 Enhancements 157
    Key Differences from WPA2 158
Transitioning to WPA3 159
    Best Practices for Transitioning 159
    Additional Wireless Security Settings 160
    Conclusion 162
Securing IoT Devices on Wireless Networks 162
Wireless Attacks 164
    1. Evil Twin Attacks 165
    2. Jamming Attacks 165
    3. Deauthentication Attacks 166
Additional Considerations 167
    Network Monitoring and Management 167
    Redundancy and Fault Tolerance 168

TABLE OF CONTENTS

  Emerging Network Threats 169
  Conclusion 169

Chapter 5: Identity and Access Management 171
  Authentication Factors: Single Sign-On, Multi-factor Authentication 172
   Single Sign-On (SSO) 172
   Multi-factor Authentication (MFA) 173
   Biometric Authentication 174
   Smart Cards 175
   Token-Based Authentication 176
   Password Authentication 177
   Certificate-Based Authentication 178
   Introduction to Federated Identity and OAuth 179
  Federated Authentication Expanded 180
   Security Assertion Markup Language (SAML) 180
   OAuth 183
   Federated Identity and Beyond 185
  Access Control Models: DAC, MAC, RBAC, ABAC 186
   Discretionary Access Control (DAC) 186
   Mandatory Access Control (MAC) 188
   Role-Based Access Control (RBAC) 190
   Attribute-Based Access Control (ABAC) 192
  Identity Management and the Cloud 195
   Cloud-Based Identity Management 195
   Single Sign-On (SSO) Across Cloud Services 196
   Federated Identity Management (FIM) 197
  Public Key Infrastructure (PKI) and Certificate Management 199
   SSL/TLS Certificates 199

TABLE OF CONTENTS

    Code Signing Certificates 201

    Email Encryption Certificates 201

  Certificate Revocation 203

    Certificate Revocation List (CRL) 203

    Online Certificate Status Protocol (OCSP) 204

  Common Identity and Access Management Solutions 205

    Identity and Access Management (IAM) Tools 206

Chapter 6: Endpoint and Application Security 211

  Endpoint Security 212

    Overview of Endpoint Security 212

    Best Practices for Endpoint Security 214

  Antivirus (AV) and Antimalware Solutions 215

    Traditional Antivirus 216

    Next-Generation Antivirus (NGAV) 217

    Endpoint Detection and Response (EDR) 219

    Application Hardening 221

    Application Whitelisting 221

  Secure System Design 223

  Configuration Baselines 223

    System Hardening 225

    Securing Applications 227

    OWASP Top Ten 228

  Patch Management 230

    Patch Management Life Cycle 230

  Automated vs. Manual Patching 231

    Automated Patching 231

    Manual Patching 233

TABLE OF CONTENTS

- Best Practices and Considerations 234
- Regularly Review and Update 236
- Maintain Documentation 236
- Educate Staff 237
- Virtualization and Cloud Security 237
  - Securing Virtual Machines (VMs) 238
  - Isolation and Segmentation 238
- Cloud Security Models 239
  - Infrastructure as a Service (IaaS) 240
  - Platform as a Service (PaaS) 241
  - Software as a Service (SaaS) 242
- Container Security 243
  - Container Orchestration Security 244
  - Securing Kubernetes 246
- Image Scanning and Hardening 247
  - Image Scanning 248
  - Image Hardening 248
- Application Security and Testing 250
  - Static Application Security Testing (SAST) 250
  - Dynamic Application Security Testing (DAST) 253
  - Integrating SAST and DAST in the SDLC 256
- Mobile Device Security: Bring Your Own Device (BYOD) Policies 257
  - Security Considerations 257
  - Mobile Device Management (MDM) Solutions 260
  - Mobile Threat Defense (MTD) 262

Chapter 7: Cryptography and Public Key Infrastructure 267

- Fundamentals of Cryptography: Symmetric vs. Asymmetric Encryption 267
- Symmetric Encryption 268

TABLE OF CONTENTS

Asymmetric Encryption 269
Hashing: Ensuring Data Integrity 271
Digital Signatures: Authenticating Data and Ensuring Non-repudiation 272
Public Key Infrastructure (PKI): Enabling Trust in Digital Communication 273
    Cryptographic Protocols and Applications 274
    Cryptography Considerations for the Security+ Exam 274
Blockchain: Beyond Cryptocurrency 275
    Applications Beyond Cryptocurrency 276
Elliptic Curve Cryptography (ECC) 278
    Advantages of ECC 278
    Conclusion 279
Hashing 280
    Key Properties of Hash Functions 280
    Common Hash Functions 281
    Applications of Hashing 282
Digital Signatures 282
    Process of Digital Signature 283
    Applications of Digital Signatures 283
    Summary 284
Certificates 284
    X.509 Certificates 285
    Types of Certificates 285
    SSL/TLS (Secure Sockets Layer/Transport Layer Security) 286
    HTTPS (Hypertext Transfer Protocol Secure) 287
    IPsec (Internet Protocol Security) 288
    Key Takeaways 288
Key Management and the Cryptographic Life Cycle 289
Phases of the Cryptographic Life Cycle 289

TABLE OF CONTENTS

    1. Key Generation 290

    2. Key Distribution 291

    3. Key Rotation 293

    4. Key Destruction 294

    Summary 295

Real-World Applications of Cryptography in Security 295

    Securing Online Transactions 296

    Cryptocurrencies and Blockchain..296

    Digital Signatures and Authentication 296

IoT Security 297

VPNs (Virtual Private Networks)..298

    Types of VPNs 298

    Encryption Protocols..299

Secure Email 299

    Encryption Protocol Examples 299

Disk Encryption 300

    Encryption Tools 300

    Encryption Methods..301

Quantum Cryptography 301

    Post-Quantum Cryptography: Current Threats.......................................302

    Preparing for the Quantum Era..302

    Quantum Key Distribution (QKD)...303

    Future Outlook 305

Chapter 8: Security Operations and Incident Response 307

    Roles and Responsibilities 308

    Incident Responders 309

    Threat Hunters 310

TABLE OF CONTENTS

The Incident Response Process 310
Preparation 310
Detection and Analysis 311
Containment 311
Eradication 312
Recovery 312
Post-incident Activities 313
Threat Hunting 313
Proactive vs. Reactive Security 313
The Role of Threat Hunting in Modern SOCs 315
Forensics and Evidence Handling 315
Chain of Custody 316
Backup Strategies 317
Full Backup 317
Incremental Backup 318
Differential Backup 319
Choosing the Right Backup Strategy 320
Log Analysis 321
Network Traffic Analysis 322
Security Information and Event Management (SIEM) Tools 322
Advanced SIEM Capabilities 323
Security Orchestration and Automated Response (SOAR) Tools 324

Chapter 9: Governance, Risk, and Compliance 327
Risk Assessments 327
Key Components of Risk Assessments 328
    Summary 331
    Risk Mitigation 332

TABLE OF CONTENTS

- Risk Management Frameworks 333
  - NIST Risk Management Framework (RMF) 333
  - ISO/IEC 27001 335
- Compliance Standards: GDPR, HIPAA, PCI-DSS 337
  - General Data Protection Regulation (GDPR) 337
  - Health Insurance Portability and Accountability Act (HIPAA) 338
  - Payment Card Industry Data Security Standard (PCI-DSS) 339
  - The Importance of Compliance 341
- Global vs. Regional Compliance 341
  - Global Compliance 341
  - Regional Compliance 342
  - Overlaps Between Global and Regional Compliance 343
  - Challenges of Global and Regional Compliance 344
  - Navigating Global and Regional Compliance 345
- Security Policies, Procedures, and Best Practices 346
  - Policy Development and Enforcement 346
  - Key Security Policies 348
  - Procedures and Best Practices 350
- Data Loss Prevention Techniques and Tools 351
  - DLP Implementation 352
  - DLP Techniques 353
  - Data Classification 354
  - User Training 355
  - Regular Audits 355
  - Conclusion 355
- Business Impact Analysis and Third-Party Risk Management 356
  - Steps in Conducting a BIA 356
  - Third-Party Risk Management 358

TABLE OF CONTENTS

Key Considerations in Third-Party Risk Management 358
Privacy Impact Analysis (PIA) and Data Protection Impact Assessments (DPIA) 360
    Privacy Impact Analysis (PIA) 361
    Components of a PIA 361
    Data Protection Impact Assessments (DPIA) 363
    Key Elements of a DPIA 363
Legal and Ethical Considerations in Cybersecurity 364
Third-Party Auditing 366

Chapter 10: Final Review and Exam Preparation 367

Domain 1: Threats, Attacks, and Vulnerabilities 367
    Malware Types 368
    Types of Attacks 370
    Threat Actors 372
    Attack Vectors 373
    Summary 374
Domain 2: Technologies and Tools 375
    Network Security Devices 376
    Secure Protocols 378
    Secure Network Design 379
    Summary 380
Domain 3: Architecture and Design 381
    Key Concepts 382
    Summary 385
Domain 4: Identity and Access Management (IAM) 386
    Authentication Mechanisms 387
    Access Control Models 389
    Identity Federation and Single Sign-On (SSO) 390

TABLE OF CONTENTS

Summary 391
Domain 5: Risk Management 392
    Risk Assessment and Analysis 393
    Business Impact Analysis (BIA) 395
    Compliance and Regulatory Standards 396
    Summary 397
Domain 6: Cryptography and PKI 398
    Cryptographic Algorithms 399
    Public Key Infrastructure (PKI) 401
    Encryption Protocols 402
    Summary 404
Domain 7: Security Assessment and Testing 404
    Security Testing 405
    Auditing and Monitoring 407
    Summary 409
Domain 8: Security Operations and Incident Response 409
    Incident Response 410
    Business Continuity and Disaster Recovery 412
    Summary 414
Practice Questions and Exam Strategies 415
    Domain 1: Threats, Attacks, and Vulnerabilities 415
    Domain 2: Architecture and Design 417
    Domain 3: Implementation 418
    Domain 4: Operations and Incident Response 420
    Domain 5: Governance, Risk, and Compliance 422
    Domain 6: Identity and Access Management (IAM) 424
    Domain 7: Cryptography and PKI 425
    Domain 8: Secure Network Design 427

TABLE OF CONTENTS

- Domain 9: Security Operations and Incident Response 432
- Domain 10: Disaster Recovery and Business Continuity 435
- Exam Strategies for Success in the Security+ Exam 438
  - Approach to Multiple-Choice Questions 438
  - Approach to Scenario-Based Questions 439
  - General Tips 439
- Time Management 440
  - Mindfulness and Relaxation Techniques 442
- Resources for Continued Learning in Cybersecurity 444
  - Advanced Certifications 445
  - Websites and Forums 446
  - Online Courses 447
  - Books and Journals 448
- Preparing for the Day of the Exam 449
  - What to Bring 449
  - What to Expect 450
  - Common Pitfalls to Avoid 451
  - Misreading Questions 451
  - Overthinking Answers 452
  - Additional Preparation Tips 452
- Conclusion and Final Thoughts 454
  - Closing Advice: Setting the Stage for Success 454
  - Encouragement: You've Got This 456
  - The Road Ahead: Your Future in Cybersecurity 458

Glossary of Key Terms 461

Index 479

About the Authors

Kodi A. Cochran is highly invested in the field of cybersecurity, something he has followed as a hobbyist for the past decade and expanded to make it his field of study and work. He has a bachelor's and master's in Cybersecurity and Information Assurance, in addition to working as an Information Systems Manager for the Networking and Infrastructure team of the Department of Human and Health Resources under the agency of the Office of Management of Information Services at the state of West Virginia.

He's responsible for networking administration, project management, system support, and site support for the state of West Virginia in all state-owned healthcare facilities, hospitals, and labs. In addition, Kodi holds the following certifications: CompTIA A+, Network+, Security+, Project+, CySA+, and Pentest+. He has completed the CASP+ (now SecurityX) and is currently working toward CISSP.

ABOUT THE AUTHORS

Kyle Reis is a cybersecurity professional and Health Information Management Analyst at Marshall Health Network, where he safeguards the confidentiality, integrity, and availability of critical healthcare data. He holds several industry-recognized certifications, including CompTIA Security+, Cloud+, and the CompTIA Advanced Security Practitioner (CASP+), now known as SecurityX, as well as is ISC2 Certified in Cybersecurity.

Kyle began his journey in cybersecurity as a hobby in 2013, sparked by a deep curiosity about digital systems and a drive to understand and secure them. Originally from Los Angeles, California, he later moved to Florida, where he worked as an electrician before shifting into the IT field. That transition continued in Huntington, West Virginia, where he supported technical operations at AT&T. He later brought his IT skillset into the healthcare industry, applying his experience in support, systems, and security to a more regulated and mission-critical environment.

His cross-industry experience and hands-on background bring a practical, grounded perspective to this book's content.

CHAPTER 1

An Introduction to Cybersecurity and CompTIA

The Importance of Cybersecurity

In today's interconnected world, cybersecurity has become a fundamental aspect of both personal and professional life. The proliferation of digital devices, online services, and cloud computing has created new opportunities but also introduced unprecedented risks. Cybersecurity refers to the practice of protecting systems, networks, and data from digital attacks, unauthorized access, or damage. As technology advances, so do the methods used by malicious actors to exploit vulnerabilities. Cybersecurity professionals are tasked with defending against these threats, ensuring the integrity, confidentiality, and availability of data.

The importance of cybersecurity cannot be overstated. Cyberattacks can result in significant financial losses, reputational damage, and even legal consequences for individuals and organizations. From protecting sensitive personal information to safeguarding critical infrastructure, the role of cybersecurity spans across every industry. The field is dynamic and

CHAPTER 1   AN INTRODUCTION TO CYBERSECURITY AND COMPTIA

constantly evolving, requiring a blend of technical skills, strategic thinking, and up-to-date knowledge of emerging threats. As the digital landscape continues to expand, the demand for skilled cybersecurity professionals is higher than ever.

As time passes and technology progresses, we are more and more entwined with technology. We are getting to an age where even our washers and dryers have wi-fi connectivity and are able to be managed "smartly." These create a tremendous sense of ease to the user, yet also introduce a significant number of vulnerabilities to even our home environments. With that in mind, cybersecurity is more relevant than ever and will only continue to stand at the front of our needs.

Introduction to CompTIA and Security+ Certification

CompTIA (the Computing Technology Industry Association) is a leading nonprofit trade association that offers vendor-neutral certifications for the IT industry. With a focus on developing foundational skills and knowledge, CompTIA certifications are recognized globally and are often the starting point for individuals entering the IT field. Among their various certifications, the CompTIA Security+ certification stands out as a critical credential for those pursuing a career in cybersecurity.

The CompTIA Security+ certification is designed to validate the baseline skills necessary for performing core security functions. It covers a wide range of topics, including threat management, cryptography, identity management, and risk mitigation. Security+ is recognized by employers and government agencies as a trusted benchmark for entry-level cybersecurity skills. Achieving this certification not only demonstrates a solid understanding of security concepts but also opens the door to various career opportunities in cybersecurity.

CHAPTER 1   AN INTRODUCTION TO CYBERSECURITY AND COMPTIA

Security+ is an ideal certification for IT professionals who want to specialize in security or advance their careers in the field. It is also suitable for those looking to transition from other areas of IT into cybersecurity. The certification serves as a foundation upon which more advanced certifications and specializations can be built, making it a critical step in a cybersecurity career path.

With that all in mind, these certifications are to establish a functional baseline level of knowledge and expertise in particular domains. Particularly at this level, it is not intended to prove mastery over a skillset but to establish a working level of knowledge in the field. It is important to both know what a certification can do for you as well as what it cannot. Certifications are wonderful proofs of work ethic, perseverance, and knowledge and I would recommend them to anyone in the field, but they do have their limitations on their purpose.

Overview of Cybersecurity and Its Importance

Cybersecurity refers to the practice of protecting systems, networks, programs, and data from digital attacks. These attacks are usually aimed at accessing, altering, or destroying sensitive information, extorting money from users, or interrupting normal business operations. With the rapid digital transformation across the globe, cybersecurity has become a critical concern for individuals, businesses, and governments alike. It encompasses a wide array of strategies, tools, and practices designed to safeguard the integrity, confidentiality, and availability of information in all its forms.

Cybersecurity is not limited to just defending against hackers; it involves a comprehensive approach to ensuring that systems are resilient to a range of threats. This includes protecting data at rest and in transit, securing communication channels, implementing strong authentication measures, and continuously monitoring for potential vulnerabilities. As the digital landscape evolves, so too does the complexity and sophistication of cyber threats, necessitating a proactive and dynamic approach to security.

The Role of Cybersecurity Professionals

Cybersecurity professionals are the guardians of the digital world, tasked with the critical responsibility of protecting organizations from cyber threats. Their roles can vary significantly, from designing and implementing security measures to responding to incidents and breaches. These professionals are involved in everything from risk management and threat analysis to compliance with regulations and incident response. Their work is essential to ensuring the security of sensitive data, maintaining the integrity of IT systems, and protecting the reputation and operational continuity of organizations.

In a typical day, a cybersecurity professional might be involved in monitoring network traffic for suspicious activity, analyzing malware, patching vulnerabilities, or educating employees about best security practices. The field requires a combination of technical expertise, analytical skills, and a deep understanding of the threat landscape. As the demand for cybersecurity professionals continues to grow, so does the importance of ongoing education and certification, such as CompTIA Security+, to stay ahead in this rapidly evolving field.

Impact of Cybersecurity on Organizations and Individuals

The impact of cybersecurity extends far beyond the IT department. For organizations, a robust cybersecurity posture is essential to avoid financial losses, legal repercussions, and damage to reputation. Cyberattacks can lead to the theft of intellectual property, exposure of confidential data, and disruption of business operations. In some cases, the consequences of a security breach can be catastrophic, leading to long-term damage and even business failure. As such, cybersecurity is not just an IT issue but a critical component of an organization's overall risk management strategy.

For individuals, cybersecurity plays a crucial role in protecting personal information from identity theft, financial fraud, and privacy breaches. With the increasing amount of personal data being shared online, from social media accounts to online banking, the risk of cyber threats has never been higher. Ensuring strong personal cybersecurity practices, such as using complex passwords, enabling two-factor authentication, and being cautious about the information shared online, is vital for safeguarding personal data.

Emerging Trends in Cybersecurity

The field of cybersecurity is constantly evolving, with new trends and challenges emerging as technology advances. One of the most significant trends is the increasing use of artificial intelligence (AI) in security. AI and machine learning are being leveraged to enhance threat detection and response, allowing for faster and more accurate identification of potential threats. However, these technologies are also being exploited by malicious actors to create more sophisticated and harder-to-detect attacks.

Another emerging trend is the growing concern over the security of the Internet of Things (IoT). As more devices become interconnected, the potential attack surface expands, creating new vulnerabilities that can be exploited by hackers. Securing IoT devices presents unique challenges due to their often limited processing power and lack of built-in security features.

Additionally, the rise of cloud computing has brought about new security considerations, such as data sovereignty, shared responsibility models, and the need for robust access controls in multi-tenant environments. As organizations continue to migrate to the cloud, ensuring that these environments are secure from both external and internal threats has become a top priority.

Finally, the increasing regulatory landscape, with laws such as GDPR, HIPAA, and CCPA, has highlighted the importance of compliance in cybersecurity. Organizations must navigate a complex web of regulations to avoid hefty fines and protect the privacy of their customers. This has led to a greater emphasis on data protection and the implementation of comprehensive security policies and practices.

Understanding CompTIA and Its Certifications

The Computing Technology Industry Association, commonly known as CompTIA, is a leading provider of vendor-neutral IT certifications that are widely recognized across the technology industry. Founded in 1982, CompTIA has become a cornerstone in the IT certification space, offering a range of certifications that cover a broad spectrum of technology-related topics. CompTIA's mission is to advance the global IT industry by providing individuals with the skills and knowledge needed to excel in their careers, while also helping organizations identify qualified professionals. From entry-level to advanced certifications, CompTIA plays a crucial role in shaping the careers of IT professionals and ensuring that they are equipped to handle the challenges of the modern digital landscape.

Why Choose CompTIA

CompTIA certifications are known for their comprehensive coverage of essential IT skills and their emphasis on practical, real-world knowledge. One of the key reasons to choose CompTIA is its vendor-neutral approach, which means that the skills you acquire through these certifications are applicable across a wide range of technologies and platforms. This flexibility makes CompTIA certifications a valuable asset for IT professionals who work in diverse environments or wish to keep their career options open. Additionally, CompTIA certifications are regularly updated to reflect the latest trends and technologies, ensuring that certified professionals remain relevant and competitive in a rapidly evolving industry.

Moreover, CompTIA certifications are designed to cater to a variety of career stages, from beginners to experienced professionals. Whether you are just starting out in IT or looking to specialize in a particular area, CompTIA offers a clear certification pathway that can help you achieve your career goals. The accessibility and affordability of CompTIA exams also make them an attractive option for individuals seeking to enhance their skills and advance their careers.

The Role and Significance of Security+ Certification

The CompTIA Security+ certification is one of the most widely recognized and respected credentials in the field of cybersecurity. It serves as a foundational certification that validates essential skills in network security, threat management, cryptography, identity management, and risk mitigation. Security+ is particularly significant because it is often seen as a stepping stone into the cybersecurity field, providing professionals with the knowledge and skills necessary to secure networks, applications, and data against a wide range of threats.

Security+ is also compliant with ISO 17024 standards and is approved by the US Department of Defense to meet directive 8140/8570.01-M requirements, making it a crucial certification for those pursuing cybersecurity roles within government or military organizations. The certification's focus on practical skills and hands-on experience ensures that certified individuals are well-prepared to handle real-world security challenges, making it a valuable asset for employers looking to strengthen their security teams.

Industry Recognition

CompTIA certifications, particularly Security+, are recognized and respected by employers worldwide. The broad acceptance of CompTIA certifications in the industry is a testament to the organization's credibility and the value that these credentials bring to the workforce. Security+ is often listed as a preferred or required qualification in job postings for security roles, reflecting its importance in the hiring process. The certification's alignment with industry standards and best practices ensures that certified professionals are equipped with the skills and knowledge that are in high demand across various sectors, including finance, healthcare, government, and more.

Career Benefits

Obtaining the CompTIA Security+ certification can open the door to a wide range of career opportunities in cybersecurity and IT. The certification not only validates your skills but also demonstrates your commitment to professional growth and development. With Security+, you can pursue roles such as security analyst, network administrator, IT auditor, penetration tester, and more. The certification also provides a solid foundation for further specialization and advanced certifications, such as CompTIA Pentest+, CompTIA Cybersecurity Analyst (CySA+), and CompTIA Advanced Security Practitioner (CASP+).

Security+ is also associated with higher earning potential, as certified professionals often command higher salaries compared to their noncertified peers. Additionally, the certification can enhance your job security by making you a more attractive candidate in a competitive job market. As cybersecurity continues to be a top priority for organizations, the demand for skilled professionals with Security+ certification is expected to remain strong, providing you with a stable and rewarding career path.

Overview of the Exam Structure and Objectives

The CompTIA Security+ exam is designed to assess your knowledge and skills in key areas of cybersecurity. The exam is divided into several domains, each covering a specific aspect of security. The following are the primary domains and their approximate weightings:

1. **Threats, Attacks, and Vulnerabilities (24%)**: This domain covers the types of threats and attacks that can affect an organization's security and how to identify and mitigate them.

2. **Technologies and Tools (22%)**: This domain focuses on the tools and technologies used in cybersecurity, including their deployment and configuration.

3. **Architecture and Design (21%)**: This domain addresses the concepts and best practices related to secure network architecture and system design.

4. **Identity and Access Management (16%)**: This domain covers the methods and technologies used to manage user identities and control access to resources.

5. **Risk Management (14%)**: This domain focuses on the principles of risk management, including risk assessment, mitigation strategies, and compliance.

6. **Cryptography and PKI (12%)**: This domain covers the principles of cryptography and the use of public key infrastructure (PKI) to secure communications.

The Security+ exam consists of a maximum of 90 questions, including multiple-choice and performance-based questions. You have 90 minutes to complete the exam, and a passing score is 750 on a scale of 100-900. The exam is available in multiple languages and can be taken at a Pearson VUE testing center or online through remote proctoring.

Understanding the exam structure and objectives is crucial for effective preparation. Each domain is weighted differently, so it's important to allocate your study time accordingly. A thorough understanding of the exam objectives will help you focus on the most critical areas and increase your chances of success.

Retake Policy

If you do not pass the Security+ exam on your first attempt, CompTIA allows you to retake the exam. There is no waiting period for the first retake, but if you fail a second time, you must wait 14 days before your next attempt. It's important to understand the retake policy so you can plan your certification journey effectively. Keep in mind that each retake requires an additional exam fee, so thorough preparation is essential to avoid unnecessary costs.

Updates and Changes to the Exam

CompTIA regularly updates the Security+ exam to reflect the latest trends, technologies, and best practices in cybersecurity. These updates ensure that the certification remains relevant and valuable in the rapidly changing field of cybersecurity. It's important to stay informed about any changes to the exam content or structure, as this can impact your study plan and preparation strategy. CompTIA typically announces updates well in advance, giving candidates ample time to adjust their preparation efforts.

CHAPTER 2

Core Concepts in Cybersecurity

In cybersecurity, mastering fundamental concepts is crucial for both new and seasoned professionals. This chapter provides an in-depth exploration of the core principles that underpin cybersecurity practices. We begin with the CIA Triad—Confidentiality, Integrity, and Availability—examining its components and practical applications. We will then move into key security models and frameworks that shape the creation of security policies, followed by an analysis of different types of security controls. The chapter will also highlight the importance of risk management and threat identification in securing systems. Finally, we will discuss Defense in Depth and Security Architecture as vital approaches to building robust and resilient security environments.

Learning Objectives

- Grasp the fundamental concepts of the CIA Triad.
- Examine different security models and frameworks.
- Differentiate various types of security controls and their uses.
- Formulate strategies for risk management and identifying threats.
- Apply Defense in Depth principles and design secure architectures.

CHAPTER 2   CORE CONCEPTS IN CYBERSECURITY

The CIA Triad: Confidentiality, Integrity, and Availability

The **CIA Triad** is a fundamental model in cybersecurity, emphasizing three key principles: **Confidentiality**, **Integrity**, and **Availability**. These pillars form the backbone of security practices and are critical for protecting information in any organization. By understanding and implementing these principles, security professionals can create comprehensive strategies to defend against a variety of cyber threats. Let's break down each component and see how it applies in practice.

Confidentiality

Confidentiality ensures that sensitive information is only accessible to those who have been explicitly granted access. This principle protects personal data, trade secrets, and other classified information from unauthorized users.

Key Techniques

- **Encryption**: This method scrambles data into an unreadable format, which can only be decrypted by users with the correct key. For instance, the Advanced Encryption Standard (AES) is widely used to protect both data at rest (e.g., files on a hard drive) and data in transit (e.g., information sent over the internet).

- **Access Controls**: Implementing mechanisms like Role-Based Access Control (RBAC) limits data access based on user roles within an organization. Biometric systems (e.g., facial recognition, fingerprints) further enhance security by ensuring only authorized personnel can access specific information.

- **Data Masking:** This involves hiding specific data elements (e.g., Social Security numbers or credit card details) to prevent exposure. Techniques like tokenization and pseudonymization replace sensitive data with nonsensitive equivalents, reducing the risk of data leaks.

Real-World Application: In the **healthcare sector**, regulations such as the Health Insurance Portability and Accountability Act (HIPAA) mandate strong confidentiality measures to protect patient data. Encryption and strict access controls are implemented to prevent unauthorized access to electronic health records (EHRs).

Integrity

Integrity focuses on maintaining the accuracy and consistency of data throughout its life cycle. It ensures that information has not been altered in unauthorized ways, whether during transmission or storage.

Key Techniques

- **Hashing:** Hash functions (like SHA-256) create a unique value or "hash" for data. Even a minor change in the data results in a completely different hash value, making unauthorized alterations easily detectable.

- **Checksums:** These involve calculating a value from a dataset to verify its integrity during transmission. If the received checksum differs from the original, it indicates that the data has been tampered with or corrupted.

- **Digital Signatures:** These cryptographic signatures authenticate the sender and ensure the data's integrity. For example, digital signatures are used to verify software updates, preventing unauthorized code modifications.

Real-World Application: In the **financial sector**, transaction integrity is paramount. Financial institutions use hashing and digital signatures to secure transactions and audit trails, ensuring that data has not been manipulated, thus preventing fraud.

Availability

Availability ensures that data and systems are accessible when needed. This principle is essential for business operations, as disruptions can lead to significant financial losses and damage to reputation.

Key Techniques

- **Redundancy**: Implementing backup systems (e.g., RAID arrays, data replication across multiple servers) ensures data is available even if a primary system fails.

- **Disaster Recovery**: Planning for unexpected events like natural disasters or cyberattacks involves creating backups, using cloud-based recovery solutions, and developing Business Continuity Plans (BCP) to quickly restore systems and data.

- **Load Balancing**: Distributing workloads across multiple servers prevents any single server from becoming a bottleneck, ensuring consistent system performance and availability even during high-traffic periods.

Real-World Application: In **e-commerce**, downtime can result in lost sales and customer trust. Companies implement load balancing and disaster recovery plans to ensure their websites remain operational, especially during peak shopping times like Black Friday.

Interconnectedness of the CIA Triad

The principles of the CIA Triad are interdependent. A breach in one area often affects the others:

- A loss of **confidentiality** (e.g., a data breach) can compromise **integrity** if unauthorized users alter the data.

- A disruption in **availability** (e.g., due to a ransomware attack) can prevent access to critical systems, impacting both **confidentiality** and **integrity**.

- Ensuring **integrity** involves methods that also protect **confidentiality** by detecting unauthorized changes that might expose sensitive information.

Conclusion

The CIA Triad serves as a foundational framework for developing robust cybersecurity strategies. By implementing measures that uphold confidentiality, integrity, and availability, organizations can better protect their data, maintain trust, and ensure compliance with regulations. This holistic approach helps address the complex and evolving challenges of the cybersecurity landscape, making the CIA Triad a crucial model for both security professionals and organizations alike.

Real-World Applications of the CIA Triad

The CIA Triad—**Confidentiality**, **Integrity**, and **Availability**—is a fundamental framework in information security. It serves as the backbone of data protection strategies across industries. By embedding these principles into their daily operations, organizations can effectively mitigate security risks, protect sensitive data, and maintain trust with customers and stakeholders. Here's how the CIA Triad is applied in the healthcare and financial services sectors, illustrating its critical role in maintaining robust security postures.

Healthcare Industry

In healthcare, safeguarding sensitive patient information and ensuring uninterrupted access to medical services are top priorities. The CIA Triad helps healthcare organizations align with legal standards like HIPAA and maintain reliable, secure operations.

Confidentiality

Application: Protecting patient data such as electronic health records (EHRs), test results, and personal health information (PHI).
   Implementation

- **Encryption**: Healthcare providers encrypt sensitive data, both at rest and in transit, using methods like AES-256 to prevent unauthorized access.

- **Access Controls**: Role-based access control (RBAC) systems ensure that only authorized medical personnel, such as doctors or nurses, can access specific patient records. Multifactor authentication (MFA) adds another layer of security.

- **Regulatory Compliance**: Compliance with HIPAA mandates that healthcare organizations implement security measures like data encryption and secure transmission protocols. This reduces the risk of data breaches and protects patient privacy.

Example

A hospital encrypts EHRs using advanced encryption standards, ensuring that even if a data breach occurs, patient information remains unreadable to unauthorized users. Strict access control policies ensure that only healthcare professionals involved in a patient's care can view their medical records.

Integrity

Application: Ensuring the accuracy and reliability of patient records to make informed medical decisions.

Implementation

- **Audit Trails**: Detailed logging of all access and changes to patient records provides traceability. Any modification made to a medical record is tracked, offering a clear edit history.

- **Data Validation**: Input validation and verification processes are employed to detect and correct potential errors in medical data.

- **Hashing**: Cryptographic hashing ensures data integrity by generating a unique identifier for each record, enabling verification that the data has not been altered.

Example

A healthcare provider uses cryptographic hashes to verify the integrity of EHRs. If a record is tampered with, the hash value will differ from the original, alerting the system to potential data corruption or unauthorized changes.

CHAPTER 2   CORE CONCEPTS IN CYBERSECURITY

Availability

Application: Ensuring uninterrupted access to healthcare systems, especially during emergencies.

Implementation

- **Disaster Recovery Plans:** Hospitals develop comprehensive disaster recovery strategies to maintain access to critical systems and data during outages.

- **Redundancy:** Redundant servers and cloud-based solutions are used to ensure continuous availability of medical records and services.

- **Load Balancing:** Traffic is distributed across multiple servers to prevent overload and ensure system reliability.

Example

A hospital implements a cloud-based EHR system with geographically distributed data centers. In case of a power outage at one center, patient data remains accessible from other locations, ensuring that healthcare providers can continue to offer seamless patient care.

Financial Services Sector

The financial services industry demands rigorous data protection due to the high risk of fraud, cyberattacks, and the potential financial and reputational damage from data breaches. The CIA Triad forms the basis of data protection strategies to safeguard customer information, secure transactions, and ensure reliable service.

Confidentiality

Application: Protecting sensitive financial data, including account numbers, transaction details, and personal information.

   Implementation

- **Encryption**: Financial institutions use strong encryption protocols like AES-256 for data protection. This helps secure information during transactions and while stored in databases.

- **Access Controls**: Implementing strict access controls, such as role-based permissions and multifactor authentication, helps limit access to sensitive data only to authorized employees.

- **Compliance**: Adherence to standards like PCI-DSS requires stringent measures to protect payment card data, including encryption and access control mechanisms.

Example

A bank employs end-to-end encryption for online transactions, ensuring that sensitive customer information, such as credit card details, is secure from unauthorized access during transmission.

Integrity

Application: Ensuring the accuracy and consistency of financial records and transactions.

   Implementation

- **Cryptographic Hashing**: Each financial transaction is hashed to create a unique identifier, making it easier to detect unauthorized modifications.

- **Audit Trails**: Comprehensive logging of all transactions and data changes helps maintain accountability and enables real-time monitoring for potential fraud.

- **Input Validation**: Automated validation checks ensure that only properly formatted and authorized transaction data is processed.

Example

A financial institution uses hashing algorithms to verify the integrity of transaction records. If a transaction's data is altered, the hash value changes, alerting the system to potential fraud or tampering.

Availability

Application: Ensuring customers have uninterrupted access to banking services, such as online transactions, ATMs, and mobile banking.

Implementation

- **High Availability Architecture**: Banks deploy geographically distributed data centers with automatic failover systems to handle outages and maintain service continuity.

- **DDoS Protection**: To guard against distributed denial-of-service (DDoS) attacks that could disrupt services, financial institutions use traffic monitoring tools and mitigation strategies.

- **Redundant Systems**: Backup servers and network redundancy help prevent single points of failure, ensuring the continuous operation of critical banking services.

Example

A bank employs a high-availability architecture with load balancing across multiple data centers. If one data center experiences an outage, traffic is rerouted to another, ensuring that customers can still access their accounts and perform transactions without interruption.

Conclusion

The CIA Triad serves as the foundation for developing comprehensive security strategies across industries. In healthcare, it ensures the protection of sensitive patient information and the continuous delivery of medical services. In financial services, it safeguards data integrity, prevents unauthorized access, and ensures uninterrupted service availability. By implementing the principles of the CIA Triad, organizations can build robust security measures, comply with regulations, and maintain trust with their customers.

Security Models and Frameworks

Security models provide essential theoretical frameworks that guide the development of security policies and systems. They are designed to be customized to the unique needs of each organization, ensuring they address specific security concerns rather than offering a universal solution. Here's an overview of key security models and how they are applied in various industries.

1. Bell-LaPadula Model

The Bell-LaPadula model is one of the most widely recognized security models, focusing primarily on the principle of confidentiality. This model is particularly important in environments where protecting classified information from unauthorized disclosure is critical.

Key Principles

- **No Read Up**: A subject at a lower security level cannot read information at a higher level. This restriction prevents lower-level users from accessing sensitive information that could compromise security.

- **No Write Down**: A subject at a higher security level cannot write data to a lower level. This prevents classified information from being inadvertently disclosed to users who lack the necessary clearance.

Industry Application

The Bell-LaPadula model is predominantly used in military, government, and defense environments where maintaining confidentiality is paramount. For example, it governs the access controls for classified documents, ensuring that sensitive military information is only accessible to personnel with the appropriate security clearance.

2. Biba Integrity Model

While the Bell-LaPadula model emphasizes confidentiality, the Biba Integrity model focuses on ensuring data integrity. This model is crucial in environments where maintaining the accuracy and reliability of information is essential.

Key Principles

- **No Write Up (Simple Integrity Property)**: A subject at a lower integrity level cannot write to a higher integrity level. This ensures that only trustworthy data can influence more critical systems.

- **No Read Down (Star Integrity Property)**: A subject at a higher integrity level cannot read data at a lower integrity level, preventing the use of potentially corrupted data.

Industry Application

The Biba Integrity model is often employed in financial institutions and healthcare organizations where data integrity is critical for accurate transactions and patient care. For example, in finance, it helps prevent unauthorized modifications to transaction data, ensuring that financial records remain reliable and trustworthy.

3. Clark-Wilson Model

The Clark-Wilson model enhances integrity and consistency through the enforcement of well-formed transactions and separation of duties. This model is essential in systems that require strict adherence to data integrity and procedural correctness.

Key Principles

- **Well-Formed Transactions**: Users must perform actions through authorized processes, ensuring that data cannot be altered improperly.

- **Separation of Duties**: This principle requires that critical tasks be divided among multiple individuals to prevent fraud and errors.

Industry Application

The Clark-Wilson model is often applied in commercial systems such as accounting, financial systems, and databases where maintaining the accuracy and consistency of data is crucial. For instance, in an accounting system, it ensures that only authorized transactions are processed, reducing the risk of fraudulent activities.

4. Brewer-Nash Model (Chinese Wall)

The Brewer-Nash model, also known as the Chinese Wall model, is designed to prevent conflicts of interest by dynamically restricting access based on the user's activity. This model is essential in environments where safeguarding sensitive information from competing interests is critical.

Key Principles

- **Dynamic Access Control**: Access to data is restricted based on a user's previous activities. For example, if a user accesses data from one company, they may be restricted from accessing data from a competing firm.

- **Prevention of Insider Threats**: By limiting access to sensitive information based on user interactions, the model mitigates the risk of unethical behavior or insider threats.

Industry Application

This model is commonly applied in consulting, legal, and financial industries, where managing conflicts of interest is vital. For example, in a legal firm, attorneys working on a case involving one client may be restricted from accessing case details for a competing client to maintain confidentiality and prevent biased decision-making.

5. Lattice-Based Model

The Lattice-Based model organizes security levels in a lattice structure, facilitating controlled access and secure information flow. This model is particularly beneficial in environments where information classification varies significantly in sensitivity.

Key Principles

- **Lattice Structure**: Security levels are arranged in a lattice format, with each level defining authorized actions and permissible data flows.

- **Controlled Access**: Users can only access data that matches their clearance level, and the model allows for secure data flow between different levels while preventing unauthorized access.

Industry Application

The Lattice-Based model is ideal for multilevel security environments, such as government and intelligence agencies, where information is classified at various levels of sensitivity (e.g., confidential, secret, top secret). It ensures that users can only access information for which they possess the necessary clearance and controls how data flows between different security levels, thus preserving the integrity and confidentiality of sensitive data.

Practical Applications of Security Models

Understanding and applying security models helps organizations develop customized security strategies to meet their unique needs and regulatory requirements. Different industries adopt specific models to target and protect the core security principles of confidentiality, integrity, and availability. Here's a closer look at how various sectors utilize these models effectively.

1. Government Agencies

Application: Use of the **Bell-LaPadula model** to manage classified data and protect sensitive information.

CHAPTER 2   CORE CONCEPTS IN CYBERSECURITY

Purpose

Government agencies prioritize confidentiality to prevent unauthorized access to classified information. The Bell-LaPadula model, which enforces strict "no read up, no write down" rules, is ideal for this setting. It ensures that individuals with lower security clearances cannot access higher-level classified data, while also preventing those with high clearance from downgrading information inappropriately.

Example

In defense and intelligence agencies, systems handling national security information are often designed around the Bell-LaPadula model. For instance, employees at lower security levels cannot access top-secret files, thus maintaining strict confidentiality. This approach helps prevent unauthorized disclosures of sensitive data related to national defense.

2. Financial Institutions

Application: Use of the **Clark-Wilson model** to ensure transaction integrity and prevent fraud.

Purpose

In the financial sector, maintaining the integrity of transactions and data is crucial to prevent fraud and unauthorized alterations. The Clark-Wilson model requires well-formed transactions and strict separation of duties, making sure that only authorized personnel can modify sensitive financial records. This helps to reduce the risk of insider fraud and operational errors.

Example

Banks implement the Clark-Wilson model in their core banking systems to safeguard the accuracy of customer account information. For example, only authorized bank employees can approve high-value transactions, and any changes to financial data must go through multiple levels of approval, ensuring transaction integrity.

3. Healthcare Providers

Application: Use of the **Biba Integrity model** to maintain data accuracy in patient records.

Purpose

For healthcare organizations, the integrity of patient data is vital to ensure accurate diagnoses and treatment plans. The Biba Integrity model, with its "no write up, no read down" policy, prevents unauthorized users from altering critical medical data, thereby maintaining the accuracy of health records.

Example

Electronic Health Records (EHR) systems in hospitals may implement the Biba Integrity model to safeguard patient data. Nurses or administrative staff with lower access levels can view patient information but cannot modify critical medical records. This helps ensure that only authorized medical personnel, such as doctors, can update sensitive patient data, preserving its integrity.

4. Consulting and Legal Firms

Application: Use of the **Brewer-Nash model (Chinese Wall)** to prevent conflicts of interest.

Purpose

Consulting and legal firms often handle sensitive information from clients who may be competitors. The Brewer-Nash model dynamically restricts access based on the user's previous actions, preventing conflicts of interest by ensuring that employees cannot access information from competing clients.

Example

In a law firm handling multiple clients within the same industry, the Brewer-Nash model might be applied to prevent a lawyer who has accessed Client A's sensitive information from viewing or working on cases for Client B. This model safeguards client confidentiality and maintains ethical boundaries, preventing biased representation.

5. Military and Defense Contractors

Application: Use of the **Lattice-Based Access Control model** to manage multilevel classified information.

Purpose

Military and defense contractors often work with highly sensitive information classified at various levels (e.g., Confidential, Secret, Top Secret). The Lattice-Based model allows for controlled access between different classification levels, providing a granular approach to information flow.

Example

In a defense contractor setting, employees are assigned clearance levels based on their role and the sensitivity of the information they need to access. For instance, an engineer with "Secret" clearance can access certain design documents but cannot view "Top Secret" materials.

The Lattice-Based model ensures that data access is strictly controlled according to clearance levels, maintaining the security of classified information.

Conclusion

Applying security models in practical scenarios helps organizations tailor their security strategies to specific needs, providing targeted solutions for protecting confidentiality, integrity, and availability. By understanding the strengths of each model, organizations in different sectors can implement effective security measures that align with their operational requirements and compliance obligations.

Types of Security Controls

Security controls play a crucial role in protecting information systems and data across organizations. Each control serves its own unique purpose, but the most effective security posture involves employing multiple controls together. These controls, when combined, create layers of defense that strengthen the overall security framework, whether at work or even in your home environment.

Categorizing Security Controls

Security controls can be categorized into three primary types: **Administrative**, **Technical**, and **Physical**. Each category focuses on different aspects of protecting an organization's assets, whether it's through policies, infrastructure, or physical deterrents.

CHAPTER 2   CORE CONCEPTS IN CYBERSECURITY

1. Administrative Controls

Administrative controls form the backbone of an organization's security framework, encompassing the policies, procedures, and guidelines that govern security efforts. These controls not only guide user behavior but also establish a secure operating environment by defining roles, responsibilities, and acceptable practices. Below is a detailed overview of key administrative controls and their applications:

1. **Policies and Procedures**
    - **Function**: Administrative controls set the rules and expectations for how users and employees should interact with the organization's resources. These guidelines are essential for maintaining a secure environment and ensuring compliance with regulatory standards.
    - **Types**
        - **Acceptable Use Policies (AUP)**: These policies establish clear guidelines on how the organization's resources, such as computers, networks, and internet access, should be used. They aim to protect both the organization and its employees from misuse and potential security threats.
        - **Data Classification Policies**: These policies define how sensitive data should be categorized and handled, ensuring that information is appropriately protected based on its level of sensitivity. For instance, data may be classified as public, internal, confidential, or restricted, with corresponding handling procedures for each classification.

- **Incident Response Plans**: These plans outline the steps to take in the event of a security breach or emergency, ensuring that all employees understand their roles and responsibilities during an incident. An effective incident response plan includes procedures for identification, containment, eradication, recovery, and post-incident analysis.

2. **Training and Awareness**

    - **Function**: Given that human error is one of the biggest threats to security, regular training sessions and awareness programs are critical. These initiatives help employees recognize potential threats and understand best practices for data security.

    - **Importance**: A well-informed workforce is better equipped to identify and respond to security threats, such as phishing attempts and social engineering attacks. Continuous education fosters a culture of security within the organization.

    - **Example**: Employees participating in annual cybersecurity awareness training to understand the latest threats, security protocols, and how to report suspicious activity. This training may include practical exercises, simulations, and real-world examples to reinforce learning.

3. **Risk Assessment and Management**
   - **Function**: Conducting risk assessments is vital for identifying vulnerabilities within the organization, assessing the likelihood of potential threats, and prioritizing security efforts based on risk levels.
   - **Process**
     - **Identification of Assets and Threats**: Determine which assets (data, systems, etc.) need protection and identify the potential threats that could impact them.
     - **Vulnerability Assessment**: Evaluate the current security posture and identify weaknesses that could be exploited by threats.
     - **Likelihood and Impact Analysis**: Assess the probability of identified threats occurring and the potential impact on the organization.
     - **Mitigation Strategies**: Develop strategies to address the identified risks, which may include implementing technical controls, revising policies, or enhancing employee training.
   - **Example**: Regular risk assessments conducted by the organization to identify and mitigate cybersecurity risks before they escalate into critical issues. These assessments might involve periodic audits, penetration testing, and reviewing incident reports to continually adapt the security framework to emerging threats.

2. Technical Controls

Technical controls (also known as logical controls) are crucial in protecting systems and data by leveraging technology. These controls are primarily infrastructure-oriented and function within the technical layers of an organization's environment, ensuring that sensitive information remains secure from unauthorized access and cyber threats. Below is an overview of key technical controls and their applications:

1. **Firewalls**
    - **Function**: Firewalls act as barriers between trusted and untrusted networks, filtering traffic based on predefined rules. They serve as a first line of defense against external threats by controlling incoming and outgoing network traffic.
    - **Types**
        - **Network-Level Firewalls**: These are typically deployed at the perimeter of the network and protect the entire network from outside threats.
        - **Application-Level Firewalls**: These focus on filtering traffic specific to applications, providing an additional layer of security for web-based applications.
    - **Example**: A perimeter firewall that blocks traffic from specific IP addresses associated with known malicious actors. This ensures that any attempts to access the network from these harmful sources are denied, effectively protecting the internal environment.

CHAPTER 2   CORE CONCEPTS IN CYBERSECURITY

2. **Encryption**

    - **Function**: Encryption transforms data into a format that is unreadable without the proper authorization, ensuring data confidentiality and integrity. It safeguards sensitive information both in transit and at rest.

    - **Standards**: Common encryption standards include Advanced Encryption Standard (AES), RSA, and others, depending on the required level of security.

    - **Example**: Encrypting emails and files containing sensitive customer information using AES-256. This ensures that only authorized users with the correct decryption keys can access the content, significantly reducing the risk of data breaches.

3. **Access Controls**

    - **Function**: Access controls ensure that only authorized users can access sensitive systems and data. They are critical for enforcing security policies and protecting information from unauthorized access.

    - **Types**
        - **Multi-Factor Authentication (MFA)**: Requires users to verify their identity through multiple means (e.g., a password combined with biometric verification), enhancing security by making it harder for unauthorized individuals to gain access.

- **Role-Based Access Control (RBAC)**: Assigns access permissions based on the user's role within the organization, ensuring that individuals only have access to the information necessary for their job functions.

- **Example**: A banking system that utilizes MFA to verify a user's identity (e.g., requiring a password and a fingerprint scan) while employing RBAC to restrict access to financial records based on job roles (e.g., tellers have different access levels than loan officers). This layered approach helps protect sensitive financial data from unauthorized access.

4. **Intrusion Detection Systems (IDS) and Intrusion Prevention Systems (IPS)**

    - **Function**: IDS and IPS are vital components of an organization's security infrastructure, monitoring network traffic to detect and respond to potential threats.

    - **Types**

        - **Intrusion Detection System (IDS)**: Monitors network traffic and alerts administrators to suspicious activities. It acts as a passive security measure, providing visibility into potential threats.

        - **Intrusion Prevention System (IPS)**: Actively blocks malicious traffic in real time, providing a more proactive approach to security by preventing attacks before they can cause harm.

CHAPTER 2   CORE CONCEPTS IN CYBERSECURITY

- **Example**: An IDS system that alerts administrators to unusual login attempts from foreign IP addresses. In contrast, an IPS might automatically block those IP addresses to prevent unauthorized access, helping maintain the security of the organization's network.

3. Physical Controls

Physical controls are a critical component of an organization's security framework, serving as the first line of defense against unauthorized access to the physical spaces where systems and data are housed. By implementing these controls, organizations can effectively deter potential threats while also establishing active defenses to protect their assets. Below is a detailed overview of key physical controls and their applications:

1. **Locks and Barriers**
    - **Function**: Locks and barriers provide simple yet effective means of securing physical spaces, preventing unauthorized individuals from gaining access to sensitive areas such as data centers, server rooms, and offices.
    - **Types**
        - **Keyed Locks**: Traditional locks that require physical keys for access. While straightforward, they can be vulnerable to picking or unauthorized duplication.
        - **Electronic Keycards**: These access control systems use electronic cards that grant access based on the user's permissions. Keycards can be easily deactivated if lost or stolen, enhancing security.

- **Biometric Scanners**: Advanced systems that require unique biological traits for access, such as fingerprints, facial recognition, or iris scans. Biometric systems provide a high level of security since they are difficult to replicate.

- **Example**: A data center that requires both a keycard and biometric scan for entry ensures that only authorized personnel can access critical infrastructure, significantly reducing the risk of unauthorized entry.

2. **Surveillance Systems**

    - **Function**: Surveillance systems enhance physical security by providing visibility into key areas of the organization. They serve both as deterrents to unauthorized activity and as tools for investigation in the event of security breaches.

    - **Components**

        - **Closed-Circuit Television (CCTV)**: Cameras positioned at strategic locations to monitor entrances, exits, and other critical areas. CCTV systems can deter criminal activity by increasing the perceived risk of detection.

        - **Monitoring Systems**: Some surveillance systems integrate with alarms and motion detectors to provide real-time alerts of suspicious activity.

- **Example**: A CCTV system installed around the perimeter of a building monitors all entrances and exits, recording activity that can be reviewed if a security incident occurs. This capability not only acts as a deterrent but also assists law enforcement in investigations.

3. **Environmental Controls**
   - **Function**: Environmental controls are essential for protecting physical assets from environmental hazards such as fire, flood, or extreme temperature changes. These controls help mitigate risks to equipment and data integrity.
   - **Types**
     - **Fire Suppression Systems**: Automated systems designed to detect and extinguish fires without damaging sensitive electronic equipment. Common systems include sprinklers, foam systems, and gas-based extinguishing systems.
     - **Climate Control**: Systems such as heating, ventilation, and air conditioning (HVAC) are critical for maintaining optimal conditions for hardware operation. Excessive heat can damage equipment, leading to downtime and data loss.
   - **Example**: Installing a fire suppression system in a server room ensures that any detected fire is automatically extinguished without causing harm to the electronics, thus protecting both the physical infrastructure and the data stored within.

CHAPTER 2   CORE CONCEPTS IN CYBERSECURITY

Importance of Layered Security

Layered security, often referred to as defense in depth, is a comprehensive approach to protecting sensitive data and systems by employing multiple layers of security controls from administrative, technical, and physical categories. This multifaceted strategy enhances the overall security posture of an organization, making it significantly more difficult for attackers to succeed. Below are several reasons why layered security is essential for effective protection against a variety of threats:

1. **Redundancy and Reliability**

    - **Function**: Layered security creates redundancy by implementing overlapping controls. If one layer is compromised, additional layers continue to provide protection.

    - **Example**: Consider a scenario where an attacker manages to bypass a firewall (a technical control). The intrusion detection system (another technical control) can still detect unusual activity, while surveillance cameras (a physical control) can monitor unauthorized access attempts. Simultaneously, administrative controls such as incident response plans can be activated to address and mitigate any breach.

2. **Comprehensive Coverage Against Diverse Threats**

    - **Function**: Different types of security threats require different types of responses. Layered security encompasses various controls that address specific vulnerabilities and threats, from malware attacks to physical intrusions.

CHAPTER 2   CORE CONCEPTS IN CYBERSECURITY

- **Example**: Technical controls like antivirus software can help protect against malware, while physical controls like locks and barriers prevent unauthorized physical access. Administrative controls, such as security training for employees, ensure that all personnel are aware of potential social engineering threats, effectively addressing a wide range of attack vectors.

3. **Enhanced Detection and Response Capabilities**

    - **Function**: By employing multiple layers, organizations can improve their ability to detect and respond to security incidents in real time. Each layer contributes to a broader understanding of potential threats and vulnerabilities.

    - **Example**: An organization that employs security information and event management (SIEM) systems alongside intrusion prevention systems (IPS) can not only identify potential threats as they occur but also automate responses to mitigate risks. Additionally, regular audits and incident response training (administrative controls) further enhance the organization's ability to react promptly and effectively.

4. **Mitigation of Human Error**

    - **Function**: Human error is a significant factor in many security breaches. Layered security helps reduce the risks associated with human mistakes by implementing processes and technologies that serve as additional safeguards.

- **Example**: An employee may inadvertently click a phishing link, exposing the organization to malware. However, if the organization has implemented technical controls such as web filtering and email security, along with administrative controls like security awareness training, the impact of that error can be significantly minimized. The training helps employees recognize and avoid such threats, while technical controls can block malicious content from entering the network.

5. **Compliance and Regulatory Requirements**

    - **Function**: Many industries are subject to strict regulatory requirements regarding data security. Layered security helps organizations meet these compliance obligations by ensuring that multiple aspects of security are addressed.

    - **Example**: Financial institutions must adhere to regulations such as the Gramm-Leach-Bliley Act (GLBA) and Payment Card Industry Data Security Standard (PCI DSS). By implementing layered security, these organizations can demonstrate compliance by showing that they have robust administrative policies, technical defenses, and physical security measures in place to protect sensitive customer information.

Relying on a single layer of security is no longer sufficient. Layered security offers a comprehensive approach that combines administrative, technical, and physical controls to create a resilient security posture. This multilayered strategy not only enhances protection against a diverse range of threats but also improves detection and response capabilities, mitigates human error, and ensures compliance with regulatory requirements. Ultimately, investing in layered security is crucial for safeguarding an organization's most valuable assets—its data, systems, and reputation.

Change Management in Cybersecurity

Change management refers to the structured approach of planning, implementing, and monitoring changes within an organization to minimize disruption, ensure proper communication, and maintain operational integrity. In cybersecurity, change management is particularly critical because every change to the IT environment—whether it's implementing new software, updating configurations, or deploying patches—can introduce potential risks if not managed properly. Effective change management ensures that these modifications are carried out securely, efficiently, and with minimal impact on operations.

The Importance of Change Management in Cybersecurity

Cybersecurity thrives on stability and predictability. Introducing changes without proper planning or oversight can inadvertently open vulnerabilities, disrupt services, or lead to misconfigurations that adversaries might exploit. Change management reduces these risks by enforcing structured processes for reviewing and approving changes before implementation. It ensures that stakeholders are aware of the changes, potential risks are mitigated, and security controls are maintained or updated as needed.

For example, patching a critical vulnerability in a system is essential for maintaining security, but untested patches can sometimes disrupt system functionality or create new vulnerabilities. A change management process allows for thorough testing in controlled environments, ensuring that the patch achieves its intended purpose without unintended consequences. This allows for version controls to be set in place for archiving and reimplementation if the need arises.

Components of an Effective Change Management Process

An effective change management process typically includes the following components:

1. **Change Request and Documentation**

   Every proposed change begins with a formal request, which outlines the details of the modification, the rationale behind it, and its potential impact on systems and operations. Proper documentation is essential for creating an audit trail and ensuring accountability.

2. **Risk Assessment and Approval**

   Before implementing changes, a thorough risk assessment is conducted to evaluate the potential security, operational, and business impacts. Based on this analysis, changes are approved or rejected by a change advisory board (CAB), which consists of stakeholders, including cybersecurity personnel.

3. **Testing and Validation**

   Changes are tested in a controlled environment to ensure they function as intended and do not introduce new vulnerabilities. This step is

CHAPTER 2   CORE CONCEPTS IN CYBERSECURITY

particularly important for updates, patches, or system reconfigurations, as it prevents disruptions in live environments.

4. **Implementation and Communication**

   Once approved and tested, the change is implemented according to a predefined schedule to minimize business impact. Clear communication with affected teams and stakeholders ensures everyone is prepared for the change and can provide input if issues arise.

5. **Monitoring and Post-Change Review**

   After implementation, the environment is monitored to ensure the change performs as expected and does not introduce new issues. A post-change review is conducted to evaluate the success of the process, identify lessons learned, and refine future change management practices.

Best Practices for Change Management in Cybersecurity

To ensure a robust change management process, organizations should adopt the following best practices:

- **Automate Whenever Possible**: Automated tools can streamline workflows, reduce human errors, and provide real-time monitoring of changes.
- **Maintain Clear Policies**: Establish policies that define who can request, approve, and implement changes, as well as the steps required for each type of change.

- **Enforce Least Privilege Principles**: Limit access to systems and data only to personnel involved in implementing and testing changes.

- **Implement Continuous Monitoring**: Post-implementation monitoring ensures that changes do not negatively impact security or operations.

- **Ensure Regular Training**: Educate staff on the importance of following change management processes to maintain security and compliance.

Benefits of Change Management in Cybersecurity

A well-implemented change management process helps organizations maintain security and operational efficiency while adapting to evolving threats and business needs. It ensures that modifications are thoughtfully planned, risks are mitigated, and security postures are preserved. By embracing change management as a cornerstone of their cybersecurity strategy, organizations can balance agility with security, reducing the likelihood of costly disruptions or breaches.

Risk Management

Risk management is a comprehensive process that involves identifying, evaluating, and addressing risks to protect an organization's critical assets. This process allows organizations to determine the potential impact of various risks, prioritize them based on their severity, and take appropriate actions. Risk management is not a one-size-fits-all solution—each organization must define its own risk appetite and tolerance, based on its specific needs, regulatory environment, and resources.

CHAPTER 2   CORE CONCEPTS IN CYBERSECURITY

Components of Risk Management

Risk management is an essential practice for any organization aiming to protect its assets, data, and reputation. It involves a structured approach to identifying, evaluating, and mitigating potential threats. Let's dive into the three main components.

1. Risk Assessment

Risk assessment is the cornerstone of risk management. It helps organizations identify, evaluate, and prioritize potential threats based on their likelihood and impact. The goal is to understand the risks an organization faces and develop strategies to manage them effectively. There are two primary methods used for conducting risk assessments:

- **Qualitative Risk Assessment**

    This method involves using subjective judgment to evaluate risks. It is often based on expert opinions, experience, and intuition rather than hard data. Risks are categorized into levels such as high, medium, or low. This approach is beneficial when precise numerical data is unavailable or when time constraints limit detailed analysis. Qualitative assessments allow decision-makers to quickly identify and prioritize the most critical risks, making it a practical choice for initial evaluations or smaller organizations.

- **Quantitative Risk Assessment**

    Unlike the qualitative approach, quantitative risk assessment relies on numerical data and statistical analysis. This method assigns concrete values to both the likelihood and impact of risks, often using historical data, financial figures, or mathematical models. Quantitative assessments provide a detailed analysis, enabling organizations to calculate potential financial losses and compare them against the costs of implementing mitigation strategies. This approach is especially useful for large enterprises where data-driven decision-making is crucial.

Outcome

The results of the risk assessment process include a prioritized list of identified risks and recommended actions for mitigation. By understanding which risks pose the greatest threat, organizations can allocate resources effectively and create tailored strategies to address vulnerabilities.

2. Risk Mitigation

Once risks have been identified and evaluated, the next step is to implement measures to reduce their likelihood and impact. Risk mitigation involves a combination of policies, technical safeguards, and ongoing audits. The objective is to minimize exposure to threats and ensure a consistent security posture.

- **Security Policies**

    Implementing robust organizational policies is fundamental to risk mitigation. Security policies, such as incident response plans, access control policies, and data protection guidelines, help establish clear expectations for behavior and response in the face of potential threats. These policies act as a framework for consistent decision-making and set the tone for a strong security culture.

- **Technical Safeguards**

    Technical controls are critical in defending against cyber threats. Examples include firewalls, which act as barriers against unauthorized access; encryption, which protects sensitive data in transit and at rest; and Intrusion Detection Systems (IDS), which monitor network traffic for signs of malicious activity. Implementing these safeguards helps protect assets and reduce vulnerabilities within the organization's infrastructure.

- **Security Audits**

    Conducting regular security audits and vulnerability assessments is essential for identifying weaknesses in systems, processes, and policies. Audits help ensure compliance with industry standards and regulations, detect emerging threats, and verify that existing controls are functioning as intended. Regular assessments provide an opportunity to address vulnerabilities proactively before they can be exploited by attackers.

Outcome

Effective risk mitigation strategies reduce both the likelihood of a threat occurring and the severity of its impact if it does. By taking a proactive approach, organizations can limit potential damage and enhance their overall resilience against cyber threats.

3. Risk Monitoring

Risk management is an ongoing process that requires continuous evaluation and adaptation. The threat landscape is dynamic, with new vulnerabilities emerging regularly as technologies evolve and threat actors develop new tactics. Continuous risk monitoring is essential to maintaining an effective security posture.

- **Regularly Update Risk Assessments**

    As business processes, technologies, and external factors change, organizations must revisit and update their risk assessments. Regular updates ensure that the risk management strategy reflects current threats and vulnerabilities. For instance, the adoption of new software or changes in business operations may introduce new risks that need to be accounted for in the assessment.

- **Monitor Threat Landscape**

    Staying informed about emerging threats is critical for proactive risk management. Organizations should leverage threat intelligence feeds, security reports, and industry updates to track changes in the threat environment. By understanding the tactics, techniques, and procedures (TTPs) used by threat actors, security teams can adjust their defenses and stay one step ahead of potential attacks.

- **Incident Response and Continuous Improvement**

    An effective incident response plan is a key component of risk monitoring. It outlines the steps to take when a security incident occurs, enabling a swift and coordinated response. After an incident, conducting a thorough analysis helps identify the root cause and provides insights into how existing controls can be improved. This cycle of monitoring, response, and improvement helps organizations adapt to evolving threats and continuously strengthen their defenses.

Outcome

Ongoing risk monitoring ensures that risk management strategies remain effective over time. By continuously evaluating and adapting their approach, organizations can maintain a robust security posture, respond to emerging threats quickly, and minimize the potential impact of security incidents.

In summary, effective risk management is a cyclical process involving risk assessment, mitigation, and monitoring. It requires a proactive mindset, a commitment to continuous improvement, and an understanding that risk is an inherent part of any business. By implementing comprehensive risk management practices, organizations can better protect their assets, minimize potential losses, and build a strong foundation for long-term success in cybersecurity.

Threat Identification

Identifying threats is a foundational element of any risk management strategy. It involves recognizing potential dangers that could exploit vulnerabilities within an organization, thereby preparing for incidents before they occur. By thoroughly understanding the various types of threats, organizations can implement targeted defenses and reduce the impact of potential attacks.

CHAPTER 2   CORE CONCEPTS IN CYBERSECURITY

1. External Threats

External threats originate outside of an organization and are typically driven by malicious actors or external forces. These threats are often targeted, deliberate, and can be highly damaging. Understanding external threats helps organizations build defenses against various attack vectors. Common examples include

- **Hackers**

    Hackers are individuals or groups who seek to exploit vulnerabilities in systems for unauthorized access. Their motives can vary from financial gain, such as stealing credit card information, to political activism, or causing disruption. Hackers can range from opportunistic attackers who exploit known vulnerabilities to advanced persistent threats (APTs), which are highly sophisticated, targeted attacks designed to infiltrate and persist within a system over a long period.

- **Malware**

    Malware, short for "malicious software," is any software designed to disrupt, damage, or gain unauthorized access to a computer system. Common forms of malware include

    - **Viruses**: Programs that attach themselves to legitimate software and spread across systems, corrupting or destroying data.

CHAPTER 2   CORE CONCEPTS IN CYBERSECURITY

- **Ransomware**: A type of malware that encrypts files and demands payment from the victim to restore access.

- **Trojans**: Malicious programs disguised as legitimate software, which, once executed, can take control of the system or steal sensitive data.

- **Phishing Attacks**

  Phishing is a form of social engineering where attackers deceive users into divulging sensitive information, such as usernames, passwords, or financial details. Phishing attacks often involve fraudulent emails that appear to come from trusted sources, tricking users into clicking malicious links or opening infected attachments. Spear phishing, a more targeted form of phishing, focuses on specific individuals or organizations, making it harder to detect.

Mitigation Strategies

To protect against external threats, organizations should implement robust firewalls, intrusion detection systems (IDS), regular software updates, and comprehensive employee training programs to recognize and respond to phishing attempts.

2. Internal Threats

Internal threats arise from individuals within the organization, such as employees, contractors, or business partners. These threats can be intentional (malicious insiders) or unintentional (accidental actions).

Despite having fewer incidents compared to external threats, internal threats can be more damaging due to insiders' familiarity with the organization's systems and processes.

- **Insider Threats**

    Insider threats involve employees or contractors who intentionally misuse their access to the organization's resources for malicious purposes, such as data theft or sabotage. This can include disgruntled employees seeking revenge or financially motivated individuals selling confidential data to competitors or cybercriminals.

- **Human Error**

    Human error is one of the most common causes of internal security breaches. Unintentional mistakes, such as misconfiguring security settings, accidentally deleting files, or sending sensitive information to the wrong recipient, can lead to significant data exposure. Despite the lack of malicious intent, the consequences of human errors can be as severe as those of intentional attacks.

- **Privilege Abuse**

    Privilege abuse occurs when individuals with high-level access rights exceed their authorized activities. For example, an employee with access to sensitive financial records may use their privileges to view or alter information for personal gain. Monitoring and controlling access rights through the principle of least privilege (POLP) can help mitigate this risk.

Mitigation Strategies

Effective measures against internal threats include strict access controls, regular employee training on cybersecurity best practices, monitoring user activity, and implementing strong policies to manage and revoke access rights.

3. Environmental Threats

Environmental threats are external, nonhuman factors that can disrupt operations or cause physical damage to infrastructure. These threats are often unpredictable and can have a wide-ranging impact on an organization's ability to maintain service continuity.

- **Natural Disasters**

    Natural disasters such as earthquakes, floods, hurricanes, and wildfires can severely damage physical infrastructure, including data centers and office buildings. The consequences may include data loss, service outages, and costly recovery efforts. Organizations located in areas prone to natural disasters must plan for these risks and have disaster recovery and business continuity plans in place.

- **Power Outages**

    Power outages, whether due to natural disasters, grid failures, or infrastructure issues, can significantly impact system availability. Prolonged power disruptions may lead to data corruption, loss of productivity, and potential damage to hardware components.

Mitigation Strategies

To reduce the impact of environmental threats, organizations should invest in disaster recovery solutions, such as offsite backups, uninterruptible power supplies (UPS), and failover systems. Additionally, business continuity plans should outline steps to maintain operations during and after a disaster.

Threat Intelligence

To effectively counter the various threats faced by organizations, it is essential to engage in continuous threat intelligence gathering and analysis. Threat intelligence helps organizations anticipate potential attacks, stay informed about emerging risks, and implement proactive defenses.

- **Threat Intelligence Feeds**

   These are real-time data streams that provide information on the latest cyber threats, including new vulnerabilities, malware campaigns, and attack vectors. By subscribing to threat intelligence feeds, organizations can stay ahead of emerging risks and respond quickly to evolving threats. Examples of popular threat intelligence sources include the Cyber Threat Alliance (CTA), AlienVault Open Threat Exchange (OTX), and MITRE ATT&CK.

- **Information Sharing Communities**

   Collaborating with industry-specific or government-led information sharing communities can enhance an organization's understanding of the threat landscape. Communities such as the Information Sharing and

Analysis Centers (ISACs) and the Cybersecurity and Infrastructure Security Agency (CISA) provide valuable insights and alerts about ongoing threats, allowing members to learn from each other's experiences and adopt best practices.

- **Threat Modeling**

  Threat modeling involves simulating potential attack scenarios to identify vulnerabilities and assess the impact of potential threats. By analyzing different attack vectors, organizations can better understand their weaknesses and develop targeted mitigation strategies. Common threat modeling frameworks include STRIDE (Spoofing, Tampering, Repudiation, Information Disclosure, Denial of Service, Elevation of Privilege) and DREAD (Damage Potential, Reproducibility, Exploitability, Affected Users, Discoverability).

Outcome

By integrating threat intelligence into their risk management practices, organizations can enhance their ability to predict, detect, and respond to potential attacks. This proactive approach helps minimize the risk of incidents and ensures a stronger defense against both known and emerging threats.

In conclusion, threat identification is a dynamic process that requires continuous attention and adaptation. By recognizing and understanding the different types of threats—external, internal, and environmental—organizations can tailor their security strategies to effectively address their unique risk landscape. Incorporating threat intelligence further strengthens this process, providing valuable insights that help organizations stay one step ahead of potential attackers.

Defense in Depth

Defense in Depth (DiD) is a comprehensive security strategy that involves implementing multiple layers of security controls to protect systems, networks, and data from a wide range of threats. The core principle behind DiD is that no single security measure can defend against every possible attack. By layering various defenses, organizations can create a robust security posture that provides multiple opportunities to detect, delay, and respond to attacks. This approach not only complicates an attacker's efforts but also increases the likelihood of identifying and mitigating threats before they cause significant harm.

1. Layered Security

The essence of Defense in Depth is its use of layered security. It combines a variety of controls—administrative, technical, and physical—to address different aspects of security. If one layer is compromised, others remain active to protect the system. Each type of control plays a unique role:

- **Administrative Controls**

    Administrative controls include policies, procedures, and training programs that guide secure behavior and establish security requirements across the organization. Examples include security awareness training, incident response plans, and access management policies. By setting clear guidelines, administrative controls help create a security-conscious culture among employees, reducing the risk of accidental or intentional security breaches.

- **Technical Controls**

    Technical controls, also known as logical controls, involve hardware and software solutions designed to prevent, detect, or respond to security threats. Examples include firewalls, encryption, intrusion detection systems (IDS), and multi-factor authentication (MFA). These controls are often the first line of defense against cyberattacks, preventing unauthorized access and protecting sensitive data from being compromised.

- **Physical Controls**

    Physical controls focus on securing the physical environment where systems and data reside. This includes measures such as surveillance cameras, security guards, access card systems, and biometric scanners. By limiting physical access to sensitive areas, these controls help prevent unauthorized individuals from tampering with hardware or stealing data directly from the source.

Example in Action

Consider a data center that uses biometric scanners (physical control) to restrict access, firewalls (technical control) to filter incoming and outgoing traffic, and security policies (administrative control) that require regular software updates. If an attacker manages to bypass the firewall, the physical security and administrative policies still serve as barriers, creating multiple points of failure for the attacker.

2. Redundancy

Redundancy is a critical component of Defense in Depth, designed to maintain system availability and minimize the impact of attacks. By duplicating critical components and systems, redundancy ensures that operations can continue even if one part fails or is compromised.

- **Backup Systems**

    Backup systems involve creating copies of critical data and storing them in separate, secure locations. These backups can be used to restore systems quickly after an attack, such as a ransomware infection, preventing significant data loss and minimizing downtime.

- **Failover Mechanisms**

    Failover mechanisms automatically switch to backup systems or alternative resources if the primary systems fail. For example, in a network environment, if the primary server goes down, a failover server takes over, maintaining service continuity without noticeable disruption to users.

Example in Action

An organization may implement a dual-datacenter setup with real-time data replication. If one datacenter experiences a catastrophic failure, the other can seamlessly take over, ensuring business continuity and reducing the risk of data loss.

Implementing Defense in Depth

Effective implementation of Defense in Depth requires a holistic approach, covering multiple areas of security. Here's how it can be applied across different layers.

CHAPTER 2   CORE CONCEPTS IN CYBERSECURITY

1. Perimeter Security

Perimeter security acts as the first line of defense, protecting the organization's external boundary from unauthorized access and malicious traffic.

- **Firewalls**

    Firewalls serve as gatekeepers, filtering traffic between internal and external networks based on predefined security rules. They block potentially harmful traffic, preventing unauthorized access and attacks like Distributed Denial of Service (DDoS).

- **Intrusion Detection and Prevention Systems (IDS/IPS)**

    IDS and IPS are designed to detect and respond to suspicious activities at the network perimeter. IDS monitors network traffic for signs of attacks and alerts security personnel, while IPS takes proactive measures to block identified threats.

- **Network Segmentation**

    Network segmentation involves dividing the network into smaller, isolated segments, reducing the impact of a breach. By segmenting the network, even if an attacker gains access to one segment, they are prevented from easily moving laterally to other parts of the network.

Example in Action

A company might use a combination of firewalls, an IDS/IPS, and VLANs (Virtual Local Area Networks) to separate sensitive financial data from other parts of the network, providing additional protection and reducing the risk of a full network compromise.

2. Endpoint Security

Endpoint security focuses on protecting individual devices, such as computers, smartphones, and tablets, which are often the first points of entry for attackers.

- **Antivirus Software**

    Antivirus programs scan devices for known malware signatures and suspicious behaviors, helping to detect and remove malicious software before it can cause damage.

- **Endpoint Detection and Response (EDR)**

    EDR solutions offer advanced monitoring and analysis of endpoint activities, allowing for real-time detection and response to malicious behavior. They provide detailed insights into potential threats and can automatically quarantine affected devices.

- **Patch Management**

    Regularly updating software to patch known vulnerabilities is crucial for endpoint security. Unpatched software is a common target for attackers seeking to exploit weaknesses, making timely updates a key defense strategy.

Example in Action

An organization that enforces strict patch management policies and deploys EDR solutions across all devices can quickly detect and respond to emerging threats, minimizing the potential damage of an attack.

3. Application Security

Application security aims to protect software applications from threats throughout their life cycle, from development to deployment and beyond.

- **Secure Development Lifecycle (SDLC)**

    The SDLC integrates security practices at every stage of software development, from initial design to testing and deployment. This proactive approach helps identify and address security flaws early, reducing the risk of vulnerabilities in the final product.

- **Regular Vulnerability Assessments**

    Conducting regular vulnerability assessments helps identify and fix weaknesses in applications before attackers can exploit them. These assessments may involve code reviews, penetration testing, and automated scanning tools.

Example in Action

A company might implement a continuous integration/continuous deployment (CI/CD) pipeline that includes automated security testing, ensuring that any newly introduced code is thoroughly checked for vulnerabilities before being released.

4. Data Security

Data security focuses on protecting the confidentiality, integrity, and availability of sensitive information, both at rest and in transit.

- **Encryption**

    Encryption transforms data into an unreadable format, protecting it from unauthorized access. Encrypting sensitive data both at rest (e.g., stored on hard drives) and in transit (e.g., sent over the internet) ensures that even if data is intercepted, it cannot be easily read or used by attackers.

- **Access Controls**

    Implementing strict access controls ensures that only authorized individuals can access sensitive data. Role-based access control (RBAC) and multi-factor authentication (MFA) are common methods for limiting data access based on user roles and identity verification.

- **Auditing**

    Regular audits help verify compliance with security policies and identify any irregularities or unauthorized access. By monitoring and reviewing access logs, organizations can detect potential security incidents and take corrective actions.

Example in Action

A financial institution might use encryption to secure customer data, enforce role-based access controls to restrict access, and conduct regular audits to ensure compliance with industry regulations like PCI-DSS.

By implementing Defense in Depth, organizations can create a resilient security posture that is difficult for attackers to penetrate. Each layer serves as an additional hurdle, reducing the likelihood of a successful attack and providing multiple opportunities for detection and response. The ultimate goal of Defense in Depth is not only to protect assets but also to provide the organization with the time and ability to react effectively to any potential breach, ensuring continued security and operational integrity.

Defining Security Architecture

Security architecture serves as the foundation for designing and implementing an organization's security measures. It is essentially the blueprint that outlines how an organization will safeguard its information systems and data against a wide array of threats. A well-defined security architecture integrates security across every layer of an organization's IT infrastructure—from network design to application development. This holistic approach ensures that all aspects of the organization's technology environment work together to maintain security and resilience.

Key Components of Security Architecture
1. Security Policies

Security policies are formal documents that define an organization's security goals, the strategies to achieve them, and the rules that must be followed to protect information assets. They serve as the backbone of the security architecture, providing direction for the implementation, maintenance, and enforcement of security measures.

- **Purpose**: To set the standards and expectations for security behavior within the organization.

- **Examples**: Acceptable use policy, data classification policy, incident response policy.

Example in Action

A financial institution may have a data protection policy that mandates encryption for all customer data, both at rest and in transit. This policy guides the implementation of encryption technologies throughout the organization.

2. Security Controls

Security controls are mechanisms or safeguards implemented to enforce security policies and protect information assets. They are categorized into three main types:

- **Technical Controls**

    These are technology-based solutions designed to prevent unauthorized access and detect malicious activities. Examples include firewalls, intrusion detection systems (IDS), encryption tools, and multi-factor authentication (MFA).

- **Procedural Controls**

    Procedural or administrative controls involve processes and procedures to manage and mitigate risks. Examples include incident response plans, change management processes, and user training programs.

- **Physical Controls**

  Physical controls aim to prevent unauthorized access to facilities and equipment. Examples include security cameras, locks, biometric access systems, and secure facility design.

Example in Action

An organization might implement a multilayered control strategy, using firewalls (technical), conducting employee security training (procedural), and securing data centers with access badges and biometric scanners (physical).

3. Security Models

Security models are theoretical frameworks that provide structured guidance on implementing security measures effectively. They define formal policies and access control mechanisms to ensure the confidentiality, integrity, and availability of information.

- **Bell-LaPadula Model**

  This model focuses on maintaining data confidentiality. It enforces strict access controls, preventing lower-security-level users from accessing higher-level data (no read up) and restricting higher-level users from sharing sensitive data with lower levels (no write down).

- **Clark-Wilson Model**

  This model emphasizes data integrity, ensuring that information is modified only in legitimate and authorized ways. It enforces well-formed transactions and separation of duties, making it suitable for environments where data accuracy is crucial, such as financial systems.

CHAPTER 2   CORE CONCEPTS IN CYBERSECURITY

Example in Action

A government agency handling classified information might use the Bell-LaPadula model to ensure that employees can only access documents aligned with their security clearance level.

4. Network Architecture

A secure network architecture involves designing the network layout in a way that protects data and prevents unauthorized access. This includes segmentation, secure protocols, and effective firewall configurations.

- **Segmentation**

    Network segmentation involves dividing the network into smaller, isolated segments or zones, such as separating public-facing web servers from internal systems. This limits the potential impact of a breach, as attackers cannot easily move laterally across the network.

- **Secure Protocols**

    Using encrypted communication protocols such as HTTPS, Secure Shell (SSH), and Virtual Private Networks (VPNs) helps protect data in transit from interception and tampering.

- **Firewall Configurations**

    Firewalls are configured to filter incoming and outgoing traffic based on security rules, blocking malicious traffic and monitoring for suspicious activities. Properly configured firewalls serve as a critical barrier against unauthorized access.

CHAPTER 2   CORE CONCEPTS IN CYBERSECURITY

Example in Action

A company might use a combination of internal and external firewalls to protect its sensitive customer databases, employing VPNs for secure remote access and segmenting the network to isolate critical systems.

5. System Architecture

System architecture involves building security into individual systems from the design phase onward. It focuses on securing the core components of systems, such as access controls, encryption, and interfaces.

- **Access Controls**

    Access controls ensure that only authorized users can access specific systems and data. This involves implementing strong authentication mechanisms (like multi-factor authentication) and authorization policies (like role-based access control).

- **Encryption**

    Encryption is used to protect sensitive data, converting it into an unreadable format that can only be decoded by authorized users with the correct decryption key. This applies to both data at rest (stored on disks) and data in transit (moving across networks).

- **Secure Interfaces**

    Designing secure Application Programming Interfaces (APIs) and system interfaces is crucial to prevent unauthorized access and data breaches. Secure coding practices, input validation, and strong authentication mechanisms help protect these interfaces.

Example in Action

An online payment platform may implement robust access controls and encrypt sensitive financial data using industry-standard algorithms like AES-256. The APIs used for transaction processing would also be secured with strict input validation and OAuth2-based authentication.

6. Security Frameworks

Security frameworks provide a structured approach for implementing and managing an organization's security practices. They offer guidelines, best practices, and standards to help organizations build a comprehensive security posture. Commonly adopted frameworks include

- **NIST Cybersecurity Framework**

    Developed by the National Institute of Standards and Technology (NIST), this framework provides a set of best practices to help organizations identify, protect, detect, respond to, and recover from cybersecurity incidents. It is widely used for building effective risk management strategies.

- **ISO/IEC 27001**

    ISO/IEC 27001 is an international standard for Information Security Management Systems (ISMS). It provides a systematic approach to managing sensitive company information, ensuring its confidentiality, integrity, and availability through a rigorous set of security controls.

CHAPTER 2   CORE CONCEPTS IN CYBERSECURITY

Example in Action

A multinational corporation may adopt the NIST Cybersecurity Framework to establish a baseline of security practices and comply with industry regulations. By following the framework's guidelines, the company can systematically identify risks and implement necessary controls to protect its digital assets.

Conclusion

Security architecture is an essential part of an organization's cybersecurity strategy. By defining a clear blueprint that encompasses policies, controls, models, and frameworks, it provides a comprehensive and structured approach to protecting information systems. A well-designed security architecture not only safeguards sensitive data but also enhances the organization's overall resilience against emerging threats. In an ever-evolving threat landscape, integrating security at every layer of the IT infrastructure is key to maintaining a strong defense and ensuring business continuity.

CHAPTER 3

Attacks, Threats, and Vulnerabilities

Chapter 3 looks into the diverse array of attacks, threats, and vulnerabilities that modern operational environments face. In today's increasingly interconnected world, understanding these risks is paramount for cybersecurity professionals. This chapter will equip you with the knowledge required to recognize, mitigate, and defend against various forms of cyber threats, from traditional attacks like phishing and malware to more advanced techniques like zero-day exploits and insider threats. A firm grasp of these attack vectors is not only essential for maintaining security but also critical for minimizing potential damage in the event of a breach.

By aligning with the CompTIA Security+ standards, this chapter serves as a comprehensive guide to mastering the fundamentals of attack types and their associated defenses. Whether dealing with network-based threats, social engineering tactics, or emerging vulnerabilities, the content here will provide the insights needed to develop effective countermeasures. You will learn how these attacks are carried out, the motives behind them, and the security measures required to protect an organization's assets.

CHAPTER 3   ATTACKS, THREATS, AND VULNERABILITIES

Ultimately, Chapter 3 aims to bolster your understanding of these core concepts, preparing you for both real-world security challenges and your journey toward Security+ certification success. By building this foundation, you'll be better positioned to respond to evolving threats, ensuring robust defense mechanisms in any cybersecurity role.

Learning Objectives

- **Understand Common Attack Types**: Recognize and differentiate between traditional and modern cyberattacks, such as phishing, malware, and ransomware.

- **Identify Emerging Threats**: Gain insights into advanced techniques like zero-day exploits, insider threats, and advanced persistent threats (APTs).

- **Analyze Attack Vectors**: Explore how network-based, social engineering, and application-layer threats are carried out and their impact on organizational security.

- **Evaluate Threat Motives**: Understand the motives behind cyberattacks, including financial gain, political objectives, or personal agendas.

- **Mitigate Risks**: Learn the strategies and tools required to defend against identified vulnerabilities and minimize the risk of exploitation.

- **Apply Security Measures**: Develop effective countermeasures to protect organizational assets against a range of threats.

- **Prepare for Real-World Scenarios**: Build the skills necessary to recognize, respond to, and recover from security breaches effectively.

- **Align with Security+ Standards**: Master the foundational knowledge required to meet CompTIA Security+ certification objectives related to threats and vulnerabilities.

This chapter equips learners with the critical understanding needed to tackle today's cybersecurity challenges effectively.

Insider Threats

Insider threats are security risks that come from within an organization, perpetrated by individuals who have legitimate access to the organization's systems, data, or facilities. Unlike external threats, insider threats can be more difficult to detect, as they often bypass traditional security defenses by using authorized credentials. Understanding and addressing insider threats is critical for protecting sensitive data and maintaining operational security.

Addressing insider threats requires a multifaceted approach that includes both technical and procedural controls. Key measures include implementing strong access controls, monitoring user activity for unusual behavior, conducting regular security training, and fostering a culture of security awareness across the organization. Proactive detection and response strategies can help mitigate the risks posed by insider threats and reduce the potential damage they can cause.

Types of Insider Threats

1. **Malicious Insiders**

    Definition: These are individuals who intentionally misuse their access to an organization's data, systems, or resources to inflict damage, steal information, or disrupt operations. Their motives can range from personal grievances to financial gain or even collaboration with external attackers.

Examples

- A disgruntled employee stealing confidential intellectual property, such as trade secrets, patents, or product designs and selling it to a competitor.
- An IT administrator purposefully sabotaging critical systems, such as deleting or corrupting essential files, after being passed over for a promotion.
- An employee with authorized access who shares sensitive information, such as customer data or corporate strategies, with third-party entities or malicious actors.

2. **Negligent Insiders**

Definition: Unlike malicious insiders, negligent insiders do not intend to harm the organization, but their careless or uninformed actions can lead to security breaches. These employees may inadvertently expose sensitive data or compromise security due to a lack of awareness, insufficient training, or failure to follow security protocols.

Examples

- An employee sending an email containing sensitive customer information to the wrong recipient due to an accidental misclick.

CHAPTER 3   ATTACKS, THREATS, AND VULNERABILITIES

- A user failing to secure their work device by leaving it unlocked or using weak passwords, making it easy for an unauthorized person to access sensitive data.

- An employee falling for a phishing attack and unknowingly providing login credentials or downloading malware onto the company's network, potentially allowing attackers to gain unauthorized access.

3. **Compromised Insiders**

   Definition: Compromised insiders are individuals whose accounts or credentials have been taken over by external attackers. These employees may be unaware that their accounts are being used maliciously. Attackers typically use tactics such as phishing, social engineering, or brute force attacks to gain access to the employee's credentials. Once in control of the account, they can access sensitive data or systems, often undetected.

   Examples

   - A cybercriminal uses stolen credentials from an employee to log into a company's network and escalate privileges, giving them access to restricted areas of the system.

   - An attacker compromises the email account of a senior executive, sending fraudulent instructions to the finance department, leading to unauthorized wire transfers.

- A hacker uses compromised credentials to create backdoor access to a system, allowing ongoing exploitation without alerting internal monitoring systems.

Mitigating Insider Threats

Effectively mitigating insider threats requires a comprehensive approach that encompasses both detection and prevention strategies. Organizations must employ a blend of technical solutions, policies, and a culture of awareness to identify and address potential risks from within. By combining behavioral analysis, robust access controls, and a security-conscious workforce, businesses can reduce the likelihood and impact of insider threats.

Strategies for Detection

1. **User Behavior Analytics (UBA)**

    Definition: UBA involves monitoring user activities, analyzing patterns of behavior, and flagging any deviations from typical patterns that could suggest an insider threat.

    Application: UBA tools can track actions such as abnormal login times, accessing files outside of job responsibilities, or transferring unusually large amounts of data. If an employee typically accesses files during business hours but starts downloading large files late at night, UBA tools can flag this behavior for further investigation.

2. **Data Loss Prevention (DLP) Tools**

   Definition: DLP tools are designed to monitor, detect, and prevent the unauthorized transmission of sensitive data both within and outside the organization.

   Application: These tools can restrict users from sharing sensitive information via email, USB drives, or cloud storage. For instance, if an employee attempts to upload confidential customer data to an external server, the DLP tool will block the transfer and alert the security team.

3. **Continuous Monitoring**

   Definition: Continuous monitoring involves real-time surveillance of user activities, system logs, and access records to detect any unusual or suspicious actions.

   Application: This strategy helps identify insider threats in real time by tracking users' interactions with critical systems. Monitoring tools can send alerts when unauthorized access or data exfiltration occurs, allowing organizations to react swiftly.

4. **Access Controls and Least Privilege**

   Definition: Implementing the principle of least privilege means granting employees the minimum level of access necessary to perform their duties.

   Application: By restricting access to sensitive systems and data, organizations can limit the potential damage an insider can cause. Regularly reviewing and adjusting access permissions ensures that employees only have access to what they need, minimizing the risk of intentional or accidental misuse.

Strategies for Prevention

1. **Security Awareness Training**

   Definition: Regular training sessions that educate employees on the latest security threats, best practices for data handling, and the importance of safeguarding sensitive information.

   Application: Training programs should cover phishing awareness, secure password practices, and the risks associated with insider threats. Employees need to understand the impact of their actions and how to recognize potential attacks. For instance, training employees to identify phishing emails can prevent credentials from being compromised.

2. **Strict Access Management**

   Definition: Implementing stringent access controls and enforcing multi-factor authentication (MFA) to secure critical systems and data.

   Application: MFA adds an additional layer of security by requiring two or more verification methods before granting access. Regular reviews of access privileges also help ensure that employees only retain the permissions they need for their current role, reducing the risk of privilege abuse.

CHAPTER 3   ATTACKS, THREATS, AND VULNERABILITIES

3. **Robust Incident Response Plan**

   Definition: Having a well-defined plan in place for quickly responding to potential insider threats and minimizing damage.

   Application: The incident response plan should outline specific steps for detecting, containing, and eradicating threats, as well as procedures for communication and recovery. It's essential to regularly test and update the plan to adapt to new threat scenarios, ensuring that the organization is prepared to act swiftly in the event of an insider attack.

4. **Employee Monitoring and Vetting**

   Definition: Conducting thorough background checks and continuously monitoring employees, especially those with access to sensitive data and systems.

   Application: Regular audits and employee vetting procedures help detect risky behaviors early. By monitoring privileged users, organizations can identify red flags such as financial distress or erratic behavior, which might indicate a higher risk of malicious activity.

5. **Encouraging a Security-Conscious Culture**

   Definition: Fostering an organizational culture where employees prioritize security and are encouraged to report potential threats without fear of retaliation.

Application: When employees understand the critical role, they play in maintaining security, they are more likely to follow best practices and report suspicious activities. Establishing a zero-tolerance policy for security violations and promoting transparency around security issues can reinforce this culture.

By combining these detection and prevention strategies, organizations can significantly reduce the risks posed by insider threats. An integrated approach that includes technical controls, awareness programs, and regular monitoring helps create a security framework that is resilient against both intentional and accidental threats from within.

Cloud-Based Threats

As organizations increasingly migrate to cloud environments for storage, processing, and collaboration, they encounter a unique set of security challenges. Cloud-based threats exploit vulnerabilities specific to cloud infrastructure, misconfigurations, and shared responsibility models. Understanding these threats is crucial for maintaining a secure cloud environment and safeguarding sensitive data.

Common Cloud-Based Threats

1. **Data Breaches**

   Definition: Unauthorized access to sensitive data stored in the cloud, resulting in data leakage or exposure.

CHAPTER 3   ATTACKS, THREATS, AND VULNERABILITIES

Causes: Cloud storage misconfigurations, inadequate access controls, or vulnerabilities in cloud applications can lead to data breaches. In multi-tenant cloud environments, data belonging to different organizations can be co-located on the same infrastructure, raising the risk of data compromise if isolation mechanisms fail.

Mitigation: Organizations should implement strong encryption for data at rest and in transit, use multi-factor authentication (MFA), and regularly audit cloud configurations to ensure proper access controls are in place.

2. **Misconfigurations**

   Definition: Incorrect settings or improper configurations in cloud environments that leave systems exposed to threats.

   Causes: Misconfigurations can arise from human error, lack of understanding of cloud security settings, or failure to properly secure cloud resources like storage buckets, virtual machines, and databases.

   Mitigation: Regular configuration audits, automated cloud security tools, and adherence to security best practices can help prevent misconfigurations. Establishing a process for reviewing and updating security settings whenever new resources are deployed is essential.

3. **Account Hijacking**

   Definition: Unauthorized access to a cloud account, often through compromised credentials, allowing attackers to manipulate cloud services, steal data, or execute malicious activities.

   Causes: Weak passwords, phishing attacks, or lack of MFA are common causes of account hijacking. Once attackers gain control of an account, they can escalate privileges and move laterally within the cloud environment.

   Mitigation: Implementing strong authentication mechanisms, including MFA, regular password changes, and monitoring for suspicious login attempts can prevent account hijacking. Educating users on phishing threats and enforcing least privilege policies are also critical.

4. **Insider Threats**

   Definition: Cloud-based threats originating from individuals within the organization, such as employees or contractors, who misuse their access to cloud services.

   Causes: Malicious insiders may intentionally exfiltrate data or disrupt services, while negligent insiders might unintentionally expose sensitive information due to lack of cloud security knowledge.

   Mitigation: Employing user behavior analytics (UBA), access monitoring, and enforcing least privilege access can detect and prevent insider threats. Regular security awareness training also helps mitigate the risk posed by negligent insiders.

CHAPTER 3   ATTACKS, THREATS, AND VULNERABILITIES

5. **Denial of Service (DoS) Attacks**

    Definition: Cloud services are overwhelmed with excessive traffic, rendering them inaccessible to legitimate users.

    Causes: Attackers exploit cloud resources by flooding them with traffic, consuming bandwidth and computing power, and preventing the cloud environment from functioning properly. Cloud services, due to their scalability, can become an attractive target for large-scale DoS attacks.

    Mitigation: Implementing rate-limiting, leveraging content delivery networks (CDNs) for traffic distribution, and utilizing cloud provider's DoS protection services can help mitigate the impact of such attacks. Regular performance monitoring also allows for early detection of traffic spikes.

6. **Insecure APIs**

    Definition: Application programming interfaces (APIs) used for interacting with cloud services can be vulnerable to attacks if improperly secured.

    Causes: Weak authentication, poor coding practices, or inadequate input validation in APIs can lead to exploits like unauthorized access, data exposure, or manipulation of cloud services. APIs are often a prime target for attackers due to their role in facilitating data exchange between systems.

    Mitigation: Securing APIs through strong authentication, implementing rate limits, and performing regular security testing (including

CHAPTER 3   ATTACKS, THREATS, AND VULNERABILITIES

penetration testing) can help protect against insecure API threats. Developers should adhere to secure coding practices, and organizations should leverage API gateways for monitoring and management.

7. **Advanced Persistent Threats (APTs)**

    Definition: APTs are sophisticated, multi-stage cyberattacks that often target cloud environments with the intent of gaining long-term access to sensitive data or cloud resources.

    Causes: APT actors typically exploit vulnerabilities, social engineering, or weak access controls to infiltrate a cloud environment. They maintain persistent access by using stealth techniques to avoid detection while gathering sensitive data or disrupting operations over time.

    Mitigation: Defending against APTs requires advanced threat detection tools, continuous monitoring of cloud environments, and regular threat intelligence updates. Implementing zero-trust architectures and network segmentation can also limit the potential impact of APTs.

8. **Data Loss**

    Definition: The loss of data in a cloud environment, either through accidental deletion, overwriting, or corruption, often without a proper backup in place.

    Causes: Human error, software bugs, or a lack of data redundancy can result in permanent data loss, particularly in environments where data is not properly backed up or archived.

Mitigation: Regularly backing up data, ensuring redundancy across multiple cloud regions, and implementing robust version control systems can mitigate the risk of data loss. Cloud providers often offer built-in backup and disaster recovery options that organizations should utilize.

9. **Compliance Violations**

    Definition: Failing to adhere to regulatory and compliance requirements related to data security, privacy, and governance in cloud environments.

    Causes: Inadequate security controls, misconfigured data access policies, or lack of understanding of regional data protection laws can lead to violations. For example, storing sensitive data in regions without proper safeguards could breach regulations like GDPR or HIPAA.

    Mitigation: Organizations must conduct regular compliance audits, work closely with cloud providers to understand shared responsibility models, and implement appropriate security controls to meet industry regulations. Encryption, data localization policies, and audit trails are essential for compliance.

Cloud Security Best Practices

1. **Shared Responsibility Model**: Understand the shared responsibility between cloud service providers (CSPs) and clients. While CSPs secure the infrastructure, clients are responsible for securing their data, applications, and user access.

2. **Encryption**: Ensure encryption of data both at rest and in transit to protect against unauthorized access. Proper key management practices are essential for safeguarding encryption keys.

3. **Identity and Access Management (IAM)**: Implement strict IAM policies to control who can access what in the cloud environment. Use role-based access control (RBAC) to limit user access and reduce attack surfaces.

4. **Regular Audits and Penetration Testing**: Continuously audit cloud security configurations and perform penetration testing to identify vulnerabilities before attackers exploit them.

5. **Backup and Disaster Recovery**: Maintain regular backups and ensure disaster recovery plans are in place to restore data and services in case of an attack or failure.

By understanding and addressing these cloud-based threats, organizations can better protect their cloud environments and maintain a secure and compliant infrastructure.

Phishing, Spear Phishing, and Whaling: Differences and Detection

Phishing, spear phishing, and whaling are all forms of social engineering attacks designed to deceive individuals into divulging sensitive information or performing malicious actions, such as clicking a malicious link or providing login credentials. While these attacks share common

CHAPTER 3   ATTACKS, THREATS, AND VULNERABILITIES

tactics, they differ in their level of sophistication, targeting, and potential impact. Understanding these differences is essential to effectively detect and prevent these threats.

1. **Phishing**

   Definition

   Phishing is a broad-based social engineering attack where attackers impersonate legitimate entities to trick large groups of people into sharing sensitive information, such as usernames, passwords, or credit card numbers.

   Characteristics

   - **Broad Targeting**: Phishing campaigns often cast a wide net, targeting hundreds or thousands of recipients simultaneously.

   - **Generic Messages**: Emails or messages used in phishing campaigns tend to be generic and non-personalized, using fear, urgency, or curiosity to entice users to act.

   - **Impersonation**: Attackers typically impersonate trusted entities like banks, social media platforms, or popular online services to lure victims.

   Examples

   - An email pretending to be from a well-known bank asking recipients to verify their account information by clicking a link.

   - A fake message from a popular online retailer claiming there is an issue with an order that requires immediate attention.

Detection and Prevention

- **Anti-phishing Software**: Deploy anti-phishing solutions that filter and block phishing emails.

- **Email Authentication Protocols**: Use Sender Policy Framework (SPF), DomainKeys Identified Mail (DKIM), and Domain-based Message Authentication, Reporting, and Conformance (DMARC) to authenticate sender addresses.

- **User Education**: Train users to recognize phishing attempts by being cautious of unsolicited emails that request personal information, contain suspicious links, or create a sense of urgency.

2. **Spear Phishing**

Definition

Spear phishing is a more targeted and sophisticated form of phishing, where attackers tailor their messages to a specific individual or organization. Unlike broad phishing attacks, spear phishing involves detailed research on the target to craft convincing and personalized emails or messages.

Characteristics

- **Targeted Attacks**: Spear phishing targets specific individuals or groups, often within an organization. Attackers gather information about the target from social media, public records, or leaked data to personalize their approach.

- **Personalized Messages**: Spear phishing emails are customized to appear as if they come from someone the target knows or trusts, such as a colleague, business partner, or superior.

- **Higher Success Rates**: Due to the personalized nature of these attacks, spear phishing campaigns have higher success rates compared to regular phishing.

Examples

- An email that appears to be from a company's IT department requesting a user to reset their password via a legitimate-looking link.

- A fake message from a colleague that includes a malicious attachment, disguised as an important work document.

Detection and Prevention

- **Behavioral Analysis**: Use user behavior analytics (UBA) to detect abnormal behavior, such as login attempts from unfamiliar locations or devices.

- **Advanced Threat Detection Tools**: Deploy solutions that can analyze and flag unusual email patterns or high-risk activities associated with spear phishing.

- **Verification Protocols**: Encourage users to verify the authenticity of unusual or unexpected emails by contacting the sender through other means before acting.

CHAPTER 3   ATTACKS, THREATS, AND VULNERABILITIES

3. **Whaling**

   Definition

   Whaling, also known as CEO fraud or executive phishing, is a type of spear phishing attack that specifically targets high-level executives, such as CEOs, CFOs, or other C-suite members. These attacks aim to steal sensitive information or convince the victim to authorize large financial transactions.

   Characteristics

   - **Targeting Senior Executives**: Whaling focuses on individuals with access to highly sensitive information or decision-making authority within an organization.

   - **Highly Personalized**: Whaling emails are carefully crafted, often using details from the executive's professional or personal life to increase credibility. The messages often mimic legitimate requests or business communications.

   - **Financial and Reputational Impact**: Due to the seniority of the targets, successful whaling attacks can result in significant financial losses and damage to the organization's reputation.

   Examples

   - An email appearing to be from a company's CEO requesting the CFO to transfer a large sum of money to an unfamiliar bank account.

- A message posing as a legal notice from an external party demanding sensitive company documents or financial information.

Detection and Prevention

- **Email Authentication:** Use email verification protocols to ensure that emails from executives are not spoofed.

- **Verification Mechanisms:** Implement multi-factor authentication (MFA) and verification steps for financial transactions or sensitive requests from executives.

- **Executive Security Training:** Provide targeted security awareness training to executives, educating them on the specific threats they face and encouraging them to be vigilant when reviewing emails or requests.

Key Differences Between Phishing, Spear Phishing, and Whaling

Aspect	Phishing	Spear Phishing	Whaling
Scope	Broad, untargeted	Narrow, specific targets	Highly specific, targets executives
Personalization	Generic	Personalized	Highly customized for senior leadership
Impact	Moderate	Can lead to data or credential theft	Financial loss, sensitive data theft

(*continued*)

CHAPTER 3   ATTACKS, THREATS, AND VULNERABILITIES

Aspect	Phishing	Spear Phishing	Whaling
Success Rate	Lower	Higher due to specificity	Very high due to authority and trust exploitation
Typical Target	General public or employees	Specific individuals or groups	C-suite executives and decision-makers

Detecting Phishing, Spear Phishing, and Whaling

1. **Email Analysis**
   - Inspect the sender's email address, domain, and reply-to address for inconsistencies.
   - Check for grammatical errors, generic greetings, or any language that creates urgency.

2. **Suspicious Links and Attachments**
   - Hover over links to verify the URL destination.
   - Be cautious of attachments, especially if unexpected or from unknown sources.

3. **Anomalous Requests**
   - Watch for unusual requests for sensitive information or financial transactions.
   - Be especially suspicious of emails requesting urgent action, particularly from executives or trusted contacts.

4. **Technical Solutions**

      - Use spam filters, email security gateways, and malware detection tools to catch suspicious emails.

      - Implement endpoint detection and response (EDR) solutions to protect against malicious payloads delivered via phishing emails.

   By understanding the nuances between phishing, spear phishing, and whaling and employing both technical solutions and user awareness, organizations can effectively mitigate these threats and reduce the risk of a successful attack.

Types of Cyberattacks

Cyberattacks can take many forms, ranging from disruptive attacks that slow or disable network functionality to more insidious attempts to steal information or damage data. These attacks exploit both technical vulnerabilities and human factors. Understanding their mechanisms and mitigation strategies is key for modern cybersecurity professionals.

Malware

Definition: Malicious software (malware) refers to any code that is designed to cause damage to a system, steal information, or otherwise harm the host or network. Malware can spread through a variety of methods, including email attachments, infected software downloads, and drive-by downloads from malicious websites.

- **Types**
  - **Viruses**: Attaches to legitimate files and spreads via user action

- **Worms**: Self-replicating malware that spreads across networks
- **Trojans**: Disguised as legitimate software, creating backdoors
- **Ransomware**: Encrypts files and demands a ransom for their release
- **Spyware**: Secretly collects user information, such as browsing habits or keystrokes
- **Adware**: Automatically downloads or displays advertisements
- **Rootkits**: Gains privileged access to a system and hides its presence
- **Bots/Botnets**: Turns devices into remotely controlled "bots" often used in coordinated attacks

- **Examples**
  - **Ransomware**: The WannaCry ransomware attack in 2017 affected organizations globally, targeting critical sectors such as healthcare by exploiting a vulnerability in the Windows OS.
  - **Worms**: The SQL Slammer worm spread so quickly that it caused a massive denial of service on some internet hosts within minutes.
  - **Spyware**: Keyloggers installed by attackers can monitor and record every keystroke a user makes to gather sensitive information like passwords.
  - **Bots/Botnets**: The Mirai botnet in 2016 caused a DDoS attack that took down major websites like Twitter, Netflix, and Reddit.

CHAPTER 3   ATTACKS, THREATS, AND VULNERABILITIES

- **Mitigation**
    - Regularly update antivirus and anti-malware software.
    - Employ network segmentation and access control lists (ACLs) to contain the spread of infections.
    - User education and awareness programs on the dangers of opening suspicious email attachments or clicking on unknown links.
    - Strong endpoint protection, firewalls, and intrusion detection/prevention systems (IDS/IPS).

Denial of Service (DoS) and Distributed Denial of Service (DDoS)

Denial of Service (DoS): A DoS attack attempts to overwhelm a system by flooding it with more requests than it can handle, rendering the service unusable for legitimate users. These attacks are typically launched from a single source.

- **Example**: SYN Flood Attacks exploit the handshake process of the TCP protocol. Attackers send a large number of SYN requests but fail to complete the connection, causing the server to become overwhelmed.
- **Mitigation**: Implement rate limiting, load balancing, and using IPS systems to detect and mitigate attacks.

Distributed Denial of Service (DDoS): Unlike a DoS attack, DDoS attacks are launched from multiple compromised systems (often a botnet). This makes it difficult to trace and mitigate due to the sheer volume of requests coming from multiple sources.

CHAPTER 3   ATTACKS, THREATS, AND VULNERABILITIES

- **Example**: In 2016, the Dyn DNS service was targeted by a massive DDoS attack orchestrated by the Mirai botnet, which used IoT devices to send millions of requests to the server, taking down major websites.
- **Mitigation**: Use services like Content Delivery Networks (CDNs) and DDoS mitigation providers. Ensure redundancy in network resources and employ strategies like traffic filtering and IP blacklisting.

Man-in-the-Middle (MITM)

A Man-in-the-Middle attack occurs when an attacker secretly intercepts and potentially alters the communication between two parties who believe they are directly communicating with each other. These attacks can take place on insecure networks, such as public Wi-Fi, or through compromised routers.

- **Example**: An attacker can intercept communication between a user and their banking website, capturing login credentials or sensitive financial information.
- **Mitigation**
    - Strong encryption protocols such as HTTPS for web traffic and VPNs to secure data in transit.
    - Using mutual authentication between communicating parties.
    - Avoiding unsecured networks and ensuring that users verify certificates before entering sensitive data.

CHAPTER 3   ATTACKS, THREATS, AND VULNERABILITIES

Rogue Access Points

Rogue access points (APs) are unauthorized wireless access points set up on a network, typically by attackers looking to intercept or manipulate traffic. These APs can be set up by malicious insiders or external attackers, creating an insecure backdoor into a supposedly secure network.

- **Example**: An attacker sets up a rogue access point in a corporate office that looks like the legitimate Wi-Fi network, allowing them to capture employee credentials and sensitive information.

- **Mitigation**
    - Implement Wireless Intrusion Detection Systems (WIDS) to detect unauthorized APs.
    - Conduct regular network scans to identify unfamiliar devices.
    - Enforce strict policies that require authentication and encryption for all wireless networks.

Cross-Site Scripting (XSS)

Cross-site scripting (XSS) is a vulnerability in web applications where an attacker injects malicious scripts into webpages viewed by other users. These scripts can be used to steal cookies, session tokens, or other sensitive information.

- **Example**: An attacker might inject a malicious script into the comment section of a blog. When another user views the comment, the script runs in their browser, stealing their session cookies.

- **Mitigation**
  - Ensure proper input validation and output encoding to prevent script injection.
  - Implement Content Security Policy (CSP) to block unauthorized scripts.
  - Use secure coding practices that sanitize user input to prevent injection attacks.

Cross-Site Request Forgery (CSRF/XSRF)

CSRF tricks users into performing actions on a web application without their consent, often while they are authenticated. This could result in unauthorized actions such as fund transfers or changing account details.

- **Example**: An attacker sends a link via email or instant message. When clicked by a user who is logged into their bank account, the link initiates a fund transfer without the user's knowledge.
- **Mitigation**
  - Use anti-CSRF tokens to validate user requests.
  - Require re-authentication for sensitive transactions.
  - Validate the origin of requests to ensure they are legitimate.

Rootkits

Rootkits are a form of malware designed to gain root (administrative) access to a system and hide their presence. Rootkits often modify system files or operating system functions to conceal their activity, making them difficult to detect and remove.

- **Example**: The Stuxnet worm, which targeted industrial control systems, used a rootkit to hide its presence while sabotaging equipment.

- **Mitigation**
  - Use rootkit detection tools that monitor for unexpected changes in system files or behavior.
  - Regularly perform system integrity checks.
  - Limit administrative privileges to reduce the attack surface.

Service Chain Attacks

Service chain attacks (also known as supply chain attacks) exploit vulnerabilities in third-party services, vendors, or suppliers to compromise a primary target. These attacks are particularly dangerous because they exploit the trust organizations place in their vendors.

- **Example**: The SolarWinds attack compromised a trusted software update, leading to the infiltration of numerous high-profile targets, including government agencies and corporations.

- **Mitigation**
  - Implement strict vendor assessments and security controls.
  - Regularly audit and monitor third-party services and software updates.
  - Employ defense-in-depth strategies to minimize the potential impact of a compromised supplier.

Social Engineering

Social engineering attacks manipulate human behavior to gain unauthorized access to systems or information. These attacks rely more on psychology than technical vulnerabilities and often exploit the natural trust people have in others or the authority of an institution.

- **Phishing**: Attackers send emails that appear to be from trusted sources to trick users into revealing sensitive information or clicking on malicious links.
  - **Example**: An email that appears to be from a bank requesting a password reset but leads to a fake website designed to steal credentials.
  - **Mitigation**: Security awareness training, email filtering tools, and multi-factor authentication.
- **Spear Phishing**: A more targeted form of phishing, where attackers tailor their messages to specific individuals or organizations.
  - **Example**: An attacker researching a company's CEO and sending a personalized email that appears to be from a trusted vendor.

- **Whaling**: A form of spear phishing that targets high-profile individuals like executives.
    - **Example**: An attacker impersonates a CEO to trick the CFO into wiring large sums of money.
- **Baiting**: Entices victims with the promise of something valuable (e.g., free software) that turns out to be malicious.
- **Pretexting**: An attacker creates a fabricated scenario to steal information or access.
- **Tailgating**: An attacker follows an authorized person into a restricted area.
- **Mitigation for All Forms of Social Engineering**
    - Security awareness training that includes phishing simulations.
    - Implementing strong authentication methods like multi-factor authentication (MFA).
    - Enforcing physical security measures like access badges and biometric scanners.

Supply Chain Attacks

In a supply chain attack, attackers target the vulnerabilities in third-party vendors, suppliers, or partners to gain access to the primary organization. This type of attack is becoming increasingly common as businesses rely more on external partners for hardware, software, and services.

- **Example**: A compromised third-party software provider introduces malware into a widely distributed software update, affecting thousands of businesses globally.

- **Mitigation**
  - Conduct thorough vendor risk assessments and audits.
  - Ensure proper segmentation between internal systems and third-party systems.
  - Regularly update and patch systems to mitigate known vulnerabilities.

Zero-Day Attacks

A zero-day attack occurs when an attacker exploits a vulnerability that has not yet been patched or publicly disclosed. These attacks are highly dangerous because there is no available defense at the time of the exploit.

- **Example**: In 2010, the Stuxnet worm used zero-day vulnerabilities in Windows to target and sabotage Iranian nuclear facilities.
- **Mitigation**
  - Maintain a robust patch management strategy.
  - Use advanced threat detection systems that can identify and stop suspicious activity, even for unknown threats.
  - Ensure that network and application monitoring tools are capable of identifying abnormal behavior that may indicate an exploit in progress.

Types of Threat Intelligence

Threat intelligence is the practice of gathering, analyzing, and interpreting information about current and potential threats to inform an organization's cybersecurity strategy. It provides insights into the evolving tactics, techniques, and procedures (TTPs) of attackers, helping organizations anticipate, prevent, and respond effectively to cyber threats. Different types of threat intelligence cater to various needs, from high-level insights for executives to actionable data for incident response teams. Below are the primary categories of threat intelligence and their distinct purposes within a security program:

1. **Strategic Threat Intelligence**

    - **Purpose**: Strategic threat intelligence offers a broad, high-level view of the cyber threat landscape, enabling executives, policymakers, and other decision-makers to understand trends that could affect the organization's cybersecurity. This intelligence is used to shape long-term security strategies, policies, and investment priorities.

    - **Characteristics**: Unlike other types, strategic intelligence is less concerned with the technical details of attacks. Instead, it focuses on macro-level trends, such as the motivations behind cyberattacks, threat actor profiles, and the potential impact of various risks on an industry or region. This type of intelligence often includes insights into geopolitical issues, economic factors, and social motivations that drive threat actors, making it essential for aligning cybersecurity efforts with organizational objectives.

- **Typical Sources**: Strategic intelligence is often gathered from industry reports, government advisories, and research institutions. Analysts also monitor news sources and track major developments affecting industries at risk.

- **Example**: A strategic report detailing how ransomware is increasingly targeting healthcare facilities globally can provide healthcare executives with critical insights into potential vulnerabilities in their infrastructure. This awareness can influence the allocation of resources to fortify defenses against ransomware.

2. **Tactical Threat Intelligence**

    - **Purpose**: Tactical threat intelligence is designed to provide security teams with information on specific TTPs used by threat actors. This type of intelligence is especially valuable for security operations center (SOC) teams, cybersecurity analysts, and administrators who work to detect, prevent, and respond to attacks.

    - **Characteristics**: Tactical intelligence offers detailed insight into the "how" behind an attack. This typically includes IOCs, such as file hashes, IP addresses, URLs, and email addresses associated with known malicious activity. These IOCs can be quickly fed into detection tools like intrusion detection systems (IDS), firewalls, and endpoint protection platforms (EPP) to bolster defenses. Tactical intelligence also includes the procedural methods attackers use to infiltrate systems,

CHAPTER 3   ATTACKS, THREATS, AND VULNERABILITIES

escalate privileges, and exfiltrate data, helping defenders recognize malicious activity within their environment.

- **Typical Sources**: Tactical intelligence is gathered from network and endpoint monitoring tools, threat analysis tools, and threat-sharing platforms like the MITRE ATT&CK framework. It's also often shared by cybersecurity vendors and government agencies.

- **Example**: A tactical intelligence report highlighting recent phishing campaign indicators could include the email addresses, sender domains, and attachment hashes associated with the campaign. SOC teams can input this information into their email filters and threat detection systems to block these indicators and prevent the phishing emails from reaching end users.

3. **Operational Threat Intelligence**

    - **Purpose**: Operational threat intelligence provides actionable insights about active or imminent threats, enabling incident response (IR) teams to anticipate attacks and respond in real time. This intelligence is often time-sensitive and vital for organizations with high-value assets that are frequently targeted.

    - **Characteristics**: Operational intelligence is focused on live and developing threats, making it instrumental for proactively defending against attacks. It includes details such as the attackers' goals, timelines, and intended targets. Operational intelligence may also contain insights gathered from sources like dark web forums, closed online communities, and encrypted chat channels used by threat actors. This intelligence helps organizations gauge whether they are in the crosshairs of a particular threat actor or attack campaign.

- **Typical Sources**: Operational intelligence is typically gathered through human intelligence (HUMINT) activities, such as infiltrating online forums where threat actors operate, as well as from automated monitoring of dark web activity and threat actor chatter. Specialized cybersecurity firms often provide operational intelligence services by monitoring threat actors on the organization's behalf.

- **Example:** A threat intelligence service detects chatter in a hacker forum indicating a planned DDoS attack against financial services firms within the next 48 hours. This intelligence allows a targeted financial institution to prepare by activating its DDoS mitigation tools, alerting key personnel, and ensuring additional monitoring is in place to counter the anticipated attack.

4. **Technical Threat Intelligence**
    - **Purpose**: Technical threat intelligence delves into the specific technical details of threats, focusing on the mechanisms, tools, and software that threat actors use in their operations. It provides security engineers and incident response teams with a deeper understanding of how malicious code and

exploitation techniques work, often aiding in the development of countermeasures and security improvements.

- **Characteristics**: Technical intelligence provides granular details about malware functionalities, command-and-control (C2) infrastructures, botnets, and vulnerabilities in software and hardware. This intelligence can be instrumental in developing detection signatures, patching systems, and designing countermeasures to thwart or mitigate specific attack methods.

- **Typical Sources**: Technical intelligence is gathered from malware analysis, reverse engineering, and penetration testing. Threat intelligence feeds, vulnerability databases, and code repositories for known malware strains are also valuable sources.

- **Example**: Security researchers reverse-engineer a new ransomware variant and discover a unique encryption algorithm it uses. By analyzing this technical intelligence, they can develop a decryption tool and disseminate it to help affected organizations recover their data without paying a ransom.

How to Apply Threat Intelligence in a Security Strategy

Effectively using threat intelligence requires its seamless integration into an organization's security framework. By embedding intelligence insights into core security functions, organizations can bolster their defense

CHAPTER 3   ATTACKS, THREATS, AND VULNERABILITIES

capabilities, refine response strategies, and ensure they stay ahead of evolving threats. Here are the key steps to applying threat intelligence in a comprehensive security strategy:

1. **Integrating Threat Intelligence into Security Operations**

    - **Contextual Awareness**: Leverage threat intelligence to gain insight into threats specifically targeting your organization or industry. Understanding the unique threat landscape helps tailor defenses to be more proactive against high-risk attack methods.

    - **Incident Response**: Incorporate threat intelligence into incident response (IR) procedures. This enables rapid detection and analysis of threats, allowing for faster mitigation. Intelligence feeds can help IR teams identify Indicators of Compromise (IOCs) and tactics, techniques, and procedures (TTPs) associated with active threats, streamlining response efforts.

    - **Threat Hunting**: Proactively hunt for potential compromises within the environment by using TTPs identified from threat intelligence. Teams can identify lurking threats or vulnerabilities by focusing on known patterns and behaviors associated with specific attackers, enhancing early detection efforts.

CHAPTER 3   ATTACKS, THREATS, AND VULNERABILITIES

2. **Enhancing Security Controls**

    - **Updating Detection Rules**: Regularly update detection systems, such as intrusion detection systems (IDS), intrusion prevention systems (IPS), firewalls, and antivirus software, with the latest IOCs and threat signatures. This keeps detection capabilities current, allowing systems to block new threats before they impact the organization.

    - **Vulnerability Management**: Prioritize patching and remediation efforts by leveraging threat intelligence to identify vulnerabilities currently under active exploitation. By focusing on high-risk vulnerabilities, organizations can close critical security gaps before attackers exploit them, effectively reducing the attack surface.

3. **Supporting Decision-Making**

    - **Risk Management**: Strategic threat intelligence provides high-level insights that inform decisions on security investments and resource allocation. By assessing the likelihood and impact of emerging threats, security leaders can prioritize risk management efforts and direct investments where they're most needed.

    - **Security Policy Development**: Align organizational security policies with the latest threat intelligence to ensure they are effective against known risks. Regular updates to policies—based on intelligence insights—help the organization adapt to emerging threats, enabling a proactive approach to cybersecurity.

4. **Collaboration and Information Sharing**

    - **Industry Collaboration:** Participate in industry threat-sharing communities, such as Information Sharing and Analysis Centers (ISACs) and other intelligence-sharing networks, to strengthen collective security. Collaborating with other organizations provides a wider intelligence pool and helps identify threats affecting multiple organizations within the same sector.

    - **Internal Communication:** Ensure threat intelligence reaches all relevant teams within the organization. This involves keeping executives, operational teams, and frontline security personnel aware of potential threats and response strategies, fostering a unified approach to threat response and mitigation.

5. **Continuous Improvement**

    - **Feedback Loops:** Establish feedback loops within your threat intelligence program to continually evaluate its effectiveness. Regular assessments help ensure that threat intelligence remains aligned with evolving organizational needs and that insights continue to provide meaningful, actionable information.

    - **Performance Metrics:** Measure the success of the threat intelligence program through metrics such as response times, the number of detected and mitigated threats, and overall security posture improvements. These metrics provide a quantitative basis for tracking progress and identifying areas for further enhancement.

CHAPTER 3   ATTACKS, THREATS, AND VULNERABILITIES

By applying threat intelligence across these dimensions, organizations can make informed security decisions, prioritize resource allocation, and ensure that their defenses remain relevant and effective against the latest cyber threats.

Indicators of Compromise (IOCs)

Indicators of Compromise (IOCs) are distinct pieces of forensic data that signal a security breach or malicious activity within a system. They act as breadcrumbs that alert security teams to the presence of potential or ongoing threats, helping to reveal patterns or anomalies indicative of a compromise. IOCs serve a critical role in security operations by helping identify, respond to, and contain security incidents. By providing evidence of suspicious activities, they enable organizations to detect and mitigate threats more quickly and accurately.

Types of Indicators of Compromise

Similar to how there are many types of vulnerabilities, risks, and components of an environment, there are various forms of Indicators of Compromise. It is always recommended that an organization review the entirety of their infrastructure regularly to ensure that there are no visible indicators of compromise on any one part. All it takes is for an intruder to compromise a single item to gain entry to the greater whole.

1. **Network IOCs**

    - **Suspicious IP Addresses**: Connections to IP addresses associated with known malicious entities may indicate unauthorized access attempts or compromised communications.

- **Unusual Domain Names**: Unexpected domains, especially those linked to phishing campaigns or command-and-control (C2) servers, often suggest malicious activity.

- **Anomalous Traffic Patterns**: High data transfer volumes or unusual traffic spikes can hint at data exfiltration or malware spreading across the network.

- **DNS Anomalies**: Requests to obscure or flagged malicious domains can reveal malware operations attempting to connect to external servers.

2. **File-Based IOCs**

    - **Malware Signatures**: Identifiable code patterns or binary sequences within files that match known malware can help detect infections.

    - **File Hashes**: Cryptographic hashes (e.g., MD5, SHA-256) of files known to be malicious allow quick comparison and identification of malicious files.

    - **Unusual File Modifications**: Unauthorized alterations to critical system files often indicate malware attempting to manipulate system behavior.

    - **Presence of Suspicious Files**: Detection of files in unexpected locations or with uncommon extensions can reveal hidden malware or illicit tools.

CHAPTER 3   ATTACKS, THREATS, AND VULNERABILITIES

3. **Host-Based IOCs**

    - **Unauthorized User Accounts**: The creation of unapproved user accounts can be a sign of unauthorized access or an attacker attempting to gain persistence.

    - **Unexpected Process Execution**: The presence of unfamiliar or malicious processes running on a host system may indicate active malware or a compromise.

    - **System Log Anomalies**: Irregularities in logs, such as repeated failed login attempts or unauthorized permission changes, may reveal brute force or privilege escalation attempts.

    - **Registry Changes (Windows)**: Unapproved changes to registry entries may indicate malware setting up persistence mechanisms.

4. **Email-Based IOCs**

    - **Phishing Email Artifacts**: Elements like suspicious headers, unusual sender addresses, and malicious links or attachments often point to phishing attempts.

    - **Compromised Email Accounts**: If legitimate accounts are used to send unauthorized or malicious emails, this is a common sign of account compromise.

    - **Unusual Email Behaviors**: Increased activity from certain accounts, especially those sending links or attachments, could indicate spamming or phishing attacks.

CHAPTER 3   ATTACKS, THREATS, AND VULNERABILITIES

How to Use Indicators of Compromise

Which of course brings us to this topic, now that we have a known indicator of compromise, what are we to do with it? There are various methods that you can follow, and there is no one-size-fit-all answer. The following are some of the most common tactics to take once an indicator of compromise has been verified.

1. **Detection and Monitoring**

    - **Integration with SIEM Tools**: Feed IOCs into Security Information and Event Management (SIEM) platforms to automate threat detection across the environment.

    - **Real-Time Alerts**: Configure automated alerts within security tools to notify security teams when IOCs are detected, ensuring a swift response to potential threats.

    - **Continuous Monitoring**: Regularly update IOC databases to reflect emerging threats, helping maintain a proactive stance in threat detection.

2. **Incident Response**

    - **IOC Analysis**: Evaluate IOCs during incidents to determine the type, severity, and scope of the compromise.

    - **Triage and Containment**: Use IOC data to focus response efforts on compromised systems, enabling efficient containment.

    - **Eradication and Recovery**: IOCs aid in locating malicious files, identifying rogue IPs, and restoring systems, facilitating a complete eradication and recovery process.

CHAPTER 3   ATTACKS, THREATS, AND VULNERABILITIES

3. **Threat Intelligence and Sharing**

    - **Community Sharing**: Contributing new IOCs to cybersecurity communities strengthens the collective defense of participating organizations.

    - **Threat Intelligence Feeds**: Subscribing to external feeds ensures access to up-to-date IOCs, enhancing threat detection capabilities.

    - **Integration with Security Tools**: By importing IOCs into security infrastructure like firewalls or IDS/IPS, organizations can reinforce defenses to detect and prevent threats.

4. **Proactive Defense**

    - **IOC-Based Hunting**: Security teams can proactively search for signs of compromise by using IOCs to identify suspicious activity within their systems.

    - **Policy Enforcement**: Implement security policies that block or quarantine actions associated with malicious files, IP addresses, or domains.

    - **Regular Updates**: Maintaining an up-to-date IOC database is essential for ensuring defenses remain effective against new and emerging threats.

Indicators of Compromise are invaluable assets for a robust security posture. By integrating IOCs into monitoring, incident response, threat intelligence sharing, and proactive defense measures, organizations can strengthen their resilience against threats and improve their ability to detect, respond to, and prevent attacks.

CHAPTER 3   ATTACKS, THREATS, AND VULNERABILITIES

Understanding Vulnerabilities and Their Impacts

Vulnerabilities are inherent weaknesses or flaws within systems, networks, or applications that can be exploited by attackers. When left unaddressed, they can compromise the confidentiality, integrity, or availability of an organization's assets, exposing critical data and systems to potential breaches, financial losses, or operational disruptions. Given their prevalence and variety, vulnerabilities represent one of the most significant risks in cybersecurity, underscoring the need for proactive identification, mitigation, and management.

Types of Vulnerabilities

Software Vulnerabilities

- **Unpatched Software**: Failure to install software patches leaves systems open to exploits. Attackers often target unpatched vulnerabilities that are publicly known, giving them an easy way to compromise systems.
  - *Example:* A widely used software application releases a patch for a security flaw, but if organizations delay the update, attackers can use the flaw to breach those systems.
- **Misconfigurations**: Weak or improper configurations, such as default passwords or excessive permissions, increase exposure to attacks. Common misconfigurations include enabling unnecessary features, neglecting encryption, or setting weak access controls.

CHAPTER 3   ATTACKS, THREATS, AND VULNERABILITIES

- *Example:* Leaving an application in "debug" mode with verbose error messages can provide attackers with detailed information about system architecture.

- **Outdated Components**: Legacy or unsupported software lacks ongoing security updates, making it susceptible to unpatched vulnerabilities. Older software components often have multiple known vulnerabilities, each providing potential entry points.

    - *Example:* Organizations still using outdated operating systems, like Windows XP, face considerable security risks, as these systems no longer receive security patches.

Hardware Vulnerabilities

- **Firmware Exploits**: Firmware, the foundational software controlling hardware, can have vulnerabilities that allow attackers low-level access, bypassing traditional security. Since firmware operates below the operating system, these vulnerabilities can be difficult to detect.

    - *Example:* A compromised firmware update on network routers could provide attackers with a persistent foothold within a network, undetectable by antivirus software.

- **Side-Channel Attacks**: These attacks exploit physical characteristics like power consumption or timing to extract sensitive data. By observing small details, attackers can retrieve encryption keys or passwords.

119

- *Example:* The Meltdown and Spectre vulnerabilities exploited CPU flaws, allowing attackers to access protected memory spaces and retrieve sensitive information.

Network Vulnerabilities

- **Open Ports and Weak Protocols**: Open ports provide entry points for attackers, and weak or outdated protocols (e.g., FTP, Telnet) lack modern security measures, making them susceptible to interception or manipulation.
    - *Example:* Leaving port 23 open for Telnet communications allows attackers to intercept or alter data due to Telnet's lack of encryption.
- **Insecure Wi-Fi Networks**: Weak Wi-Fi configurations can be exploited by attackers for man-in-the-middle (MITM) attacks or unauthorized access. Open or poorly protected Wi-Fi networks are especially vulnerable.
    - *Example:* Using outdated security protocols like WEP instead of WPA3 can expose a network to unauthorized access attempts and interception.
- **Denial of Service (DoS)**: Network vulnerabilities can be exploited to flood systems with traffic, leading to service disruptions. Weak rate limiting and improper firewall rules contribute to these vulnerabilities.
    - *Example:* An attacker floods a web server with traffic, exploiting the lack of rate limiting to cause a DoS attack, making the site inaccessible to legitimate users.

CHAPTER 3   ATTACKS, THREATS, AND VULNERABILITIES

Human Vulnerabilities

- **Phishing and Social Engineering:** Attackers use psychological manipulation to trick individuals into revealing confidential information or clicking on malicious links. Phishing remains one of the most effective initial vectors for breaches.

  - *Example:* An employee receives an email claiming to be from IT support, urging them to reset their password on a fake website, giving attackers access to the employee's account.

- **Insider Threats:** Authorized personnel with legitimate access can, either intentionally or unintentionally, misuse their access. Insiders often have a deeper understanding of organizational processes, making their actions more difficult to detect.

  - *Example:* A disgruntled employee may leak sensitive data or grant access to unauthorized personnel, causing significant security incidents.

Operational Vulnerabilities

- **Weak Passwords and Authentication:** Using weak passwords or inadequate authentication measures increases the risk of unauthorized access. Effective password policies and multi-factor authentication (MFA) are essential to mitigate this risk.

  - *Example:* An employee's password is simply "password123," making it easily guessable, thereby compromising security.

- **Inadequate Backup Procedures**: Without proper backups, organizations are vulnerable to data loss, whether from ransomware, accidental deletion, or hardware failure. Backup policies ensure data is available for restoration in the event of a compromise.
  - *Example:* A ransomware attack encrypts all critical files, but without a recent backup, the organization has no way to restore its data.
- **Insufficient Monitoring**: Lacking robust monitoring and alerting means that suspicious activities or potential threats might go undetected. Effective monitoring includes anomaly detection and logging that helps quickly identify security incidents.
  - *Example:* Failing to monitor login attempts or file access patterns might allow an attacker to operate undetected within a network.

Why Addressing Vulnerabilities Matters

The impact of vulnerabilities varies but can be devastating if exploited. Unaddressed vulnerabilities can lead to

- **Data Breaches**: Sensitive information, like customer data or proprietary information, may be exposed.
- **Operational Disruptions**: Ransomware or denial-of-service attacks can bring business operations to a standstill.

- **Financial Losses**: Costs from regulatory fines, recovery efforts, and reputational damage can be substantial.

- **Legal and Regulatory Risks**: Compliance violations may lead to legal consequences, especially when handling sensitive information.

Addressing vulnerabilities is essential in building a robust security posture. Through regular assessments, patching, updating security configurations, and employee training, organizations can significantly reduce the risk of exploitation, enhancing their defenses against today's evolving threats.

Reducing the Attack Surface

Reducing the attack surface—meaning the number of potential entry points for an attacker—is a core strategy in vulnerability management. By limiting system exposure, organizations can decrease the likelihood of successful attacks. Key methods for reducing the attack surface include

- **Restricting Access**: Only providing users and devices with access to necessary systems minimizes exposure.

- **Network Segmentation**: Isolating critical systems limits the spread of an attack within a network, should one occur.

- **Disabling Unused Services**: Eliminating unnecessary services and protocols reduces the number of exploitable points.

CHAPTER 3   ATTACKS, THREATS, AND VULNERABILITIES

Assessing the Severity of Vulnerabilities

Not all vulnerabilities are equal; some represent minor issues, while others could severely impact the organization. Evaluating vulnerabilities involves considering various factors, including exploitability, potential impact, and exposure.

1. **Exploitability**

    - **Ease of Exploitation**: Assess whether the vulnerability can be exploited by an unskilled attacker or if it requires a sophisticated approach.

    - **Public Availability**: A vulnerability with a widely available exploit poses a significantly higher risk.

2. **Potential Impact**

    - **Business Criticality**: Evaluate the importance of the affected system to organizational operations. A vulnerability in a critical system, like payment processing, warrants a high-severity rating.

    - **Scope of Impact**: Vulnerabilities that affect multiple systems or users carry a higher severity due to their broader risk.

3. **Exposure and Visibility**

    - **Internet-Facing Systems**: Vulnerabilities in publicly accessible systems, such as web servers, are at higher risk of attack.

    - **Internal vs. External**: While internal vulnerabilities are dangerous, they typically require attackers to breach the network first, making them harder to exploit.

CHAPTER 3   ATTACKS, THREATS, AND VULNERABILITIES

Mitigating Vulnerabilities

Mitigation is the process of implementing measures to reduce the impact of vulnerabilities. The most effective strategies include

1. **Regular Patch Management**: Apply software updates promptly to minimize risk from known vulnerabilities.

2. **Network Segmentation**: Isolate critical systems to limit exposure and prevent lateral movement by attackers.

3. **Strong Authentication and Access Controls**: Implement multi-factor authentication (MFA) and role-based access controls to protect sensitive systems.

4. **Employee Training and Awareness**: Regular training can reduce human vulnerabilities, such as susceptibility to phishing.

5. **Security Audits and Vulnerability Scanning**: Conduct periodic audits and scans to identify and address potential weaknesses proactively.

Common Vulnerability Scoring System (CVSS): How Vulnerabilities Are Rated

The Common Vulnerability Scoring System (CVSS) is an industry-standard framework for evaluating vulnerability severity. CVSS provides a consistent, numerical score ranging from 0 to 10 to reflect the level of risk associated with a vulnerability, helping organizations prioritize their responses. Scores are categorized into four levels:

- **Low (0.1-3.9)**: Minor impact vulnerabilities that pose minimal risk.

- **Medium (4.0-6.9)**: Moderate impact vulnerabilities that require timely remediation.

- **High (7.0-8.9)**: Significant impact vulnerabilities needing prompt attention.

- **Critical (9.0-10.0)**: Severe vulnerabilities demanding immediate action.

Components of CVSS

CVSS scores are derived from three main metric groups: Base, Temporal, and Environmental. Each reflects a different aspect of the vulnerability:

1. **Base Metrics**

    - **Exploitability**: Includes metrics such as Attack Vector (how a vulnerability can be accessed), Attack Complexity (difficulty of exploitation), Privileges Required, and User Interaction.

    - **Impact Metrics**: These include Confidentiality, Integrity, and Availability impacts, indicating the potential effect of a successful exploit.

2. **Temporal Metrics**

    - Reflects the current state of the vulnerability, such as the availability of exploit code or patches. Examples include

        - **Exploit Code Maturity**: Indicates the development stage of exploit techniques

- **Remediation Level**: Details the availability of patches or fixes
- **Report Confidence**: Measures confidence in the vulnerability's existence and technical details

3. **Environmental Metrics**
   - Adapt the Base score to the specific environment. For instance, vulnerabilities affecting highly sensitive systems may have their scores adjusted to reflect the higher risk.

Effective Vulnerability Management Strategies

Effective vulnerability management goes beyond identifying and scoring vulnerabilities; it involves prioritizing, mitigating, and continuously monitoring them. Core practices include

- **Asset Management**: Maintain a detailed inventory of systems, software, and hardware, identifying which assets require higher security measures.
- **Prioritization and Risk Assessment**: Focus on vulnerabilities that pose the highest risk based on CVSS scores, business criticality, and exposure.
- **Automated Patching and Updates**: Automation ensures that critical patches are applied promptly across systems.
- **Incident Response Planning**: Have a response plan in place, detailing steps for containment, remediation, and recovery if a vulnerability is exploited.

By understanding vulnerabilities in the context of the organization and taking systematic action, cybersecurity professionals can minimize risks and strengthen defenses against evolving threats. CVSS offers a standardized framework for assessing vulnerabilities, but effective risk management ultimately depends on prioritizing response actions in line with organizational needs and continuously adapting defenses.

Using CVSS in Vulnerability Management

Organizations rely on the Common Vulnerability Scoring System (CVSS) as an integral part of their vulnerability management strategy. CVSS offers a standardized approach to assess and prioritize vulnerabilities based on their severity and potential impact, allowing security teams to systematically address risks. Here's how CVSS supports various aspects of vulnerability management.

Prioritization

1. **CVSS Scores for Severity**

    CVSS scoring enables organizations to classify vulnerabilities based on severity, assisting in prioritization efforts. Vulnerabilities rated as critical (9.0–10.0) require urgent action—such as immediate patch application or workarounds—to protect against severe impacts on confidentiality, integrity, or availability. This allows teams to systematically address the most pressing issues first, optimizing resource allocation.

CHAPTER 3   ATTACKS, THREATS, AND VULNERABILITIES

2. **Alignment with Organizational Priorities**

   CVSS scores are adaptable to reflect an organization's unique priorities. By adjusting the base score using environmental metrics, vulnerabilities affecting high-value assets, such as customer databases or financial systems, can be given higher priority. This ensures that even medium-rated vulnerabilities receive heightened focus if they could significantly impact critical systems.

Risk Assessment

1. **Contextualized Risk**

   CVSS provides a multidimensional view of vulnerability risk by incorporating base, temporal, and environmental metrics. This framework enables security teams to understand both the likelihood of exploitation and the potential consequences if a vulnerability is exploited. By offering this comprehensive perspective, CVSS helps organizations align remediation efforts with the actual level of threat posed.

2. **Informed Decision-Making**

   CVSS metrics, such as attack vector, attack complexity, and exploit code maturity, aid in evaluating whether a vulnerability requires immediate remediation or if it can be mitigated through compensating controls. For instance, if a vulnerability has a low likelihood of being exploited externally, organizations might opt to address it in the next patch cycle rather than deploying an urgent fix, thus allowing for effective resource distribution.

Patch Management

1. **Patch Prioritization**

    The CVSS score informs the urgency with which patches should be applied. High or critical CVSS-rated vulnerabilities are given precedence during patch management cycles, ensuring that essential updates are deployed first to protect systems against the highest risks. This prioritization process helps to minimize exposure time for vulnerabilities with the potential to cause the most damage.

2. **Remediation Timeline**

    CVSS scores serve as a guide for setting internal service-level agreements (SLAs) related to patching. Higher CVSS scores may warrant shorter remediation timelines, prompting organizations to develop tighter schedules for critical updates. By establishing clear SLAs based on CVSS, organizations can maintain consistent patching standards and reduce the window of opportunity for exploitation.

Communication

1. **Standardized Language**

   The CVSS scoring system provides a standardized way to discuss vulnerabilities across different stakeholders. With numerical scores and associated severity levels, security teams, management, and vendors can communicate risk consistently. This common language streamlines conversations around vulnerability impact and prioritization, ensuring all parties understand the level of urgency and the necessary actions.

2. **Executive Reporting**

   Security leaders can leverage CVSS-based assessments to communicate risk to nontechnical stakeholders, including executives and board members. By presenting CVSS scores within a business context, security teams can illustrate the potential impacts on operations, revenue, and reputation, helping executives understand why specific vulnerabilities require attention and support for remediation efforts.

Incorporating CVSS into an organization's vulnerability management strategy enables security teams to prioritize vulnerabilities effectively, streamline patch management, and facilitate clear communication across technical and nontechnical teams. This approach strengthens the organization's overall security posture by ensuring vulnerabilities are systematically assessed, prioritized, and addressed based on their potential business impact.

CHAPTER 3   ATTACKS, THREATS, AND VULNERABILITIES

Overview of Security Assessment Tools

Security assessment tools are critical assets that allow organizations to identify, prioritize, and mitigate vulnerabilities within their IT infrastructure. By regularly conducting assessments, organizations gain insights into existing weaknesses, helping them stay ahead of potential threats. These tools vary in functionality, depth of analysis, and application but all contribute to a comprehensive security posture. Key types of security assessment tools include vulnerability scanners, penetration testing platforms, configuration management tools, and additional frameworks designed to enhance network resilience and protection.

Vulnerability Scanners

Vulnerability scanners play a fundamental role in identifying security weaknesses across devices, applications, and systems. These automated tools assess systems for known vulnerabilities by comparing the organization's software and configurations against an extensive database of vulnerabilities.

Types of Vulnerability Scanners

1. **Network Scanners**: Tools like **Nessus** and **Qualys** focus on identifying vulnerabilities in network infrastructure, such as misconfigurations, outdated software, and open ports.

2. **Web Application Scanners:** Tools like **Acunetix** and **Burp Suite** specialize in detecting vulnerabilities specific to web applications, including SQL injection, cross-site scripting (XSS), and insecure API calls.

3. **Cloud Vulnerability Scanners:** Tools like **AWS Inspector** and **Microsoft Defender for Cloud** target vulnerabilities within cloud infrastructure, assessing configurations, storage permissions, and access management across cloud environments.

Real-Time Detection and Reporting

Vulnerability scanners provide real-time or scheduled scanning, allowing security teams to continuously monitor the organization's security posture. Reports generated by these scanners detail the identified vulnerabilities, their severity, and suggested remediation steps, providing a roadmap for prioritizing patching efforts.

Limitations and Considerations

While scanners are invaluable, they only detect known vulnerabilities. New or complex zero-day threats, for example, may evade detection, underscoring the need for additional assessment techniques.

Penetration Testing Tools

Penetration testing (pen testing) tools simulate real-world attacks to reveal how systems would respond under actual threat conditions. These tools go beyond vulnerability scanning by actively exploiting vulnerabilities to understand potential consequences if an attacker gained unauthorized access.

CHAPTER 3   ATTACKS, THREATS, AND VULNERABILITIES

Common Penetration Testing Tools

1. **Metasploit**: A widely used framework for pen testing that enables the creation, customization, and automation of exploit tests.

2. **Nmap (Network Mapper)**: Primarily a network discovery tool but also used to find open ports, running services, and possible security risks across a network.

3. **Burp Suite Pro**: Known for its web application testing capabilities, it allows testers to detect vulnerabilities in complex applications by manipulating requests and analyzing server responses.

4. **Wireshark**: A packet analyzer used to monitor network traffic and identify potential vulnerabilities by examining how data travels across the network.

Assessing Exploitability and Real-World Risks

Pen testing provides insight into how easily an attacker could exploit certain vulnerabilities. By successfully exploiting these vulnerabilities, security teams can see firsthand the types of data or systems that may be compromised, thus clarifying the actual risk level.

Customized Testing

Pen testing tools can be tailored for specific environments or applications, allowing testers to focus on critical assets and high-value systems. However, given the manual effort involved, pen testing is typically performed periodically rather than continuously.

Reporting and Documentation

Penetration tests culminate in detailed reports that include exploited vulnerabilities, successful attacks, and recommended mitigations. These reports are instrumental for development teams, helping them understand and address root causes.

Configuration and Compliance Management Tools

Configuration management tools ensure that systems adhere to baseline configurations, security policies, and regulatory requirements. By assessing and enforcing these standards, these tools prevent configuration drift, reduce misconfigurations, and maintain security compliance.

Common Configuration and Compliance Tools

1. **Chef InSpec**: A tool for creating compliance policies that define and assess system configurations, enabling automated auditing and adherence to standards.

2. **Microsoft System Center Configuration Manager (SCCM)**: Manages endpoint configurations across networks, ensuring that software updates and security policies are consistently applied.

3. **Puppet and Ansible**: Primarily used for automated system configuration, these tools help enforce standard configurations across servers, improving consistency and reducing security gaps.

CHAPTER 3   ATTACKS, THREATS, AND VULNERABILITIES

Risk Management and Compliance

Configuration tools play a critical role in maintaining compliance with regulations like HIPAA, PCI-DSS, and GDPR, which often mandate strict configuration and patching standards. By detecting deviations from baseline configurations, these tools alert security teams to potential security risks and compliance violations.

Real-Time Monitoring and Reporting

Tools like SCCM and Chef InSpec provide continuous monitoring and reporting capabilities, enabling teams to detect and correct unauthorized changes promptly. This reduces the window of exposure and maintains a more consistent security posture across the environment.

Security Information and Event Management (SIEM) Tools

SIEM tools collect, analyze, and correlate security-related data from across an organization's IT environment, providing a centralized view of security events and potential threats. By combining real-time monitoring with advanced analytics, SIEM tools allow teams to detect anomalies, identify potential attacks, and respond quickly.

Popular SIEM Solutions

1. **Splunk**: Offers extensive data analysis and correlation capabilities, providing comprehensive event logging, reporting, and real-time threat detection.

2. **IBM QRadar**: Known for its advanced correlation rules and analytics, QRadar helps detect complex, multi-step attacks across large environments.

3. **Azure Sentinel**: A cloud-native SIEM from Microsoft that integrates well with cloud workloads and other Microsoft products.

Enhanced Threat Detection

SIEM tools help organizations detect threats that may otherwise go unnoticed, such as insider threats, anomalous behavior, and advanced persistent threats (APTs). By analyzing patterns over time, these tools offer insights into sophisticated attack techniques that may evade other defenses.

Compliance and Forensics

In addition to threat detection, SIEM tools provide valuable auditing capabilities. By archiving logs and security events, they help organizations meet compliance requirements and conduct forensic investigations in the event of a breach.

Reporting and Alerting

SIEM solutions offer customizable alerts and dashboards, allowing security teams to track key metrics, investigate suspicious activities, and provide executive-level reporting on security posture and incidents.

CHAPTER 3   ATTACKS, THREATS, AND VULNERABILITIES

Additional Security Assessment Frameworks

Several frameworks complement the use of tools by providing structured approaches to assessing and enhancing security. Frameworks like the National Institute of Standards and Technology (NIST) Cybersecurity Framework (CSF) and the MITRE ATT&CK® Framework offer guidelines that help organizations standardize their assessment practices and identify coverage gaps in their defenses.

1. **NIST Cybersecurity Framework (CSF)**
   - NIST CSF outlines five core functions (Identify, Protect, Detect, Respond, Recover) that guide organizations in creating and maintaining effective security programs. Using NIST CSF as a baseline helps organizations organize their security efforts and assess their capabilities in a structured manner.

2. **MITRE ATT&CK Framework**
   - MITRE ATT&CK provides a detailed matrix of adversary tactics and techniques based on real-world observations. Security teams use ATT&CK to assess their defensive coverage against specific techniques and tactics used by threat actors, enabling them to tailor their defenses effectively.

3. **CIS Controls**
   - The Center for Internet Security (CIS) provides a prioritized list of security controls designed to help organizations implement effective defenses. The controls cover areas like secure configurations, access management, and malware defenses, offering a checklist for comprehensive security.

Integrating Security Tools into a Cohesive Assessment Strategy

Using a combination of tools, frameworks, and methodologies allows organizations to create a robust and comprehensive security assessment strategy. While individual tools offer significant value, combining their outputs provides a more holistic view of organizational security. For instance, vulnerability scanners can identify weaknesses, penetration testing can validate those weaknesses, and SIEM solutions can monitor for related suspicious activity.

By integrating these tools within a continuous assessment program, organizations can maintain a proactive stance against emerging threats and better protect their assets. Adopting standardized frameworks such as NIST CSF or MITRE ATT&CK further enhances this strategy, allowing organizations to benchmark their security capabilities against best practices and industry standards. Ultimately, combining these resources allows organizations to proactively identify, prioritize, and address vulnerabilities, continuously improving their resilience against cyber threats.

Manual Penetration Testing: Importance and Limitations

While automated scanning tools provide efficient coverage of common vulnerabilities, manual penetration testing brings essential depth and context to security assessments. It leverages human intuition, creativity, and real-world judgment, which are often necessary to uncover complex or nuanced issues that automation might miss. A comprehensive security assessment strategy integrates both automated and manual methods to enhance vulnerability detection and overall security.

CHAPTER 3   ATTACKS, THREATS, AND VULNERABILITIES

Importance of Manual Penetration Testing

1. **Human Expertise**

    - **Why It's Important**: Automated tools rely on pre-programmed rules and patterns, which limits their ability to detect vulnerabilities requiring more nuanced analysis. Human testers, however, can apply creativity and experience to uncover vulnerabilities that may not fit traditional patterns.

    - **Example**: Skilled pen testers can chain multiple low-risk vulnerabilities, creating a high-impact attack pathway (chained exploit). For example, combining a low-risk file disclosure vulnerability with weak file permissions could allow a tester to obtain sensitive information that automated tools might overlook.

2. **Contextual Understanding**

    - **Why It's Important**: Manual testers assess vulnerabilities within the context of the organization's operations, helping prioritize findings based on potential impact. They consider how vulnerabilities might affect critical assets and provide recommendations grounded in the specific business environment.

    - **Example**: A vulnerability on an internal server might be considered low risk in some cases but could have significant consequences if that server connects to critical infrastructure or contains sensitive customer data.

CHAPTER 3   ATTACKS, THREATS, AND VULNERABILITIES

3. **Exploiting Complex Vulnerabilities**

    - **Why It's Important**: Some vulnerabilities, such as logic flaws, race conditions, and authentication bypasses, are complex and difficult for automated tools to detect. These flaws often require critical thinking and creativity to exploit, making human expertise essential.

    - **Example**: A manual tester might identify a logical flaw in a multi-step process, such as a shopping cart system, that allows a user to bypass payment by manipulating request sequences—something that automated tools would likely miss.

4. **Customization**

    - **Why It's Important**: Manual penetration testing can be tailored to an organization's unique risk profile, allowing for a targeted approach that aligns with the organization's threat landscape. This customization enables testing to focus on high-risk areas, such as systems handling sensitive data, critical infrastructure, or specific threat scenarios like insider attacks.

    - **Example**: A pen test could focus on systems that store financial information, testing for complex vulnerabilities specific to those applications, ensuring sensitive data is protected in line with the organization's highest risks.

Limitations of Manual Penetration Testing

1. **Time-Consuming**

    - **Why It's a Limitation**: Manual testing involves careful planning, execution, and analysis, which can extend over days, weeks, or even months. This can hinder the rapid detection and mitigation of widespread vulnerabilities, especially in large-scale environments.

    - **Mitigation**: Organizations can focus manual testing efforts on high-priority systems while using automated tools for continuous scans across the rest of the environment to maintain coverage.

2. **Resource-Intensive**

    - **Why It's a Limitation**: Skilled penetration testers are in high demand and can be costly, making it challenging for some organizations to conduct thorough, regular manual testing. This is especially true in complex environments where expertise and time requirements increase.

    - **Mitigation**: Reserve manual testing for the most critical systems or sensitive areas, leveraging automated tools to scan other systems. This allows organizations to optimize resources while covering the majority of their attack surface.

3. **Limited Coverage**

    - **Why It's a Limitation**: Manual tests are often conducted in specific, high-risk areas rather than across the entire environment. As a result, other areas may not receive the same level of scrutiny, which could leave undetected vulnerabilities.

    - **Mitigation**: Implement a hybrid approach, using automated tools to scan the entire environment routinely and focusing manual testing on critical systems and sensitive applications.

4. **Potential for Human Error**

    - **Why It's a Limitation**: Even experienced testers are prone to errors, such as overlooking certain vulnerabilities due to time constraints or simple oversight. Human error can reduce the comprehensiveness and accuracy of test results.

    - **Mitigation**: Employ peer review and team-based testing processes, where multiple testers verify and analyze each other's findings to improve accuracy and reduce the likelihood of overlooked vulnerabilities.

The Hybrid Approach: Combining Automated and Manual Testing

To maximize vulnerability management, organizations should adopt a hybrid approach, leveraging both automated tools and manual penetration testing. Automated scanning tools are ideal for regular, comprehensive scans that quickly detect known vulnerabilities across large networks.

Manual testing complements this by focusing on high-risk areas, uncovering complex vulnerabilities, and providing contextual insights that only human expertise can offer.

Advantages of the Hybrid Approach

- **Broad Coverage**: Automated tools provide widespread, continuous monitoring, ensuring that the majority of the organization's environment is regularly assessed.

- **Depth of Analysis**: Manual testing allows for an in-depth focus on critical or high-risk assets, detecting vulnerabilities that require human intuition and creativity to uncover.

- **Enhanced Prioritization**: Combining both methods enables organizations to prioritize remediation efforts effectively, addressing both common and complex vulnerabilities based on real-world risk.

- **Improved Security Posture**: This balanced approach ensures that vulnerabilities are not only identified but fully understood, enabling the organization to strengthen defenses based on comprehensive assessments.

In conclusion, combining automated scanning with manual penetration testing provides a well-rounded security assessment, helping organizations detect vulnerabilities with both breadth and depth. This hybrid strategy ultimately strengthens the organization's resilience against cyber threats by ensuring a robust security posture built on comprehensive coverage and real-world contextual analysis.

CHAPTER 4

Network Security

Network security encompasses a variety of strategies, protocols, and best practices designed to protect networks from unauthorized access, misuse, or damage. The rise of interconnected systems has made networks a prime target for cyberattacks. Organizations must therefore implement multilayered security measures to safeguard their network infrastructure and prevent breaches.

Key Objectives

- **Confidentiality**: Ensuring that sensitive information is only accessible to authorized users.

- **Integrity**: Protecting information from unauthorized modification.

- **Availability**: Ensuring that network services are available when needed by legitimate users.

Secure Network Architecture and Design

Network security architecture and design are essential to building resilient and secure systems. This section outlines strategies and methods to enhance network security through segmentation, device placement, and deployment of security technologies.

CHAPTER 4   NETWORK SECURITY

Network Segmentation and Segregation

Network segmentation refers to dividing a network into smaller, manageable subnetworks to enhance security, performance, and management.

Benefits

- **Enhanced Security**: Segmentation limits the spread of threats within a network by isolating potentially compromised areas.

- **Improved Performance**: Reduces congestion and improves traffic flow by localizing traffic within segments.

- **Simplified Management**: Smaller, segmented networks are easier to monitor and manage.

Implementation Strategies

- **Virtual LANs (VLANs)**: Logical separation within a single physical network that groups devices as if they were on different networks.

- **Subnetting**: Dividing a larger network into smaller subnetworks to improve performance and control access.

- **Physical Separation**: Using distinct hardware devices for network segmentation to enforce strict separation.

- **Logical Separation**: Implementing segmentation using software controls like firewalls and access control lists (ACLs).

CHAPTER 4   NETWORK SECURITY

Microsegmentation

Microsegmentation takes network segmentation to a more granular level, often controlling traffic between individual devices or applications within the same network.

- **Software-Defined Networking (SDN):** Allows for dynamic and centralized control over network traffic, enhancing segmentation and security.

- **Policy Enforcement:** Automated, policy-based segmentation that ensures security is maintained at a granular level across the network.

Demilitarized Zones (DMZ)

A **Demilitarized Zone (DMZ)** is a perimeter network that isolates an organization's external-facing services from the internal network. The primary goal is to limit access to critical internal systems and reduce the risk of external threats.

Purpose

- **Isolate External Services:** Public-facing servers such as web, email, and DNS are placed in the DMZ, reducing exposure of internal systems.

Configuration

- **Firewall Rules:** Strict rules govern traffic flow between the DMZ, the internal network, and the internet. Only necessary services are permitted.

- **Placement of Services:** Web servers, DNS servers, and email servers are typically hosted in the DMZ to limit exposure of internal systems to outside threats.

147

CHAPTER 4   NETWORK SECURITY

Network Security Devices

A comprehensive network security strategy involves deploying various security devices to monitor, filter, and control traffic. This section outlines the major security devices used to protect networks.

Firewalls

Firewalls are devices or software applications that monitor and control network traffic based on pre-established security rules.

- **Stateful vs. Stateless Firewalls**
  - **Stateful Firewalls**: Monitor the state of active connections and decide based on the context of the traffic (e.g., tracking TCP handshakes).
  - **Stateless Firewalls**: Filter packets purely based on header information (e.g., source/destination IP, port numbers), without considering the state of the connection.
- **Next-Generation Firewalls (NGFWs)**
  - **Advanced Features**: NGFWs integrate additional capabilities like **intrusion prevention, deep packet inspection**, and **application awareness**.
  - **Use Cases**: NGFWs provide enhanced protection against advanced threats, allow granular policy enforcement, and can manage encrypted traffic.

- **Firewall Rules and Best Practices**
    - **Rule Creation**: Establish precise, least-privilege rules to minimize exposure.
    - **Policy Management**: Regularly review firewall policies, remove outdated rules, and update configurations to maintain optimal security.

Intrusion Detection and Prevention Systems (IDS/IPS)

IDS/IPS are crucial for identifying and responding to suspicious or malicious activity on the network. These can be utilized individually or in tandem with one another to add additional layers of security. It is common to find these as a 2-in-1 combination product.

- **Detection Methods**
    - **Signature-Based**: Matches traffic against known attack signatures, such as specific malware or exploits.
    - **Anomaly-Based**: Detects deviations from established patterns of normal network behavior.
    - **Hybrid Approaches**: Combine signature-based and anomaly-based methods to enhance accuracy and reduce false positives.
- **Deployment Options**
    - **Network-Based IDS/IPS**: Monitors traffic across a network segment, often placed at critical junctions like network perimeters.

- **Host-Based IDS/IPS**: Monitors the activity on individual systems, providing detailed insight into threats targeting specific hosts.
- **Tuning and Maintenance**
  - **Regular Updates**: Keep detection signatures and algorithms up to date to address emerging threats.
  - **False Positive/Negative Management**: Fine-tune detection sensitivity to reduce false alerts while ensuring that real threats are identified.

Proxies

Proxies serve as intermediaries between clients and servers, providing various security and performance benefits.

- **Types of Proxies**
  - **Forward Proxies**: Intermediaries that handle client requests to external servers, often used to enforce content filtering and anonymity.
  - **Reverse Proxies**: Intermediaries for servers, handling requests from clients, typically used for load balancing and securing public-facing services.
  - **Transparent Proxies**: Operate without requiring client-side configuration, often used for content filtering and monitoring without user knowledge.

- **Use Cases**
    - **Caching**: Improve performance by storing frequently accessed content and serving it to users without needing to re-fetch from the original source.
    - **Content Filtering**: Block harmful or inappropriate content, ensuring compliance with corporate policies.
    - **Anonymity**: Hide the client's IP address to protect privacy and obscure internal network structures.

Designing a secure network architecture requires careful consideration of various strategies, devices, and protocols. By utilizing network segmentation, DMZs, and critical security devices like firewalls, IDS/IPS, and proxies, organizations can effectively reduce their attack surface and enhance overall security. Additionally, ongoing tuning, rule management, and adopting advanced technologies like microsegmentation and NGFWs ensure networks remain resilient against evolving threats.

Secure Protocols and VPNs

Secure communication protocols and Virtual Private Networks (VPNs) are essential components of network security. These technologies ensure the confidentiality, integrity, and authentication of data in transit across both internal and external networks.

CHAPTER 4   NETWORK SECURITY

Importance of Secure Communication Protocols

- **Confidentiality**: Both **TLS/SSL (Transport Layer Security/Secure Sockets Layer)** and **SSH (Secure Shell)** encrypt data during transmission, protecting it from interception and eavesdropping.

- **Integrity**: These protocols ensure that data has not been altered or tampered with during transmission, safeguarding against man-in-the-middle attacks.

Implementation Considerations

- **Certificate Management**: For TLS/SSL, proper management of digital certificates is crucial, including the issuance, renewal, and revocation of certificates to maintain secure connections.

- **Key Exchange Mechanisms**: The secure establishment of communication sessions is achieved using key exchange protocols such as **Diffie-Hellman** or **RSA**, ensuring a secure initial handshake.

VPN Types

Virtual Private Networks (VPNs) create secure, encrypted connections over potentially insecure networks like the internet, ensuring secure remote communication.

- **Site-to-Site VPNs**
  - **Purpose**: Connects two or more networks securely over the internet, commonly used to link different office locations or branch networks.

- **Protocols: IPSec (Internet Protocol Security)** and **GRE (Generic Routing Encapsulation)** are commonly used to secure the communication between sites.

- **Remote Access VPNs**
    - **Purpose**: Allows individual users to securely access the corporate network from remote locations, typically from home or while traveling.
    - **Protocols: PPTP (Point-to-Point Tunneling Protocol), L2TP (Layer 2 Tunneling Protocol)**, and **IPSec** are commonly used for remote access connections.

- **SSL VPNs**
    - **Simplified Access**: Offers secure remote access using just a web browser, eliminating the need for specialized VPN client software.
    - **Use Cases**: Ideal for remote access for users on a variety of devices, including mobile phones and tablets.

Advanced Network Security Protocols

To further enhance network security, advanced protocols for authentication, authorization, and accounting (AAA), as well as network access control, are essential.

CHAPTER 4 NETWORK SECURITY

RADIUS and TACACS+

- **RADIUS (Remote Authentication Dial-In User Service)**: Provides centralized authentication, authorization, and accounting for users and devices connecting to a network. Often used in wireless networks and VPNs.

- **TACACS+ (Terminal Access Controller Access-Control System Plus)**: Offers enhanced command-level authorization, making it more suitable for managing administrative access to network devices.

Comparison and Use Cases

- **RADIUS**: Primarily used for controlling access to the network itself (e.g., VPN and wireless authentication).

- **TACACS+**: Preferred for device management due to its ability to provide more granular control over commands and actions executed on network devices.

802.1X

- **Purpose**: 802.1X ensures that only authenticated devices can connect to the network, using credentials like usernames and passwords or certificates before granting network access.

- **Integration with NAC (Network Access Control) Solutions**: When combined with NAC, 802.1X provides dynamic access control, allowing organizations to apply security policies based on the compliance and security status of the connecting devices.

CHAPTER 4   NETWORK SECURITY

Network Address Translation (NAT) and Port Address Translation (PAT)

NAT and **PAT** are methods used to translate internal IP addresses to public IP addresses for communication with external networks. This enhances security and optimizes the use of IP addresses.

Static NAT vs. Dynamic NAT

Differences and Use Cases

- **Static NAT**: Provides a one-to-one mapping between an internal IP address and a public IP address. This is useful for services that require constant, publicly reachable IP addresses (e.g., web servers).

- **Dynamic NAT**: Maps multiple internal IP addresses to a pool of external IP addresses, using available public IP addresses dynamically. This is typically used when the number of devices inside a network is greater than the available external IP addresses.

Security Implications

- **Address Obfuscation**: NAT helps by hiding internal IP addresses from external networks, enhancing security by reducing direct exposure.

- **Resource Allocation with PAT: Port Address Translation (PAT)** extends NAT by allowing multiple internal IP addresses to share a single public IP address, with different port numbers distinguishing the internal devices.

Secure communication protocols like TLS/SSL and SSH, along with robust VPN solutions, ensure that data remains protected when transmitted across networks. Advanced authentication protocols (RADIUS, TACACS+), network access controls like 802.1X, and technologies like NAT and PAT further enhance security by controlling access and managing resources. Implementing these technologies is critical for maintaining a secure and efficient network infrastructure.

Zero Trust Networks

The **Zero Trust Architecture** (ZTA) is a modern security framework that challenges the traditional perimeter-based approach by assuming that no entity, internal or external, can be inherently trusted. This approach requires constant verification and strict access control to maintain security across all network layers.

Zero Trust Architecture

- **Never Trust, Always Verify**: All access requests, whether from inside or outside the network, must be authenticated and authorized. No entity is assumed to be trustworthy.

- **Least Privilege**: Users and devices are granted only the minimum level of access necessary to perform their tasks, reducing the potential impact of a breach.

CHAPTER 4   NETWORK SECURITY

Implementation

- **Identity and Access Management (IAM)**: Centralized control over access rights, ensuring that only authenticated and authorized users and devices gain access to network resources.

- **Continuous Monitoring**: Access is continuously monitored, and verification of users and devices is conducted throughout their sessions to detect anomalies or potential threats.

Securing Wireless Networks: WPA3 and Wireless Security Settings

Wireless networks are critical components of modern IT infrastructure, but they are also frequent targets for cyberattacks. With the proliferation of devices, including IoT (Internet of Things) gadgets, ensuring the security of these networks has become more important than ever. Modern wireless security protocols like **WPA3** (Wi-Fi Protected Access 3) provide enhanced protection compared to previous standards, making them vital for securing contemporary networks.

WPA3 Enhancements

WPA3 is the latest version of the Wi-Fi Protected Access protocol, designed to address the vulnerabilities found in its predecessor, **WPA2**. It introduces several key improvements to enhance security, making it the recommended standard for protecting both home and enterprise wireless networks.

CHAPTER 4   NETWORK SECURITY

Key Differences from WPA2

1. **Stronger Encryption**

    - **WPA3 Enterprise** uses a 192-bit encryption key for enterprise networks, significantly enhancing the security of the encryption process. **WPA3 Personal** uses 128-bit-AES-GCM.

    - This stronger encryption standard protects against brute-force attacks, making it much more difficult for attackers to crack passwords by guessing them repeatedly.

2. **Protection Against Brute-Force Attacks**

    - One of the significant upgrades in WPA3 is the use of **Simultaneous Authentication of Equals (SAE)**, which replaces the **Pre-Shared Key (PSK)** protocol found in WPA2.

    - SAE provides a more secure handshake process that prevents attackers from capturing and analyzing network traffic to perform offline dictionary attacks.

    - Unlike PSK, where attackers can attempt to guess passwords without interacting with the actual network, SAE requires real-time interaction, greatly reducing the feasibility of such attacks.

3. **Forward Secrecy**

    - Forward secrecy is a key feature of WPA3, ensuring that even if encryption keys are compromised in the future, previous communications cannot be decrypted.

CHAPTER 4   NETWORK SECURITY

- This is achieved by generating a unique encryption key for each session, rather than relying on a single key for all data. This way, past sessions remain secure even if current keys are exposed.

Transitioning to WPA3

While the benefits of WPA3 are clear, transitioning from WPA2 requires careful planning and consideration, particularly in environments with a mix of modern and legacy devices.

Best Practices for Transitioning

- **Gradual Rollout**
    - Implementing WPA3 across an organization's network should be done gradually to minimize disruptions. Start by upgrading access points (APs) and routers to support WPA3, and then test the new setup with various devices.
    - This phased approach helps identify compatibility issues early, allowing for troubleshooting before a full deployment.
- **Compatibility with Legacy Devices**
    - Not all devices, especially older ones, may support WPA3 natively. During the transition phase, consider enabling **WPA3/WPA2 mixed mode** on access points.

- This mode allows devices that support WPA3 to use its enhanced security features, while legacy devices can still connect using WPA2. However, this is a temporary solution, as it maintains some vulnerabilities of WPA2.

- **IT Staff Training**
    - As with any new technology, IT staff need to be trained on WPA3 features, potential issues, and troubleshooting techniques. Understanding how SAE works, for instance, can help in resolving connectivity problems with devices that have older wireless adapters.

- **Testing Across Diverse Devices**
    - Given the variety of devices that may connect to the network, from smartphones and laptops to IoT gadgets, comprehensive testing is crucial.
    - Pay special attention to **IoT devices**, as they often have limited update capabilities and may not be compatible with WPA3. In such cases, consider isolating them on a separate, secured network.

Additional Wireless Security Settings

Securing a wireless network goes beyond just implementing WPA3. To maximize protection, consider the following additional settings:

1. **Disabling WPS (Wi-Fi Protected Setup)**
    - Although WPS was designed to simplify device connections, it is prone to brute-force attacks. Disabling WPS helps prevent unauthorized access attempts.

2. **MAC Address Filtering**

    - Implementing MAC address filtering can add an extra layer of security by allowing only pre-approved devices to connect to the network.

    - However, be aware that MAC addresses can be spoofed, so this should be used as a complementary measure rather than a primary defense mechanism.

3. **Network Segmentation**

    - Segmenting the network, especially when dealing with IoT devices, helps reduce the potential attack surface. For instance, place IoT devices on a separate VLAN with restricted access to critical systems.

    - This isolation minimizes the impact if an IoT device is compromised, preventing attackers from easily accessing sensitive data or internal systems.

4. **Regular Firmware Updates**

    - Ensure that all access points, routers, and connected devices are running the latest firmware. Manufacturers frequently release updates to patch vulnerabilities and improve security features.

    - Setting up automatic updates or periodically checking for new firmware can help maintain a secure environment.

5. **Disabling SSID Broadcasting (if feasible)**

    - Hiding the SSID (Service Set Identifier) of your network can make it less visible to casual users or potential attackers.

    - However, this is not foolproof, as determined attackers can still detect hidden networks using specialized tools. It should be used as part of a broader security strategy rather than as a standalone measure.

Conclusion

Transitioning to WPA3 and optimizing wireless security settings are essential steps for safeguarding modern networks. By implementing WPA3, organizations can benefit from stronger encryption, improved protection against attacks, and enhanced overall security. However, the full benefits of WPA3 are only realized when combined with other best practices, such as proper device management, regular updates, and layered security measures. Together, these efforts help create a robust and resilient wireless network, capable of defending against evolving cyber threats.

Securing IoT Devices on Wireless Networks

The rapid adoption of **IoT (Internet of Things)** devices in enterprise environments has introduced new security challenges. These devices often lack robust built-in security, making them attractive targets for attackers seeking entry points into the network. To address this, organizations must implement tailored security measures that account for the unique constraints of IoT devices.

Unique Challenges

1. **Limited Processing Power**

    - Many IoT devices have minimal processing capabilities, which restricts their ability to use strong encryption methods or complex security protocols. This limitation can make them vulnerable to attacks if not properly secured.

2. **Weak Default Security**

    - IoT devices are often shipped with **default configurations** that include weak, hardcoded passwords and minimal security measures. These settings are rarely updated by users, leaving devices vulnerable to common attacks, such as brute-force login attempts.

Solutions

1. **Network Segmentation**

    - By isolating IoT devices on a separate **VLAN (Virtual Local Area Network)** or **subnet**, organizations can limit the risk of lateral movement within the network. If an IoT device is compromised, this segmentation prevents attackers from easily accessing critical systems or data.

2. **Device Management**

    - Securely configuring IoT devices and ensuring they are regularly updated is vital. Use strong authentication methods like **digital certificates** or **secure onboarding processes** to verify and manage devices on the network. This approach helps maintain the integrity and security of the connected devices.

3. **Secure Firmware Updates**

    - IoT devices often suffer from outdated firmware, leaving them exposed to known vulnerabilities. Supporting **secure firmware updates**, which are signed and verified, helps protect against malicious updates and ensures devices remain patched against security flaws.

4. **Zero Trust Architecture**

    - Implementing a **Zero Trust** model, where every device must continuously authenticate and validate its identity, enhances security by reducing the trust placed on any single device. This approach is particularly beneficial for networks with a diverse array of IoT devices.

Wireless Attacks

Wireless networks are susceptible to a variety of attacks due to their open nature and reliance on radio signals. Understanding these threats and implementing effective countermeasures is crucial to maintaining a secure network.

CHAPTER 4   NETWORK SECURITY

1. Evil Twin Attacks

How They Work

- In an **Evil Twin** attack, an attacker creates a rogue access point that mimics the SSID and credentials of a legitimate network. When unsuspecting users connect to this fake access point, the attacker can intercept and monitor their traffic, capturing sensitive information like login credentials and personal data.

Countermeasures

- **Wireless Intrusion Detection Systems (WIDS)**
    - Deploying WIDS can help detect rogue access points by continuously monitoring the wireless environment and identifying unauthorized devices.
- **User Education**
    - Educate users to recognize suspicious networks, avoid connecting to unknown or unsecured Wi-Fi, and verify the legitimacy of networks, especially in public areas.

2. Jamming Attacks

Types

- **Frequency Jamming**
    - Attackers broadcast disruptive signals on the same frequency as the target network, creating interference that prevents legitimate communication.

165

- **Protocol Jamming**
    - This method exploits weaknesses in wireless protocols by manipulating timing or sending incorrect signals, causing disruptions in network operations.

Mitigation Strategies

- **Spectrum Analysis**
    - Using spectrum analyzers helps identify the frequencies under attack. Network administrators can then adjust the wireless settings to operate on a less congested or jammed frequency.
- **Redundant Communication Paths**
    - Setting up multiple communication channels or frequencies can mitigate jamming attacks by providing alternative routes for data transmission, ensuring continued connectivity.

3. Deauthentication Attacks

How They Operate

- In **Deauthentication attacks**, attackers send fake deauthentication frames to disconnect devices from a wireless network. This can lead to a **Denial-of-Service (DoS)** attack or force users to reconnect, potentially to a rogue network set up by the attacker.

Countermeasures

- **WPA3's SAE**
  - The use of **Simultaneous Authentication of Equals (SAE)** in WPA3 helps prevent deauthentication attacks by employing mutual authentication and stronger encryption.
- **Monitoring for Abnormal Disconnection Patterns**
  - Network monitoring tools can detect unusual disconnection patterns, which may indicate an ongoing deauthentication attack, allowing administrators to respond quickly.

Additional Considerations

Securing wireless networks requires a combination of technical defenses and strong management practices to ensure resilience against threats.

Network Monitoring and Management

1. **Simple Network Management Protocol (SNMP)**
   - SNMP enables administrators to monitor network devices in real time, helping detect issues like unauthorized access or unusual traffic patterns.
2. **NetFlow**
   - Using protocols like **NetFlow** helps in analyzing traffic patterns, identifying potential bottlenecks, and troubleshooting issues by providing detailed insights into network performance.

3. **SIEM Integration**
   - Integrating wireless network logs with **Security Information and Event Management (SIEM)** systems provides a centralized view of network activity. This integration enables real-time alerts and comprehensive analysis of potential threats.

Redundancy and Fault Tolerance

1. **Redundant Network Paths**
   - Implementing multiple pathways for data transmission ensures that even if one link fails, communication can continue through an alternative path, improving overall reliability.

2. **Load Balancing**
   - Distributing traffic across multiple devices or servers prevents bottlenecks and enhances performance by ensuring no single device is overwhelmed with traffic.

3. **Failover Mechanisms**
   - Automatic failover systems switch to backup resources when a failure occurs, minimizing downtime and maintaining service continuity.

CHAPTER 4   NETWORK SECURITY

Emerging Network Threats

1. **5G Networks**

    - The introduction of **5G** has brought increased speeds and lower latency but also introduced new risks due to its distributed architecture and a massive increase in connected devices. Ensuring strong security measures for 5G deployments is crucial.

2. **SD-WAN Vulnerabilities**

    - While **Software-defined WAN (SD-WAN)** offers flexible and efficient network management, its reliance on software and cloud infrastructure can introduce vulnerabilities. Secure configurations and continuous monitoring are essential to protect SD-WAN deployments from potential threats.

Conclusion

Wireless networks face sophisticated threats such as **Evil Twin**, **jamming**, and **deauthentication** attacks. Addressing these threats requires a blend of technical countermeasures, such as **WIDS**, **spectrum analysis**, and **WPA3**, alongside strong user education and monitoring practices. Furthermore, with the rise of **5G** and **SD-WAN**, staying aware of emerging vulnerabilities and implementing proactive security measures will be key to maintaining robust wireless network security. By addressing the unique challenges of IoT devices and employing a **Zero Trust** approach, organizations can significantly enhance their overall security posture and resilience against evolving cyber threats.

CHAPTER 5

Identity and Access Management

Chapter 5 focuses on the critical domain of Identity and Access Management (IAM), a cornerstone of modern cybersecurity practices. In today's digital landscape, ensuring that only authorized individuals have access to the right resources at the right time is essential for maintaining security and reducing the risk of unauthorized access. This chapter will introduce you to the key concepts, tools, and techniques necessary to effectively manage identities, control access, and enforce security policies across systems and networks. From understanding authentication methods to implementing robust access control mechanisms, this chapter is designed to provide a comprehensive foundation in IAM.

Aligned with CompTIA Security+ standards, Chapter 5 will guide you through the various elements of identity management, such as multi-factor authentication (MFA), single sign-on (SSO), and the principles of least privilege. You'll learn how to implement secure authentication protocols, enforce access control policies, and manage user identities throughout their life cycle. By mastering these concepts, you'll be able to protect sensitive information, ensure regulatory compliance, and reduce the risk of insider threats or privilege escalation attacks.

As you work through the material in this chapter, you'll gain the skills necessary to design and maintain secure identity and access management systems, an essential component of any organization's cybersecurity strategy. With a strong understanding of IAM, you will not only enhance your Security+ exam preparation but also improve your ability to protect systems from unauthorized access, ensuring the security and integrity of critical data and resources.

Authentication Factors: Single Sign-On, Multi-factor Authentication

Authentication is one of the cornerstones of Identity and Access Management (IAM) and serves as the foundation for secure access control in any organization. In Chapter 5, we explore the various forms of authentication, focusing on how modern enterprises implement secure access to sensitive resources. The chapter delves into single sign-on (SSO), multi-factor authentication (MFA), and the numerous authentication methods available today. Understanding the strengths, limitations, and proper usage of these methods is critical for both IT professionals and organizations looking to enhance security while ensuring usability.

Single Sign-On (SSO)

Single Sign-On (SSO) is an authentication method that allows users to log in once and gain access to multiple applications or systems without being prompted to log in again for each one. SSO is especially beneficial in environments where users need to access various resources frequently, such as cloud services, on-premises applications, and remote systems.

- **Example**: Microsoft's Azure Active Directory (Azure AD) provides SSO for Office 365 and other enterprise applications.

- **Pros**

  - **Convenience**: Users can access multiple systems with just one login, reducing the number of credentials they must remember.

  - **Streamlined User Experience**: SSO improves productivity by reducing the need to log in repeatedly, thus minimizing friction in workflows.

  - **Centralized Management**: Administrators have centralized control over user access, enabling more straightforward policy enforcement and deprovisioning.

- **Cons**

  - **Single Point of Failure**: If the SSO system fails or is compromised, users could lose access to all associated systems.

  - **Complexity**: Implementing SSO can be complex in environments with legacy applications or diverse authentication systems.

Multi-factor Authentication (MFA)

Multi-Factor Authentication (MFA) is an authentication method that requires two or more verification factors to confirm a user's identity. The three common factors are something the user knows (like a password), something the user has (like a smart card), and something the user is (biometric data).

- **Example**: Google's 2-Step Verification uses a password (something you know) and a code sent to your mobile device (something you have).

- **Pros**
  - **Enhanced Security**: By requiring multiple factors, MFA greatly reduces the likelihood of unauthorized access due to compromised credentials.
  - **Flexibility**: MFA can combine various methods, making it adaptable to different use cases and environments.
- **Cons**
  - **User Friction**: Adding more authentication steps can create a cumbersome user experience, especially if the process is not streamlined.
  - **Cost and Complexity**: Deploying MFA across an organization requires additional infrastructure and management overhead, such as mobile device support or biometric systems.

Biometric Authentication

Biometrics involves identifying users based on unique physical characteristics. This method is increasingly used due to its ability to provide high-security authentication without the need for passwords or physical tokens. These are commonly referred to as "Something you Are" in regard to an access control, as these have to do with you as an individual.

- **Types of Biometrics**
  - **Fingerprint Scanning**: Analyzes the unique patterns of ridges and valleys on a finger.
  - **Facial Recognition**: Uses facial geometry, such as the distance between eyes and the shape of cheekbones, to verify identity.

CHAPTER 5   IDENTITY AND ACCESS MANAGEMENT

- **Iris Scanning**: Maps the complex patterns in the colored part of the eye, offering very high accuracy.
- **Voice Recognition**: Identifies individuals based on the unique characteristics of their voice.

- **Pros**
  - **High Security**: Biometrics are difficult to replicate, making them highly secure compared to traditional methods like passwords.
  - **Convenience**: Users don't need to remember anything or carry physical items, simplifying the login process.
- **Cons**
  - **Privacy Concerns**: Storing biometric data raises significant privacy issues, as it can be stolen or misused if not properly protected.
  - **False Positives/Negatives**: Biometric systems may misidentify users, leading to either access denial or unauthorized access.

Smart Cards

Smart cards are physical devices that contain an embedded chip, storing cryptographic keys and other authentication data. They are commonly used in combination with a PIN for two-factor authentication. In authentication, these are referred to as "Something you Have," as you must physically have this on your person, whether it is physical or digital.

- **Example**: Many organizations use smart cards for secure building access or to authenticate to a corporate network.

- **Pros**
  - **Two-Factor Authentication:** Combining the physical smart card with a PIN enhances security by requiring both something you have and something you know.
  - **Secure Data Storage:** The smart card's embedded chip securely stores encryption keys and credentials, minimizing the risk of data theft.
- **Cons**
  - **Cost and Infrastructure:** Organizations need to invest in smart card readers and management systems, which can be expensive to deploy and maintain.
  - **Risk of Theft or Loss:** If a smart card is lost or stolen, unauthorized individuals could use it unless it's protected by a secondary measure like a PIN.

Token-Based Authentication

Tokens are physical or software-based devices that generate one-time passwords (OTPs) for authentication. These passwords are typically time-sensitive and only valid for a short period. In authentication, these are referred to as "Something you Have," as you must physically have this on your person, whether it is physical or digital.

- **Types of Tokens**
  - **Hardware Tokens:** Devices like RSA SecurID generate OTPs independent of the user's device.
  - **Software Tokens:** Applications like Google Authenticator generate OTPs on mobile devices, providing a convenient alternative to hardware tokens.

- **Pros**

  - **Dynamic Authentication**: OTPs are time-based or event-based, making it extremely difficult for attackers to replicate or predict valid credentials.

  - **Wide Application**: Tokens are versatile and can be used for various authentication scenarios, such as VPN access, secure websites, or corporate networks.

- **Cons**

  - **Hardware Tokens**: These can be lost, damaged, or stolen, and replacing them can be a logistical challenge for organizations.

  - **Software Tokens**: If the user's device is compromised, attackers could gain access to OTPs, making security reliant on the integrity of the device itself.

Password Authentication

Although passwords are the most common authentication method, they are also one of the least secure due to their susceptibility to various attacks, such as brute force or phishing. However, they remain an integral part of most authentication systems. Within this scope, this is known as "Something you Know," as a password is created by the end user and is to be remembered for their personal verification.

- **Pros**

  - **Simplicity**: Passwords are easy to implement and use, making them accessible for all users.

- **Cons**
    - **Vulnerability**: Weak or reused passwords are often compromised in data breaches, and sophisticated attacks can crack even complex passwords over time.
    - **User Management**: Users must regularly update their passwords, leading to friction and the potential for poor password management practices.

Certificate-Based Authentication

Certificate-based authentication uses digital certificates issued by a trusted authority to verify a user's identity. This method is often used in environments that require high levels of security, such as government agencies or financial institutions. These also fall to the "Something you Have" category, as you must be able to present them whether physically or electronically.

- **Example**: Public Key Infrastructure (PKI) systems use digital certificates to authenticate users and devices.
- **Pros**
    - **High Security**: Digital certificates are difficult to forge, and the use of public/private key pairs ensures strong encryption and authentication.
    - **Automation**: Certificates can be used for automated authentication, eliminating the need for manual password entry.

- **Cons**
    - **Complexity**: Setting up and maintaining a PKI infrastructure is complex and resource-intensive.
    - **Expiration Management**: Certificates have expiration dates and must be renewed regularly, requiring diligent management.

Introduction to Federated Identity and OAuth

Federated identity systems allow users to authenticate across multiple organizations or services using a single set of credentials. OAuth is a widely used framework for this, enabling users to grant third-party services access to their resources without sharing their credentials.

- **Example**: OAuth allows users to log into third-party websites using their Google or Facebook credentials.
- **Pros**
    - **Convenience**: Users only need to remember one set of credentials to access multiple systems.
    - **Security**: OAuth allows secure delegation of access without exposing the user's credentials to the third-party service.
- **Cons**
    - **Third-Party Dependence**: If the identity provider is compromised, it could result in access being granted to unauthorized users across multiple services.

Through a combination of traditional and modern authentication methods, organizations can build a layered security approach that minimizes risk while balancing usability. Chapter 5 covers not just the technical aspects of authentication but also the strategic decisions necessary to implement a secure and effective IAM system. By understanding the advantages, challenges, and ideal use cases for each method, readers will gain a comprehensive view of authentication's critical role in cybersecurity.

Federated Authentication Expanded

Federated Authentication is a critical component of modern identity and access management (IAM) systems, allowing users to access multiple services across different organizations or domains without needing to create separate login credentials for each one. It streamlines access control while maintaining strong security protocols, particularly in environments where users interact with numerous independent systems. Two of the most widely used frameworks in federated authentication are **Security Assertion Markup Language (SAML)** and **OAuth**. Each framework has its strengths, use cases, and operational intricacies, making them indispensable tools in both enterprise and consumer-facing environments.

Security Assertion Markup Language (SAML)

An XML-based framework designed to enable Single Sign-On (SSO) across different domains by exchanging authentication and authorization data between an **Identity Provider (IdP)** and a **Service Provider (SP)**. In a federated system, SAML allows users to authenticate with a central authority (the IdP) and then access various services (SPs) without needing to re-authenticate. This process is facilitated through "assertions," which carry the necessary information to verify the user's identity and permissions.

CHAPTER 5   IDENTITY AND ACCESS MANAGEMENT

- **Purpose and Function**
  - SAML serves as a bridge between the Identity Provider (like an enterprise's central directory) and multiple Service Providers (such as web apps or cloud services), enabling seamless SSO across various applications.
- **Use Cases**
  - **Web-Based Applications:** SAML is commonly used to provide SSO for web-based applications, reducing the need for users to manage multiple sets of credentials for different services. For instance, users logging into a corporate network can access internal apps, CRM platforms, and email systems without needing to log in separately for each.
  - **Enterprise Environments:** Large organizations benefit greatly from SAML by integrating numerous internal and third-party applications, simplifying access control and reducing IT overhead. Centralized authentication allows organizations to implement and monitor strong security policies across a wide array of services.
- **Advantages**
  - **Improved User Experience:** SAML enhances the user experience by eliminating the need for multiple logins and reducing the frustration associated with managing numerous usernames and passwords.

- **Enhanced Security**: By centralizing authentication and delegating it to a trusted Identity Provider, SAML enables consistent enforcement of security policies, including multi-factor authentication (MFA), password strength rules, and session management.

- **Scalability**: SAML is highly scalable and can be implemented across a wide range of applications and services, making it an ideal solution for organizations that utilize multiple cloud or web-based platforms.

- **Compliance**: Centralized logging and auditing capabilities through SAML assist in meeting regulatory and compliance requirements by providing detailed visibility into user access and authentication events.

- **Challenges**

  - **Complex Implementation**: SAML can be complicated to implement, especially in legacy systems or environments where service providers lack standardized support for SSO.

  - **Latency**: Depending on the complexity of the systems involved, SAML authentication can introduce latency, which may affect user experience in environments requiring rapid authentication.

CHAPTER 5   IDENTITY AND ACCESS MANAGEMENT

OAuth

Another popular framework that operates differently from SAML. While SAML focuses on authentication (verifying who the user is), **OAuth** is primarily concerned with **authorization**—providing third-party applications limited access to a user's data without revealing the user's password. OAuth is a token-based authorization framework that allows services to interact with each other securely on behalf of a user, particularly in environments that require interaction between systems and APIs.

- **Purpose and Function**
  - OAuth allows users to grant third-party applications access to specific resources (like files, profiles, or settings) without exposing their passwords. It uses access tokens to delegate authority, enabling more granular control over what third-party applications can access.

- **Use Cases**
  - **Social Media Integration**: A common OAuth use case is social media login and authorization. For example, users can allow third-party applications (like a photo-sharing app) to post to their Facebook or Twitter account without sharing their login credentials with the app itself. Instead, the app receives an access token that grants it specific, limited permissions.
  - **API Access**: Developers use OAuth extensively to secure API endpoints. Applications like mobile apps, microservices, and websites can authenticate

to an API without needing to handle or store user credentials directly. OAuth enables API access while ensuring user credentials remain secure.

- **Advantages**

    - **Granular Access Control**: OAuth provides highly granular access control by issuing tokens that are scoped for specific actions or resources. For instance, an app might be allowed to read a user's email but not send messages or manage contacts.

    - **User Privacy**: OAuth improves privacy by allowing users to grant third-party services access to only the specific data they choose, without revealing their full set of credentials. This minimizes the risk of unauthorized data access or misuse.

    - **Widespread Adoption**: OAuth is widely adopted across industries, making it a trusted solution for third-party authentication and authorization. Platforms like Google, Facebook, and GitHub extensively use OAuth for secure access delegation.

- **Challenges**

    - **Token Management**: OAuth relies on tokens, and managing these tokens (e.g., expiration, revocation, refresh) can be complex, especially in large-scale environments. Compromised tokens can also lead to unauthorized access.

    - **User Confusion**: The user consent process (granting access to third-party apps) can be confusing for nontechnical users.

Misunderstanding the scopes of permission granted to third-party apps can lead to accidental exposure of sensitive data.

- **Phishing and Token Theft**: If attackers gain access to OAuth tokens, they can potentially access sensitive resources without needing the user's credentials. Thus, securing the token itself is crucial.

Federated Identity and Beyond

SAML and OAuth represent two different approaches to federated authentication—one focusing on user authentication (SAML) and the other on service authorization (OAuth). However, they can also complement each other in hybrid environments where secure access to multiple services is required while maintaining tight control over permissions and data sharing.

Beyond SAML and OAuth, there are additional standards and protocols that enhance federated identity management, such as

- **OpenID Connect (OIDC)**: Built on top of OAuth 2.0, OIDC adds an identity layer to OAuth, enabling clients to verify the user's identity and obtain basic profile information. OIDC is widely used for Single Sign-On, especially in mobile and web applications.

- **WS-Federation**: A protocol similar to SAML, WS-Federation allows different security realms to federate user identities and access resources across organizational boundaries. It is often used in conjunction with Microsoft Active Directory Federation Services (ADFS) in enterprise environments.

- **Kerberos**: Although Kerberos is more of an authentication protocol than a federated identity solution, it plays an essential role in environments like Windows domains, where it provides mutual authentication between a user and a service through ticket-granting mechanisms.

Federated authentication models continue to evolve, enabling secure access across complex ecosystems of applications, services, and organizations. Understanding the roles, use cases, and advantages of SAML and OAuth equips cybersecurity professionals with the knowledge necessary to build robust, scalable, and secure identity solutions.

Access Control Models: DAC, MAC, RBAC, ABAC

The Security+ exam emphasizes the understanding of various **Access Control Models**, each with distinct mechanisms to control how resources are accessed. These models define how permissions are assigned and enforced in different environments, balancing security needs with usability and scalability. Key models to focus on are **Discretionary Access Control (DAC)**, **Mandatory Access Control (MAC)**, **Role-Based Access Control (RBAC)**, and **Attribute-Based Access Control (ABAC)**. Each has its pros and cons, and choosing the right one depends on the organization's structure, security needs, and operational requirements.

Discretionary Access Control (DAC)

A flexible access control model where the **resource owner** has the authority to grant or revoke access to their resources. Access permissions are generally based on user identities or groups, meaning that a resource owner (such as a file owner) can determine who else has access.

- **Definition and Function**
  - DAC enables resource owners (like a user who creates a file or database) to manage who can access, modify, or delete their resources. Access rights are often assigned through **Access Control Lists (ACLs)**, which specify the permissions granted to individual users or groups.
- **Use Cases**
  - **Personal File Sharing**: Common in environments like file-sharing systems or local workstations where resource ownership is clear, and there is minimal need for strict access control.
  - **Small Teams**: DAC is often used in smaller, less formal teams where resource ownership and control are straightforward.
- **Advantages**
  - **Flexibility**: Resource owners can quickly modify permissions, granting or revoking access as needed. This flexibility makes DAC well-suited for environments where users frequently share data.
  - **Ease of Implementation**: DAC is easy to implement in systems with straightforward resource ownership and small-scale environments, such as personal or departmental file storage.
  - **User Empowerment**: Resource owners have direct control over access to their data, which can be useful in dynamic or creative environments.

- **Challenges**
  - **Security Risks**: DAC is prone to security weaknesses, as resource owners may not always follow strict access policies, resulting in improper permissions that could expose sensitive data to unauthorized users.
  - **Scalability Issues**: In large organizations, managing access permissions manually becomes cumbersome and error-prone, increasing the risk of access control misconfigurations.
  - **Lack of Central Control**: Because resource owners control access, centralized enforcement of security policies is limited, making compliance with security standards difficult.

Mandatory Access Control (MAC)

A highly secure access control model where access to resources is determined by a **central authority** based on predefined security labels. In this model, users cannot change access permissions themselves, and the system enforces access controls based on **classification levels** (e.g., **Top Secret, Secret, Confidential**). MAC is typically used in environments requiring the highest level of security, such as military or government organizations.

- **Definition and Function**
  - In MAC, access decisions are based on **security labels** assigned to both users and resources. Access is only granted when a user's security clearance level matches or exceeds the classification of the resource they are trying to access.

- **Use Cases**
  - **Government and Military Environments**: MAC is commonly used in environments where the protection of sensitive data is paramount. Security labels ensure that only authorized personnel can access classified information.
  - **Highly Regulated Industries**: Organizations like healthcare, finance, or law enforcement may use MAC to control access to critical data, such as patient records or financial information, ensuring compliance with strict regulations.
- **Advantages**
  - **High Security**: MAC offers a high level of security by enforcing strict access controls that cannot be overridden by individual users. It ensures that access is based on predefined rules, reducing the likelihood of human error.
  - **Centralized Management**: Access rights are managed by a central authority, ensuring that security policies are applied consistently across the organization.
  - **Compliance**: MAC helps organizations meet regulatory requirements by ensuring that sensitive data is only accessible to users with the appropriate security clearance.

- **Challenges**
  - **Complexity**: Implementing MAC can be resource-intensive and requires careful planning. Security labels must be carefully assigned and maintained, and the system can become complex in large organizations.
  - **Limited Flexibility**: The rigid nature of MAC makes it unsuitable for environments where access needs frequently change, as modifying security labels or classifications can be slow and cumbersome.
  - **User Frustration**: Since users cannot modify their own permissions, MAC can lead to frustration in environments where users require more dynamic access to resources.

Role-Based Access Control (RBAC)

An access control model where permissions are assigned based on **roles**, which correspond to specific job functions or responsibilities within an organization. Rather than assigning permissions to individual users, access is granted based on the user's role, making this model highly scalable and easy to manage.

- **Definition and Function**
  - In RBAC, users are assigned one or more roles, and each role is associated with a set of permissions. These roles are typically aligned with job functions (e.g., administrator, manager, HR staff) and define what resources users in those roles can access.

CHAPTER 5   IDENTITY AND ACCESS MANAGEMENT

- **Implementation**
  - **Role Definition**: Define roles based on job functions and responsibilities. Each role should have the appropriate level of access to perform necessary tasks without being over-privileged.
  - **Hierarchy**: Some RBAC implementations establish role hierarchies, where higher-level roles inherit permissions from lower-level roles, streamlining permission assignment.
  - **Separation of Duties (SoD)**: Implement SoD to ensure that conflicting duties are not assigned to the same role, preventing fraud or errors. For example, the same person should not have access to both approve and process financial transactions.
- **Use Cases**
  - **Enterprise Environments**: RBAC is widely used in large organizations to manage permissions across departments or functions, reducing the administrative burden of managing individual user accounts.
  - **Cloud Services**: RBAC is often used in cloud environments to control access to various services based on predefined roles, ensuring that users only have access to the resources they need.
- **Advantages**
  - **Scalability**: RBAC is highly scalable, allowing organizations to easily manage access for large numbers of users by assigning them to roles rather than managing individual permissions.

- **Consistency**: By aligning access rights with job functions, RBAC ensures that users have appropriate access based on their roles, reducing the risk of unauthorized access or privilege escalation.

- **Auditability**: RBAC provides a clear structure for auditing permissions, making it easier to track and review access rights for compliance purposes.

- **Challenges**
  - **Role Explosion**: In large organizations, the number of roles can grow rapidly, leading to **role explosion**, where managing and maintaining too many roles becomes complex and burdensome.
  - **Role Conflicts**: Ensuring that roles do not overlap or conflict requires careful planning and regular review. Poorly defined roles can lead to over-privileged users or gaps in access control.
  - **Initial Setup**: The initial definition of roles and the assignment of users can be time-consuming, especially in organizations with complex job structures or responsibilities.

Attribute-Based Access Control (ABAC)

Is a dynamic and highly flexible access control model that grants access based on multiple attributes, such as **user characteristics** (e.g., job title, department), **resource attributes** (e.g., classification level), and **environmental conditions** (e.g., time of day, location). ABAC evaluates these attributes in real time to determine whether access should be granted.

CHAPTER 5   IDENTITY AND ACCESS MANAGEMENT

- **Definition and Function**

  - ABAC uses **attributes** to define access control policies. These attributes can pertain to the user, the resource, the environment, or the action being requested. Access is granted when the evaluated attributes match the predefined policy for accessing a resource.

- **Use Cases**

  - **Complex Environments**: ABAC is ideal for environments that require fine-grained access control, such as cloud services or cross-organizational collaborations, where access needs are based on a wide range of factors.

  - **Cloud and Remote Work**: In cloud environments, where resources and users are highly distributed, ABAC can account for various dynamic factors like user location, device type, and network status to provide contextual access control.

- **Advantages**

  - **Granularity**: ABAC provides more precise control over access by considering multiple attributes, allowing for finely tuned access policies that adapt to specific scenarios.

  - **Flexibility**: ABAC adapts to dynamic environments where access needs frequently change, such as in cloud computing or in organizations with complex user structures.

193

- **Contextual Access**: ABAC allows for real-time evaluation of attributes to make context-aware access decisions, such as granting access only during certain hours or from specific geographic locations.
- **Challenges**
  - **Complexity in Policy Management**: ABAC requires a robust policy framework to manage the numerous attributes and conditions that influence access decisions. The complexity can make it difficult to implement and maintain, especially in large organizations.
  - **Performance Overheads**: Evaluating attributes in real time can introduce performance overheads, particularly in environments with high traffic or complex attribute-based policies.
  - **Implementation Costs**: ABAC's flexibility comes at the cost of increased complexity and resource requirements, which can lead to higher implementation and operational costs.

Understanding the key differences between **DAC**, **MAC**, **RBAC**, and **ABAC** is crucial for addressing security needs and regulatory requirements in any organization. Each model has its strengths, with **DAC** offering flexibility, **MAC** ensuring strict security, **RBAC** providing scalability, and **ABAC** enabling dynamic, fine-grained access control. The choice of an access control model depends on the organization's security posture, size, and operational environment.

Identity Management and the Cloud

Identity Providers and Cloud Integration are critical in ensuring secure and seamless access to cloud services. With the growing reliance on cloud computing, managing user identities effectively becomes a key component of maintaining security, user convenience, and operational efficiency.

Cloud-Based Identity Management

Cloud-based identity management centralizes control over user identities in cloud environments, allowing organizations to manage authentication and access across multiple cloud services efficiently.

Advantages

- **Scalability**: Cloud identity management easily scales to accommodate the growth of users and services, ensuring that organizations can adapt to changing requirements without substantial infrastructure changes.

- **Centralized Management**: By providing a single point of control for managing user identities, this approach simplifies identity management and enhances security by maintaining consistent policies across services.

- **Cost Efficiency**: Cloud-based solutions reduce the need for expensive on-premises infrastructure and related maintenance, making them a cost-effective option for managing identities.

CHAPTER 5   IDENTITY AND ACCESS MANAGEMENT

Single Sign-On (SSO) Across Cloud Services

Single Sign-On (SSO) allows users to authenticate once and gain access to multiple cloud services without the need to log in to each service individually.

Benefits

- **User Convenience**: SSO improves the user experience by minimizing the number of logins required, reducing password fatigue, and streamlining access to various services.

- **Security**: With fewer credentials to manage, SSO reduces the risk of password reuse and related security issues, enhancing the overall security posture.

Implementation Considerations

- **Integration**: Seamless integration between SSO solutions and existing cloud services is essential for optimal functionality.

- **Security Protocols**: Using industry-standard security protocols such as **SAML (Security Assertion Markup Language)** and **OAuth** ensures secure authentication and authorization across services.

Examples of Cloud-Based Identity Providers

1. **Microsoft Azure Active Directory (Azure AD)**
   - **Overview**: Azure AD is a cloud-based identity and access management service that offers SSO, multi-factor authentication (MFA), and conditional access for Microsoft Azure and other cloud applications.

- **Key Features**: Integration with Microsoft 365, support for federated identity, and advanced threat protection capabilities.

2. **Google Identity Platform**
   - **Overview**: A suite of identity management tools that supports SSO, OAuth 2.0, and OpenID Connect, allowing developers to integrate secure authentication into their applications.
   - **Key Features**: Easy integration with Google services, support for multiple authentication methods, and comprehensive developer resources.

Federated Identity Management (FIM)

Federated Identity Management (FIM) enables multiple organizations or systems to share and trust user identity information, allowing users to access resources across different domains seamlessly. FIM supports SSO across various organizations by allowing a user authenticated in one domain to access resources in another without the need to re-authenticate.

Standards Supporting FIM

- **Security Assertion Markup Language (SAML)**: A widely used protocol for implementing SSO across domains by enabling secure exchange of authentication and authorization data.
- **OpenID Connect**: Built on OAuth 2.0, OpenID Connect allows clients to verify user identities based on authentication performed by an authorization server, facilitating SSO.

- **OAuth**: Primarily an authorization protocol, OAuth can also support federated identity by allowing users to grant access to resources hosted across different systems.

Benefits of FIM

- **Seamless User Experience**: FIM enhances the user experience by allowing users to access resources across multiple domains without re-authenticating.

- **Improved Security**: Centralized authentication reduces the risks associated with password reuse and ensures consistent enforcement of security policies across systems.

- **Efficiency**: FIM simplifies the administrative process of managing user identities across different systems by leveraging a federated approach.

Challenges of FIM

- **Trust Management**: Establishing trust between federated systems or organizations requires careful management, including the use of digital certificates and secure communication.

- **Complexity**: Managing FIM can be challenging, particularly in environments where multiple identity providers and service providers are involved.

- **Compliance**: Ensuring that federated identity solutions comply with regulations such as GDPR or HIPAA can be complex, especially when sharing user data across borders.

In conclusion, **Identity Management in the Cloud** is essential for modern organizations, offering a combination of centralized control, security, scalability, and user convenience. **SSO** and **FIM** are integral components, ensuring that users can securely and easily access services across cloud platforms and organizational boundaries. However, the implementation of these systems requires careful planning, especially when considering trust management, integration, and compliance with regulations.

Public Key Infrastructure (PKI) and Certificate Management

Public Key Infrastructure (PKI) forms the backbone of secure digital communications by enabling encryption, authentication, and data integrity. Certificates, issued as part of PKI, are crucial for establishing trust in online interactions. Below is an overview of key certificate types and their respective functions, use cases, and benefits.

SSL/TLS Certificates

SSL (Secure Sockets Layer) and TLS (Transport Layer Security) certificates are used to secure communication between clients (e.g., web browsers) and servers by encrypting the data exchanged and ensuring the integrity and authenticity of the connection.

Types of SSL/TLS Certificates

- **Domain Validation (DV)**
    - **Overview**: DV certificates confirm that the applicant controls the domain but do not validate the organization behind it.

- **Use Cases:** Suitable for personal websites or low-risk applications where encryption is required, but a high level of trust isn't essential.

- **Organization Validation (OV)**
  - **Overview:** OV certificates verify both domain control and the organization's identity, offering greater legitimacy than DV certificates.
  - **Use Cases:** Commonly used by business websites and e-commerce platforms where the legitimacy of the organization needs to be assured to users.

- **Extended Validation (EV)**
  - **Overview:** EV certificates provide the highest level of trust by thoroughly verifying the organization's legal, operational, and physical existence. These certificates display a green address bar or similar visual indicators to users.
  - **Use Cases:** Ideal for banking, financial institutions, and high-profile websites that handle sensitive user information and require maximum user trust.

Importance of SSL/TLS

- **Data Encryption:** Protects sensitive information (e.g., passwords, payment details) by encrypting data in transit, preventing interception by attackers.

- **Authentication:** Ensures that users are connecting to the legitimate server, safeguarding against phishing or man-in-the-middle attacks.

- **SEO Benefits:** Search engines like Google prioritize websites with HTTPS, boosting their rankings and enhancing user trust.

Code Signing Certificates

Code signing certificates allow developers to digitally sign their software or applications, ensuring the software's authenticity and integrity. This helps users verify that the software has not been altered since it was signed.

Importance

- **Authenticity**: Confirms that the software originates from a trusted developer or organization, reducing the risk of users downloading malicious or counterfeit applications.

- **Integrity**: Guarantees that the code has not been modified or corrupted after it was signed, providing assurance that the software remains secure and unaltered.

Use Cases

- **Software Developers**: Developers use code signing certificates to sign software, drivers, scripts, and apps, ensuring their products are trusted by end users and reducing security warnings during installation.

- **Enterprises**: Organizations often require code-signed applications to meet compliance and security standards within their IT environments.

Email Encryption Certificates

Email encryption certificates, such as **S/MIME (Secure/Multipurpose Internet Mail Extensions)** certificates, are used to secure email communications by encrypting the email content and digitally signing messages to verify the sender's identity.

Importance

- **Confidentiality**: Encrypts email content, ensuring sensitive information (e.g., financial data, intellectual property) is protected from interception by unauthorized parties.

- **Authentication**: Digitally signs emails to verify the sender's identity, enabling recipients to trust the authenticity of the message.

- **Integrity**: Ensures that the content of the email has not been altered during transmission, maintaining the integrity of the information.

Use Cases

- **Corporate Communications**: Businesses use email encryption to secure sensitive information exchanged between employees, clients, or third parties, protecting data from unauthorized access.

- **Regulated Industries**: Sectors like healthcare, finance, and government often require email encryption to comply with strict privacy and data protection regulations (e.g., HIPAA, GDPR) that mandate the safeguarding of sensitive communications.

These certificate types are essential to the secure functioning of modern digital infrastructure. From encrypting web traffic with SSL/TLS certificates to verifying the authenticity of software with code signing certificates, and securing email communications with S/MIME, certificate management plays a critical role in upholding trust and security across digital platforms. PKI ensures that these certificates are issued, managed, and validated in a manner that fosters secure and reliable interactions in various use cases.

Certificate Revocation

Certificate revocation is a crucial process within Public Key Infrastructure (PKI) that ensures the integrity and security of digital communications by invalidating compromised or untrustworthy certificates before their expiration date. This is achieved primarily through two mechanisms: the Certificate Revocation List (CRL) and the Online Certificate Status Protocol (OCSP). A CRL is a periodically updated list of revoked certificates maintained by a Certificate Authority (CA), but it can introduce latency and performance issues, especially with large lists. Conversely, OCSP offers real-time certificate status checking, providing immediate validation and reducing overhead. However, implementing OCSP stapling can further enhance performance and privacy, albeit with compatibility challenges.

The importance of effective certificate revocation lies not only in bolstering security against potential attacks but also in ensuring compliance with industry regulations. By actively managing certificate life cycles and revocation processes, organizations can maintain a robust security posture and protect sensitive data from unauthorized access.

Certificate Revocation List (CRL)

A Certificate Revocation List (CRL) is an essential tool for managing certificate validity, maintained by a Certificate Authority (CA). It is a publicly accessible list that includes certificates that have been revoked before their scheduled expiration dates. Regularly updated, CRLs allow users and systems to verify whether a specific certificate is still trustworthy.

Challenges with CRLs

- **Latency**: Since CRLs are updated at set intervals, there may be a time lag between the revocation of a certificate and its update in the CRL. This delay can expose users to security risks if they unknowingly rely on a revoked certificate.

- **Performance Impact**: Downloading and processing large CRLs can strain system resources and slow down operations, especially in environments with numerous certificates. This can affect user experience and system efficiency.

Online Certificate Status Protocol (OCSP)

This provides a real-time method for checking the revocation status of a certificate. Instead of downloading an entire CRL, clients can send a query to an OCSP server to verify if a certificate is still valid.

Advantages of OCSP

- **Real-Time Validation**: OCSP delivers immediate feedback on the status of a certificate, significantly reducing the risk of utilizing a revoked certificate. This timely information is crucial for applications that rely on secure communications.

- **Reduced Overhead**: OCSP requests are generally smaller and quicker to process than downloading a full CRL, leading to improved performance. This efficiency is especially beneficial in high-traffic environments where speed is critical.

Challenges with OCSP

- **OCSP Stapling**: To enhance efficiency and privacy, OCSP responses can be "stapled" to the SSL/TLS handshake, eliminating the need for separate OCSP requests. However, not all servers or clients support this feature, which can limit its effectiveness.

Importance of Certificate Revocation

- **Security**: Revocation is vital for preventing the use of compromised or otherwise untrustworthy certificates, safeguarding users and systems against potential threats. By ensuring that revoked certificates cannot be used, organizations can maintain the integrity of their digital communications.

- **Compliance**: Many industries are governed by strict regulations that mandate effective certificate management practices, including timely revocation. Adhering to these standards is crucial for maintaining compliance and avoiding potential legal repercussions.

Common Identity and Access Management Solutions

Identity and Access Management (IAM) solutions are critical for organizations seeking to safeguard their digital environments by effectively managing user identities, access rights, and security policies. These tools enable organizations to streamline user authentication and authorization processes, ensuring that only authorized individuals can access sensitive information and resources. Major IAM solutions, such as Microsoft Active Directory (AD), Okta, and Ping Identity, offer features like Single Sign-On (SSO), Multi-Factor Authentication (MFA), and federated identity management, allowing organizations to implement robust security measures while enhancing user experience.

By leveraging these solutions, organizations can not only meet compliance requirements and reduce security risks but also adapt to evolving IT environments, including hybrid and cloud-based infrastructures. Ultimately, effective IAM is essential for protecting organizational assets and maintaining trust in digital interactions.

CHAPTER 5   IDENTITY AND ACCESS MANAGEMENT

Identity and Access Management (IAM) Tools

IAM tools play a crucial role in managing user identities, access rights, and security protocols within organizations. Here are some key IAM solutions widely used in various sectors:

1. **Microsoft Active Directory (AD)**
   - **Overview**: Active Directory is a centralized directory service primarily used in Windows environments for managing user identities, authentication, and resource access.
   - **Key Features**
     - **User and Group Management**: Administrators can efficiently manage user accounts, define user roles, and assign permissions to ensure appropriate access to resources. This is critical for maintaining security and operational efficiency.
     - **Group Policy Management**: Provides a framework for enforcing security policies, software installations, and configurations across the organization. This feature ensures compliance with organizational standards.
     - **Integration**: Active Directory integrates seamlessly with other Microsoft services, such as Exchange, SharePoint, and Teams, offering a cohesive user experience.

CHAPTER 5   IDENTITY AND ACCESS MANAGEMENT

- **Use Cases**
  - **Enterprise Environments**: AD is widely utilized in large enterprises to manage a high volume of users and resources effectively, streamlining administration and improving security.
  - **Hybrid Cloud Deployments**: Organizations with both on-premises and cloud infrastructures can leverage AD to manage identities and access consistently across both environments.

2. **Okta**
   - **Overview**: Okta is a robust cloud-based IAM solution that provides identity management, Single Sign-On (SSO), and Multi-Factor Authentication (MFA) tailored for organizations of all sizes.
   - **Key Features**
     - **Single Sign-On (SSO)**: Allows users to log in once and gain access to multiple applications, simplifying the user experience and enhancing security by reducing the number of credentials to manage.
     - **Multi-Factor Authentication (MFA)**: Supports various authentication methods, including SMS, email, push notifications, and biometric options, thereby strengthening security against unauthorized access.
     - **Integration**: Okta offers broad integration capabilities with various cloud applications, making it an excellent choice for organizations with diverse IT environments.

CHAPTER 5   IDENTITY AND ACCESS MANAGEMENT

- **Use Cases**
  - **Cloud-First Organizations**: Ideal for companies embracing a cloud-first approach, Okta provides a flexible, scalable IAM solution that adapts to growing needs.
  - **Remote Workforces**: Okta's cloud-based architecture facilitates secure access for distributed teams, enabling remote work without compromising security.

3. **Ping Identity**
   - **Overview**: Ping Identity delivers an enterprise-grade IAM solution focused on identity federation, Single Sign-On (SSO), and adaptive authentication.
   - **Key Features**
     - **Federated Identity Management**: Enables organizations to manage user identities across multiple domains, facilitating seamless access to resources regardless of their location or provider.
     - **Adaptive Authentication**: Uses risk-based analysis to dynamically adjust the level of authentication required for each user, effectively balancing security measures with user experience.
     - **API Security**: Protects application programming interfaces (APIs) by enforcing stringent authentication and access control policies, ensuring that sensitive data remains accessible only to authorized users.

- **Use Cases**
  - **Large Enterprises**: Designed for organizations with complex IT infrastructures, including those with multiple identity providers and service providers, ensuring comprehensive identity management.
  - **Regulated Industries**: With its advanced security features, Ping Identity is particularly suited for sectors like finance, healthcare, and government, where compliance with regulations is critical.

CHAPTER 6

Endpoint and Application Security

In an era where remote work is increasingly prevalent and the digital landscape is continuously expanding, the need for robust endpoint and application security has never been more critical. Endpoints—ranging from laptops and desktops to smartphones and tablets—serve as gateways to an organization's sensitive data and resources. As these devices become more integrated into everyday business operations, they also present attractive targets for cybercriminals. This chapter explores the multifaceted domain of endpoint and application security, highlighting the strategies and technologies essential for protecting these critical components of the IT ecosystem.

We will review all aspects of endpoint security, examining the tools and techniques that can help safeguard devices from a wide range of threats, including malware, ransomware, and phishing attacks. Additionally, we will address the importance of securing applications, as vulnerabilities within software can lead to significant security breaches. By understanding the interplay between endpoint and application security, organizations can develop a comprehensive security posture that mitigates risks and enhances overall resilience against cyber threats.

Throughout this chapter, we will provide insights into best practices, emerging trends, and essential tools that can empower organizations to implement effective security measures. Whether you are an IT

CHAPTER 6   ENDPOINT AND APPLICATION SECURITY

professional, a security practitioner, or a business leader, this chapter will equip you with the knowledge necessary to navigate the complexities of endpoint and application security in today's dynamic threat landscape.

Endpoint Security

Endpoint security is all about protecting end-user devices—like laptops, desktops, tablets, and smartphones—from the ever-evolving landscape of cybersecurity threats. As remote work becomes more common and mobile devices are increasingly integrated into our daily lives, the need for robust endpoint security has never been more important. This part of your security strategy focuses on ensuring that each device accessing your network is secure, reducing the risk of data breaches and unauthorized access.

We'll explore the essential components and strategies that make up effective endpoint security, highlighting the importance of not just detection but also proactive measures to defend against a variety of threats.

Overview of Endpoint Security

Endpoint security is crucial in today's cybersecurity landscape, focusing on protecting endpoints—devices such as laptops, desktops, smartphones, and tablets—from various threats. With more devices connecting to networks, the risk of cyberattacks targeting these endpoints has increased significantly. Cybercriminals employ tactics like malware, ransomware, and phishing attacks to exploit vulnerabilities, often leading to serious data breaches that can compromise sensitive information and harm an organization's reputation.

To effectively safeguard endpoints, organizations must implement a comprehensive set of security measures designed to prevent unauthorized access, detect threats, and respond to incidents as they occur. This includes using technologies like endpoint detection and response (EDR), antivirus software, firewalls, and intrusion prevention systems. Additionally, many modern endpoint security solutions leverage machine learning and behavioral analysis to identify unusual activity that could signal a developing threat.

However, endpoint security isn't just about technology; it requires a proactive approach that encompasses continuous monitoring, regular updates, and educating users about security best practices. By establishing clear security policies and fostering a culture of security awareness, organizations can empower employees to recognize potential threats and adhere to safe computing practices.

As remote work and mobile access become increasingly common, endpoint security evolves from a simple IT concern to a vital aspect of organizational resilience. By investing in robust endpoint security measures, organizations can not only protect their data but also ensure business continuity in a complex digital environment. A strong endpoint security strategy allows employees to work securely and efficiently while safeguarding the organization's digital assets.

Key Components of Endpoint Security

1. **Antivirus and Anti-malware Solutions**

    - These tools help detect, quarantine, and remove malicious software from endpoints. Regular updates and scans are essential to ensure protection against the latest threats.

2. **Endpoint Detection and Response (EDR)**

    - EDR solutions provide real-time monitoring and analysis of endpoint activities to detect suspicious behavior. They can respond to threats by isolating infected devices or removing malicious files.

3. **Data Loss Prevention (DLP)**
   - DLP technologies help prevent sensitive data from being transmitted outside the organization or accessed by unauthorized users. They monitor data in use, in transit, and at rest to enforce data protection policies.

4. **Encryption**
   - Encrypting data stored on endpoints and during transmission ensures that even if devices are compromised, sensitive information remains protected from unauthorized access.

5. **Access Control**
   - Implementing strict access controls, such as role-based access and least privilege principles, limits user access to only the resources necessary for their roles, reducing the risk of unauthorized access.

6. **Patch Management**
   - Regularly updating and patching software and operating systems is crucial for addressing known vulnerabilities that could be exploited by attackers. Automated patch management solutions can simplify this process.

Best Practices for Endpoint Security

- **User Education and Awareness**
  - Training employees to recognize phishing attempts, suspicious downloads, and other security threats is vital for reducing the risk of human error.

- **Multi-factor Authentication (MFA)**
    - Implementing MFA adds an additional layer of security, requiring users to provide multiple forms of identification before accessing endpoints and sensitive data.
- **Remote Wipe Capabilities**
    - Organizations should have the ability to remotely wipe data from lost or stolen devices to protect sensitive information from falling into the wrong hands.
- **Regular Security Audits**
    - Conducting routine audits and assessments of endpoint security measures helps identify vulnerabilities and areas for improvement.

In summary, endpoint security is essential in today's digital landscape, where cyber threats continue to evolve and target end-user devices. By implementing comprehensive security measures and best practices, organizations can effectively mitigate risks and protect their valuable assets.

Antivirus (AV) and Antimalware Solutions

In today's threat landscape, antivirus (AV) and antimalware solutions are essential components of endpoint security. Acting as the first line of defense, these tools safeguard systems from a wide array of malware, including viruses, worms, and trojans. They play a pivotal role in protecting sensitive data and maintaining the integrity of organizational systems. However, not all antivirus solutions are created equal. Understanding the differences between traditional and next-generation options is crucial for selecting the right tool for your organization.

CHAPTER 6   ENDPOINT AND APPLICATION SECURITY

Traditional antivirus software primarily relies on signature-based detection, scanning files and applications for known malware patterns. While this method can effectively neutralize well-documented threats, it often struggles against newer, polymorphic malware that modifies its code to avoid detection. Moreover, the resource-intensive nature of these scans can impact system performance, making them less suitable for high-demand environments.

Next-generation antivirus (NGAV) solutions, on the other hand, leverage advanced technologies such as machine learning, behavioral analysis, and threat intelligence. These tools are designed to identify and block a broader range of threats, including zero-day exploits that traditional AV may miss. By analyzing the behavior of applications in real time, NGAV solutions provide a more proactive defense against evolving cyber threats.

Choosing the right antivirus solution requires a thorough understanding of your organization's unique needs, potential threats, and operational environment. By weighing the benefits and limitations of both traditional and next-generation options, you can ensure that your endpoint security strategy is robust and capable of adapting to the ever-changing landscape of cyber threats.

Traditional Antivirus

Traditional antivirus (AV) software has long been a staple in the cybersecurity landscape, providing foundational protection for endpoints. It operates primarily by scanning files and applications for known malware signatures—specific patterns or code snippets associated with identified threats. This signature-based detection method enables traditional AV solutions to identify and neutralize a range of common malware, including viruses, worms, and trojans, before they can inflict damage.

While traditional antivirus software serves as a critical first line of defense, it has its limitations. The reliance on known signatures means that it may struggle against new, emerging, or polymorphic malware that alters its code to evade detection. Additionally, the resource-intensive nature of regular scanning can impact system performance, leading to slower response times and diminished user experience.

Despite these challenges, traditional AV remains relevant as a baseline protection layer, particularly in environments with less sophisticated threat vectors. Organizations often employ traditional AV alongside more advanced solutions, creating a multi-layered security approach that leverages the strengths of each technology. By combining traditional antivirus with next-generation defenses, organizations can enhance their overall security posture, ensuring that they are better equipped to face the ever-evolving landscape of cyber threats.

Limitations: While effective for many well-known viruses, signature-based detection has its weaknesses. New, polymorphic, or sophisticated malware can easily bypass traditional methods, and the resource-intensive scans can impact system performance.

Use Cases: Despite its limitations, traditional antivirus still serves as a valuable baseline protection layer, especially in environments that deal with less sophisticated threat vectors.

Next-Generation Antivirus (NGAV)

Next-generation antivirus (NGAV) solutions represent a significant advancement over traditional antivirus (AV) systems, providing a more robust defense against a wide array of cyber threats. Unlike their predecessors, which primarily relied on signature-based detection methods to identify known malware, NGAV utilizes advanced technologies such as machine learning, behavioral analysis, and threat intelligence to enhance its detection capabilities. This shift enables NGAV to identify and block not only traditional malware but also sophisticated attacks, including zero-day exploits, which often evade conventional detection methods.

CHAPTER 6 ENDPOINT AND APPLICATION SECURITY

The power of NGAV lies in its ability to analyze the behavior of files and applications in real time. By monitoring for unusual activities—such as unexpected file modifications or unauthorized network communications—NGAV can detect potential threats even if they do not match existing signatures. This proactive approach significantly increases the chances of thwarting advanced malware, ransomware, and fileless attacks before they can inflict damage.

Moreover, NGAV solutions often integrate with broader security ecosystems, allowing organizations to create a layered security strategy. This integration enhances threat intelligence sharing and facilitates rapid incident response. However, deploying NGAV solutions may require more complex configuration and tuning to minimize false positives, ensuring that legitimate activities are not mistakenly flagged as threats. Ultimately, NGAV serves as a vital component of modern endpoint security, empowering organizations to defend against the evolving landscape of cyber threats effectively.

Benefits

- **Behavioral Analysis**: NGAV monitors the behavior of files and applications in real time, allowing it to spot malicious activity even if the software doesn't match any known signature.

- **Advanced Threat Detection**: This capability enables NGAV to identify sophisticated attacks like fileless malware and ransomware, which are designed to evade traditional security measures.

Considerations: While NGAV solutions offer powerful protection, they may require more complex configuration to minimize false positives. Many of these tools also integrate well with broader security ecosystems, enhancing your overall security posture.

Key Vendors: Some of the leading vendors in this space include CrowdStrike Falcon, SentinelOne, and Cylance.

Endpoint Detection and Response (EDR)

As cyber threats continue to evolve in complexity and persistence, organizations increasingly require advanced tools that can respond effectively. Endpoint Detection and Response (EDR) solutions play a crucial role in this landscape by offering continuous monitoring, detection, and response capabilities specifically designed for endpoints. These solutions focus on identifying and mitigating threats in real time, enabling organizations to stay ahead of potential attacks. EDR tools provide detailed insights into endpoint activities, allowing security teams to detect suspicious behaviors or indicators of compromise (IOCs) that may indicate a security breach.

The importance of EDR cannot be overstated. It allows organizations to detect sophisticated and persistent threats that traditional security measures might overlook. By capturing detailed logs and event data, EDR solutions facilitate thorough post-incident analysis, helping organizations understand the attack vectors used by adversaries and improve future defenses. Furthermore, EDR tools often integrate seamlessly with Security Operations Centers (SOCs), enhancing overall incident response effectiveness and streamlining the workflow for security teams. However, deploying EDR solutions comes with its challenges; they can be complex to manage and may require significant computing resources on endpoints, potentially impacting system performance. Nonetheless, the advanced threat detection and rapid response capabilities they provide make EDR a vital component of modern endpoint security strategies.

Key Features

- **Real-Time Monitoring:** EDR solutions continuously monitor endpoint activities, looking for suspicious behavior or indicators of compromise (IOCs).

- **Incident Response**: They equip organizations with the tools necessary to isolate infected endpoints, investigate incidents, and remediate threats quickly.

- **Forensic Capabilities**: EDR tools capture detailed logs and event data, which aids in post-incident analysis and helps organizations understand the nature of attacks.

Benefits

- **Advanced Threat Detection**: EDR excels at identifying sophisticated threats that might slip past traditional defenses.

- **Rapid Response**: With EDR, organizations can swiftly contain and mitigate threats, reducing the potential damage of a successful attack.

- **Integration with Security Operations Centers (SOC)**: EDR tools often work seamlessly with SOC platforms, enhancing incident response effectiveness.

Limitations

- **Complexity**: Deploying and managing EDR solutions can be complicated, requiring specialized skills and resources.

- **Resource Intensive**: These solutions can be demanding on computing resources, which may affect endpoint performance.

Key Vendors: Examples include Carbon Black, Microsoft Defender for Endpoint, and Symantec Endpoint Protection.

Application Hardening

Application hardening is a crucial part of endpoint security that aims to secure applications against potential exploitation. This process involves implementing various security measures to reduce vulnerabilities within applications, making them less attractive targets for attackers. By focusing on hardening, organizations can significantly decrease the risk of security breaches and data leaks. This includes updating applications to the latest versions, applying patches, and configuring security settings to limit exposure to known vulnerabilities.

Additionally, organizations can employ techniques such as input validation, output encoding, and the principle of least privilege to further bolster the security posture of their applications. With cyber threats continually evolving, a robust application hardening strategy becomes indispensable in safeguarding sensitive data and maintaining the overall integrity of the organization's IT environment.

Application Whitelisting

Application whitelisting is a proactive security strategy that allows only pre-approved (or "whitelisted") applications to execute on a system, effectively blocking all unauthorized software by default. This approach significantly enhances security by minimizing the risk of running malicious applications, which can compromise sensitive data or disrupt operations. Whitelisting serves as a gatekeeper, ensuring that only trusted applications, which have undergone thorough vetting, can be installed and run.

This not only prevents the execution of known malware but also helps maintain compliance with regulatory standards that may require strict control over software installations. However, implementing application whitelisting requires careful policy development, including criteria for approving applications and an efficient process for updating the whitelist as organizational needs evolve. While this approach can enhance security significantly, it is essential to balance it with user needs, as overly restrictive whitelisting can lead to frustrations and potentially encourage unauthorized software installations, known as shadow IT.

Importance

- **Preventing Unauthorized Software Execution**: By restricting the applications that can run, organizations can effectively prevent the execution of malicious or unauthorized software.

- **Compliance**: Many regulatory frameworks require application whitelisting as part of their security standards.

- **Attack Surface Reduction**: Whitelisting significantly reduces the number of potential applications that attackers can exploit.

Implementation

- **Policy Development**: Organizations need to establish clear policies for application approval, specifying criteria for adding or removing applications from the whitelist.

- **Integration with Endpoint Security Solutions**: Many EDR and NGAV solutions incorporate application whitelisting features, simplifying deployment.

- **Maintenance**: Keeping the whitelist up to date is essential and requires regular reviews to reflect the organization's current needs.

Challenges

- **User Frustration**: Users may find it frustrating to be unable to install or run new software without prior approval, which can lead to shadow IT practices.

- **Maintenance Overhead**: Regularly updating the whitelist can be resource-intensive, particularly in dynamic environments.

Secure System Design

Secure system design is foundational for safeguarding an organization's infrastructure against cyber threats. By prioritizing security from the initial design phase, organizations can substantially mitigate risks and vulnerabilities that might otherwise be exploited by malicious actors. This section delves into several critical elements of secure system design, including configuration baselines, system hardening, secure coding practices, and patch management. Each of these components plays a vital role in fortifying an organization's security posture and ensuring compliance with industry standards and regulations.

Configuration Baselines

Configuration baselines are integral to maintaining a secure computing environment. They consist of a set of predefined and standardized settings that organizations apply to systems and applications to ensure they are securely configured from the outset. Establishing these baselines allows organizations to create a uniform security standard that reduces the likelihood of misconfigurations, which are often targeted by attackers.

CHAPTER 6   ENDPOINT AND APPLICATION SECURITY

Purpose of Configuration Baselines

- **Consistency**: Configuration baselines promote uniformity across all systems within an organization. This consistency is crucial because variations in configurations can lead to security gaps that cybercriminals might exploit. By having a well-documented baseline, IT teams can ensure that every system adheres to the same security standards, thus minimizing risks.

- **Security**: A configuration baseline establishes a known secure state that systems should consistently adhere to. When systems are configured according to these standards, they are inherently less vulnerable to attacks. This proactive approach helps to identify and mitigate potential weaknesses before they can be exploited.

- **Compliance**: Many compliance frameworks, such as PCI-DSS, HIPAA, and NIST, require organizations to define and adhere to configuration baselines as part of their security protocols. Failing to maintain these baselines can lead to compliance violations, resulting in penalties or legal repercussions.

Examples of Configuration Baselines

- **CIS Benchmarks**: The Center for Internet Security (CIS) provides comprehensive configuration guidelines for various operating systems, applications, and cloud services. These benchmarks offer organizations a clear roadmap to follow in securing their systems effectively.

- **Vendor Guidelines**: Software and hardware vendors often provide their own best practices and baseline configurations to secure their products. These guidelines help organizations understand the specific configurations that maximize the security of their technologies.

Implementing configuration baselines not only enhances security but also streamlines the process of managing and auditing systems. Regular audits against these baselines can help organizations quickly identify deviations that could indicate security issues, ensuring that they can respond promptly and effectively.

System Hardening

System hardening is a vital process that involves applying a series of security measures designed to reduce vulnerabilities and bolster defenses against potential attacks. This goes beyond simply applying secure configurations; it encompasses a comprehensive approach to fortifying systems and applications.

Techniques for System Hardening

- **Disabling Unnecessary Services**: By reducing the number of active services on a system, organizations can minimize the attack surface. Each service running on a system can introduce vulnerabilities, so disabling those that are not essential to business operations is a crucial step in hardening.

- **Patch Management**: Regularly updating systems with the latest security patches is critical for protecting against known vulnerabilities. Organizations must stay informed about available patches and updates and implement them as part of their routine maintenance.

- **Implementing Security Controls**: Additional security measures, such as host-based firewalls, intrusion detection systems (IDS), and application whitelisting, can further protect systems from threats. These controls act as an extra layer of defense, helping to monitor and restrict potentially harmful activities.

Hardening Guides

- **CIS Benchmarks**: These comprehensive guides provide step-by-step instructions for hardening various systems and applications. They offer detailed recommendations on configurations and security settings that align with best practices.

- **Vendor-Specific Guidelines**: Many vendors produce their own hardening recommendations tailored to their products. Utilizing these guidelines ensures that organizations are maximizing the security features provided by their technology partners.

Challenges in System Hardening

- **Balancing Security and Usability**: One of the primary challenges organizations face is finding the right balance between security and usability. Over-hardening a system can led to reduced functionality or user dissatisfaction, as legitimate users may encounter difficulties accessing necessary resources.

- **Maintenance**: Continuous monitoring and regular updates are necessary to maintain a hardened state, especially as new vulnerabilities emerge. Organizations must be vigilant and proactive in assessing their systems to ensure they remain secure over time.

Through diligent system hardening practices, organizations can significantly reduce their exposure to threats and create a robust security posture that can withstand attacks.

Securing Applications

Securing applications is a critical component of an organization's overall cybersecurity strategy. As applications often serve as the interface through which users interact with data, they can be prime targets for attackers. Implementing secure coding practices and leveraging frameworks like the OWASP Top Ten can significantly reduce vulnerabilities and protect applications throughout their life cycle.

Secure Coding Practices

- **Overview**: Secure coding practices involve writing software code in a way that minimizes vulnerabilities and ensures that security considerations are integrated throughout the development process.

- **Key Practices**

  - **Input Validation**: It is essential to validate all user inputs to prevent injection attacks, such as SQL injection or cross-site scripting (XSS). Proper validation ensures that inputs conform to expected formats, reducing the risk of malicious data being processed.

  - **Error Handling**: Implementing effective error handling mechanisms helps prevent sensitive information from being exposed through error messages. Developers should ensure that error messages do not reveal any details about the underlying system or application logic.

- **Code Review**: Conducting regular code reviews helps identify and rectify security issues early in the development process. Peer reviews can uncover vulnerabilities that a single developer might overlook and foster a culture of security awareness.

- **Secure API Development**: When developing APIs, it's crucial to incorporate robust authentication and authorization measures. Proper data validation and sanitation are also key to ensuring that APIs do not become a vector for attacks.

OWASP Top Ten

The **OWASP Top Ten** is a renowned list compiled by the Open Web Application Security Project (OWASP) that outlines the most critical web application security risks. Familiarity with these risks is essential for developers and security professionals alike.

- **Common Vulnerabilities**
  - **Injection:** This includes attacks where untrusted data is sent to an interpreter as part of a command or query, potentially compromising the application.
  - **Broken Authentication:** Flaws in authentication mechanisms that allow attackers to compromise user credentials or session tokens can lead to unauthorized access.
  - **Sensitive Data Exposure:** Failure to adequately protect sensitive data—such as encryption keys, passwords, or personal information—leaves applications vulnerable to data breaches.

- **Cross-Site Scripting (XSS)**: This occurs when malicious scripts are injected into web pages viewed by other users, which can lead to data theft or session hijacking.

- **Mitigation Strategies**

  - **Use Prepared Statements**: To guard against SQL injection, developers should utilize prepared statements and parameterized queries. This approach ensures that user inputs are treated as data rather than executable commands.

  - **Implement Strong Authentication**: Utilizing multi-factor authentication and secure session management can prevent broken authentication attacks. These measures add additional layers of security that protect user accounts from unauthorized access.

  - **Encrypt Sensitive Data**: To safeguard sensitive information, it's essential to encrypt data both in transit and at rest. This ensures that even if data is intercepted or accessed, it remains unreadable without the appropriate decryption keys.

By prioritizing secure coding practices and being mindful of the OWASP Top Ten risks, organizations can significantly reduce their vulnerability to application-layer attacks.

CHAPTER 6   ENDPOINT AND APPLICATION SECURITY

Patch Management

Patch management is a crucial process that involves systematically identifying, acquiring, testing, and deploying patches to address vulnerabilities in software and systems. Effective patch management helps organizations stay ahead of threats by ensuring that their systems are equipped with the latest security updates.

Patch Management Life Cycle

The patch management life cycle is a structured approach that organizations can follow to ensure timely and efficient patching of their systems.

- **Stages**
  - **Discovery**: The first step in the patch management life cycle is identifying which systems and applications require patches. Automated tools can assist in scanning for missing updates and ensuring that organizations maintain visibility into their patch status.
  - **Assessment**: Once patches are identified, organizations must evaluate their importance and potential impact. Prioritizing patches that address critical vulnerabilities is essential to mitigate risk effectively.
  - **Testing**: Before deploying patches to production systems, organizations should test them in a controlled environment. This helps ensure that patches do not introduce new issues or conflicts with existing configurations, minimizing the risk of downtime or functionality loss.

- **Deployment**: After successful testing, patches can be rolled out to production systems. Automated deployment tools are often used to ensure consistency and reduce the risk of human error during this phase.

- **Validation**: Finally, organizations must verify that patches have been successfully applied and that systems are functioning as expected post-patching. Regular checks can help identify any issues that arise from the patching process.

Automated vs. Manual Patching

Patching is a critical aspect of cybersecurity, as it ensures that software and systems remain secure against known vulnerabilities. Organizations can choose between two primary approaches to patch management: automated patching and manual patching. Each method has its strengths and weaknesses, and the choice between them often depends on the organization's specific needs, resources, and risk tolerance.

Automated Patching

Automated patching refers to the use of software tools to automatically download, test, and install patches across systems without significant human intervention. This approach can significantly streamline the patch management process, making it more efficient and consistent.

Advantages

- **Efficiency**: Automated patching systems can deploy patches to numerous machines simultaneously, significantly reducing the time required for the patching process. This efficiency is especially beneficial for large organizations with extensive IT infrastructures.

- **Consistency**: Automation ensures that patches are applied uniformly across all relevant systems, minimizing the chances of human error that could lead to inconsistent patch applications. This consistency is crucial for maintaining a strong security posture.

- **Timeliness**: Automated patching allows organizations to respond quickly to newly discovered vulnerabilities. Automated systems can be set to download and install patches as soon as they are available, reducing the window of exposure to potential threats.

- **Reduced Labor**: By minimizing the need for manual intervention, automated patching frees up IT personnel to focus on more strategic initiatives. This can lead to better resource allocation and improved overall productivity.

Challenges

- **Testing Limitations**: Automated systems may not fully test the impact of patches on all applications and configurations. This could lead to potential compatibility issues, where a patch might cause existing applications to malfunction or behave unexpectedly.

- **Lack of Control**: Organizations may feel a loss of control over the patching process, as automated systems operate based on predefined rules. This can result in patches being applied without adequate consideration of their specific implications for the organization's unique environment.

- **False Sense of Security**: Relying solely on automation can lead to complacency. Organizations may assume that automated processes guarantee security, overlooking the need for ongoing monitoring and manual intervention when necessary.

Manual Patching

Manual patching involves IT personnel manually reviewing, downloading, testing, and installing patches on systems. This hands-on approach allows for a more tailored patch management process.

Advantages

- **Thorough Testing**: Manual patching enables organizations to conduct thorough testing of patches before deployment. IT staff can assess potential impacts on specific applications and configurations, allowing for a more controlled and careful implementation.

- **Greater Control**: Organizations maintain greater control over the patching process, enabling them to prioritize critical patches based on their specific risk assessments and operational needs. This tailored approach can lead to better alignment with business objectives.

- **Personalized Documentation**: Manual patching allows IT teams to document the reasoning behind patch decisions more comprehensively. This documentation can help in audits, compliance reviews, and future troubleshooting efforts.

Challenges

- **Time-Consuming**: Manual patching is labor-intensive and can take considerable time, particularly in larger organizations with numerous systems to manage. This can lead to delays in addressing vulnerabilities, potentially increasing the risk of exploitation.

- **Inconsistencies**: With multiple personnel involved in the patching process, there is a risk of inconsistencies in how patches are applied. Variations in judgment and interpretation of priority can lead to unequal levels of security across systems.

- **Human Error**: Manual processes are prone to human errors, such as overlooking critical patches, failing to apply patches consistently, or misconfiguring settings during installation. Such errors can create vulnerabilities that attackers may exploit.

Best Practices and Considerations

To maximize the benefits and mitigate the challenges of both automated and manual patching approaches, organizations can adopt best practices that enhance their overall patch management strategy:

- **Hybrid Approach**: Many organizations benefit from a hybrid patching strategy that combines automation for routine patching with manual oversight for critical applications and systems. This allows for the efficiency of automation while retaining control and thorough testing where necessary.

- **Regular Audits**: Conduct regular audits of the patch management process to identify gaps, assess compliance, and evaluate the effectiveness of both automated and manual approaches. This can help organizations refine their strategies over time.

- **Risk-Based Prioritization**: Establish a risk-based approach to prioritize which patches to deploy first based on the severity of the vulnerabilities they address. High-risk vulnerabilities should be patched promptly, while lower-risk patches can be scheduled for deployment during routine maintenance windows.

- **Training and Awareness**: Ensure that IT staff are trained on the patch management process and the importance of staying up to date with security patches. Promoting a culture of security awareness can help mitigate the risks associated with human error in manual patching.

- **Incident Response Planning**: Develop a robust incident response plan to address any issues that arise from patching, whether automated or manual. This ensures that organizations can quickly and effectively respond to any unforeseen complications.

In summary, both automated and manual patching approaches have their advantages and challenges. By understanding these differences and implementing best practices, organizations can create a comprehensive patch management strategy that effectively reduces vulnerabilities and enhances their cybersecurity posture.

CHAPTER 6   ENDPOINT AND APPLICATION SECURITY

Regularly Review and Update

Establishing a routine for reviewing and applying patches is critical for maintaining system security. Organizations should prioritize this process based on the criticality of the vulnerabilities addressed by the patches. This includes regularly assessing the patch landscape for newly released updates and security fixes. Frequent reviews help organizations stay proactive rather than reactive, ensuring that systems remain up-to-date and resilient against emerging threats. It's important to create a schedule that aligns with the organization's operational needs—whether that means weekly, monthly, or quarterly assessments—while remaining flexible enough to address urgent patches as they arise. Automated tools can assist in monitoring vulnerabilities and scheduling updates, but human oversight is necessary to evaluate the implications of each patch and to prioritize their application based on the organization's unique risk profile.

Maintain Documentation

Keeping thorough documentation of all patch management activities is crucial for accountability, compliance, and operational efficiency. Documentation should include details about which patches were applied, when they were deployed, and the impact of those changes on system functionality and security. This comprehensive record not only serves as a historical reference but also aids in auditing processes, ensuring that organizations can demonstrate compliance with industry standards and regulatory requirements. Additionally, detailed documentation can assist in troubleshooting any issues that may arise from patching, enabling IT teams to quickly identify and resolve problems. A centralized documentation system, possibly integrated with the organization's change management process, can enhance accessibility and organization of this critical information.

Educate Staff

Training staff on the importance of patch management and the specific procedures they need to follow is essential for fostering a culture of security awareness within the organization. This education can take various forms, including workshops, online courses, and regular briefings on current cybersecurity trends and vulnerabilities. Empowering teams with knowledge about the risks associated with unpatched systems and the role they play in maintaining security can significantly enhance the overall security posture of the organization. Furthermore, by encouraging staff to take ownership of their systems and report vulnerabilities or concerns, organizations can create an environment where security is a shared responsibility. Regular updates on patch management practices and any changes in protocols will ensure that all employees remain informed and vigilant.

By implementing these best practices for patch management strategies, organizations can effectively safeguard their systems against known vulnerabilities. A proactive and well-documented approach, combined with ongoing education for staff, ensures that organizations are not only defending against current threats but are also prepared to adapt to the increasingly complex cybersecurity landscape. In this way, patch management becomes not just a reactive measure but an integral part of the organization's overall security strategy.

Virtualization and Cloud Security

As businesses increasingly adopt virtualization and cloud services, securing these environments is crucial to protecting sensitive data and ensuring operational integrity. Virtualization introduces unique risks related to the management and isolation of virtual machines (VMs), while cloud computing requires understanding the shared responsibility between providers and customers.

Securing Virtual Machines (VMs)

Virtual machines (VMs) are software-based representations of physical machines, providing flexibility and scalability. However, they also introduce specific security challenges that need to be addressed.

Isolation and Segmentation

Isolation and segmentation are fundamental to securing VMs, as they help prevent attacks from spreading within a virtual environment. By isolating VMs and creating distinct segments, organizations can contain potential threats and minimize the risk of lateral movement by attackers.

Techniques

1. **Virtual Network Segmentation**

    - **Description**: This involves creating virtual LANs (VLANs) or virtual networks to separate different types of traffic. By isolating critical applications from general user traffic, the risk of unauthorized access and lateral movement by attackers is significantly reduced.

    - **Benefits**: Helps to compartmentalize traffic, reduces the attack surface, and improves overall security.

2. **Hypervisor Security**

    - **Description**: The hypervisor, or virtual machine monitor (VMM), is the software that manages VMs. Its security is paramount because a compromised hypervisor could grant attackers control over all hosted VMs.

- **Techniques**: Implement strict access controls, monitor hypervisor activity, and regularly update and patch hypervisor software to address vulnerabilities.

Best Practices

- **Limit Access to Hypervisor**
    - Only authorized administrators should have access to the hypervisor. Strong authentication methods, such as multi-factor authentication (MFA), should be used to secure access.

- **Regular Patching**
    - Keep the hypervisor and all VMs up-to-date with the latest security patches. This mitigates known vulnerabilities that attackers could exploit.

- **Network Security Monitoring**
    - Implement monitoring tools, such as intrusion detection systems (IDS) and intrusion prevention systems (IPS), to detect and respond to suspicious activity within the virtual environment. Monitoring can provide visibility into network traffic and help identify potential threats early.

Cloud Security Models

Cloud computing offers various service models, each with distinct security considerations. The three main models are **Infrastructure as a Service (IaaS)**, **Platform as a Service (PaaS)**, and **Software as a Service (SaaS)**.

CHAPTER 6   ENDPOINT AND APPLICATION SECURITY

Infrastructure as a Service (IaaS)

IaaS provides virtualized computing resources over the internet, such as servers, storage, and networking. It offers flexibility and control over the infrastructure, but customers must manage security at various levels.

Security Considerations

- **Shared Responsibility Model**
    - In IaaS, security responsibilities are divided between the cloud provider and the customer. The provider typically handles the physical infrastructure security, while the customer is responsible for securing the applications, data, and virtual networks they deploy.

- **Data Encryption**
    - Encrypt data both at rest (stored data) and in transit (data being transferred) to protect against unauthorized access. This ensures confidentiality even if the data is intercepted.

- **Access Controls**
    - Implement strong access controls using Identity and Access Management (IAM) tools to limit who can manage and interact with cloud resources. Adhere to the principle of least privilege, granting users only the necessary permissions.

Challenges

- **Misconfigurations**
  - Misconfigured cloud resources, such as open storage buckets or improperly secured virtual networks, can expose sensitive data to unauthorized access. Regular audits and configuration checks can help prevent such issues.

- **Visibility**
  - Gaining visibility into cloud environments can be challenging. Organizations may need specialized tools and expertise to monitor cloud activities and detect potential security incidents.

Platform as a Service (PaaS)

PaaS provides a platform for developing, running, and managing applications without the need to manage the underlying infrastructure. It streamlines the development process but requires attention to application-level security.

Security Considerations

- **Secure Development Practices**
  - Developers should follow secure coding practices, such as input validation and error handling, to minimize vulnerabilities. Regularly updating application dependencies and libraries helps reduce exposure to known security flaws.

- **Data Protection**
    - Ensure that sensitive data processed by PaaS applications is encrypted and protected using robust encryption protocols. This safeguards data from unauthorized access during storage and transmission.
- **Identity and Access Management (IAM)**
    - Use IAM tools to manage access to PaaS resources effectively. Enforce the principle of least privilege and implement strong authentication methods to control access to the development and production environments.

Software as a Service (SaaS)

SaaS delivers software applications over the internet, typically on a subscription basis. The provider manages the underlying infrastructure, allowing customers to focus on using the application rather than maintaining it.

Security Considerations
- **Data Privacy**
    - Understand how the SaaS provider handles and protects customer data. This includes data encryption methods and privacy policies that govern the processing and storage of user information.

- **User Access Controls**
  - Implement strong authentication mechanisms, such as MFA, and use role-based access control (RBAC) to limit access to sensitive features and data within the SaaS application.

- **Compliance**
  - Ensure that the SaaS provider complies with relevant industry regulations and standards, such as the General Data Protection Regulation (GDPR) or the Health Insurance Portability and Accountability Act (HIPAA). Regularly review compliance documentation and audit reports from the provider.

By addressing these aspects of **Virtualization and Cloud Security**, organizations can better protect their virtual environments and cloud-based resources from evolving threats. Employing robust security practices for VMs and understanding the shared responsibility model across cloud services are essential steps in maintaining a secure infrastructure.

Container Security

Container security is a crucial aspect of modern application deployment, particularly as containerized environments become standard for building and scaling applications. Containers offer several benefits, such as portability and resource efficiency, but also introduce unique security challenges that must be addressed to ensure a secure infrastructure.

CHAPTER 6   ENDPOINT AND APPLICATION SECURITY

Container Orchestration Security

Container orchestration platforms like **Kubernetes** and **Docker Swarm** manage the deployment, scaling, and operation of containerized applications. These platforms help automate processes but require robust security practices to protect against threats.

Security Considerations

1. **Cluster Security**

    - **Description**: The container orchestration cluster is the backbone of the containerized environment. Securing this cluster involves protecting the underlying infrastructure and controlling access to sensitive components.

    - **Key Practices**

        - **Restrict Access**: Limit access to the cluster's control plane and nodes using firewalls and strong authentication mechanisms.

        - **Network Segmentation**: Use network policies to isolate different components of the cluster, minimizing the risk of lateral movement by attackers.

        - **Harden Infrastructure**: Ensure the underlying operating system and Kubernetes nodes are secured with the latest patches and configurations.

2. **Container Isolation**

    - **Description**: Containers should be isolated to prevent a compromise in one from affecting others. Proper isolation enhances security by limiting the blast radius of any potential breach.

CHAPTER 6   ENDPOINT AND APPLICATION SECURITY

- **Techniques**
    - Use namespaces and control groups (cgroups) to isolate container resources.
    - Employ security features like AppArmor or SELinux to enforce additional constraints on container processes.

3. **Role-Based Access Control (RBAC)**
    - **Description**: RBAC restricts access based on user roles, ensuring that only authorized users or applications have the necessary permissions.
    - **Implementation**
        - Define specific roles and permissions aligned with the principle of least privilege.
        - Regularly review and update roles to align with changes in user responsibilities and application requirements.

4. **Pod Security Policies** (Kubernetes-specific)
    - **Description**: Pod Security Policies (PSPs) define security requirements for pods in a Kubernetes cluster, such as restricting the use of privileged containers or disallowing host networking.
    - **Best Practices**
        - Use PSPs to enforce policies like disallowing root user access in containers or limiting capabilities.
        - Migrate to the Kubernetes Pod Security Standards as Kubernetes phases out PSPs in favor of built-in security controls.

CHAPTER 6   ENDPOINT AND APPLICATION SECURITY

Securing Kubernetes

Kubernetes is the most popular container orchestration platform, but its complexity requires specific security measures:

- **API Server Security**
  - **Description**: The API server is the central control point of a Kubernetes cluster. Unauthorized access can lead to full control over the cluster.
  - **Best Practices**
    - Restrict access using network policies and ensure strong authentication and authorization mechanisms are in place.
    - Use API server audit logs to track access and identify suspicious activities.
- **Network Policies**
  - **Description**: Network policies define rules for how pods communicate with each other and external services.
  - **Implementation**
    - Use Kubernetes Network Policies to limit traffic between pods based on factors like namespace or labels, reducing the risk of lateral movement by attackers.
- **Secrets Management**
  - **Description**: Kubernetes Secrets manage sensitive information, such as passwords and API keys.

- **Tools**
    - Use tools like HashiCorp Vault or external secret managers to securely store and manage secrets.
    - Ensure secrets are encrypted both at rest and in transit.

Monitoring and Auditing

- **Overview**: Regular monitoring and auditing of container activities help detect security incidents early and maintain compliance.
- **Best Practices**
    - Use monitoring tools like Prometheus or Grafana for real-time visibility.
    - Implement logging solutions like Fluentd or ELK Stack to collect and analyze logs for suspicious activities.
    - Conduct regular audits of cluster configurations and access controls.

Image Scanning and Hardening

Container images serve as the blueprint for containers, making their security integral to preventing vulnerabilities from being introduced into the containerized environment.

Image Scanning

Image scanning involves analyzing container images for known vulnerabilities, misconfigurations, and outdated components before deployment. This process helps identify security issues early in the development pipeline.

Tools

- **Popular Image Scanning Tools**
    - **Clair**: An open source project for the static analysis of vulnerabilities in application containers.
    - **Trivy**: A comprehensive and easy-to-use vulnerability scanner for container images.
    - **Docker Security Scanning**: Part of Docker's suite of security tools, providing automated image scanning integrated into the CI/CD pipeline.

Challenges

- **Resource Intensity**: Regularly scanning large images can consume significant computational resources.
- **False Positives**: Scanning tools may flag non-issues, requiring manual verification to avoid unnecessary actions.

Image Hardening

Image hardening involves applying security best practices to reduce the attack surface of container images, focusing on minimizing unnecessary components and enforcing secure configurations.

CHAPTER 6 ENDPOINT AND APPLICATION SECURITY

Principles

1. **Least Privilege**

    - **Description**: Limit the software and components included in container images to only what is necessary for the application to function.

    - **Techniques**

        - Remove unnecessary tools, services, and packages.

        - Avoid running containers with elevated privileges (i.e., as the root user).

2. **Base Image Selection**

    - **Description**: Choosing a minimal and trusted base image helps reduce vulnerabilities by limiting the number of components that could be exploited.

    - **Best Practices**

        - Use official or well-maintained images from trusted repositories.

        - Regularly update base images to incorporate the latest security patches.

3. **Regular Updates**

    - **Description**: Ensuring container images are up-to-date with the latest security patches is critical to maintaining a secure environment.

- **Techniques**
    - Automate the process of checking for updates and rebuilding images when patches are available.
    - Integrate image scanning and updates into the CI/CD pipeline for continuous security.

By implementing these strategies, organizations can build and maintain a secure containerized environment, reducing risks and enhancing the overall security posture of their applications. Container security requires a multi-layered approach, focusing on both the orchestration platform and individual container images to protect against emerging threats.

Application Security and Testing

Application Security and Testing aim to identify and mitigate vulnerabilities in software applications before they can be exploited. It involves a blend of automated tools, manual code reviews, and testing techniques to ensure that the application is secure from design to deployment. This process is a key part of **DevSecOps**, where security is integrated into every phase of the development pipeline.

Static Application Security Testing (SAST)

SAST is a white-box testing method that analyzes an application's source code, bytecode, or binary code to identify potential security vulnerabilities without actually executing the application. It typically reviews the code for common security flaws, such as **SQL injection**, **cross-site scripting (XSS)**, **buffer overflows**, and **insecure deserialization**.

Key Features of SAST

- **Code Analysis**: SAST tools evaluate the code at rest, meaning they do not run the application but instead review its structure and content for vulnerabilities.

- **Developer Integration**: These tools are often integrated directly into integrated development environments (IDEs) or CI/CD pipelines, enabling continuous and automated code analysis.

Benefits

1. **Early Detection**

   - Identifying vulnerabilities during the early stages of development reduces the cost and complexity of fixing issues. Catching bugs early minimizes the risk of introducing severe vulnerabilities later in the production stage.

2. **Comprehensive Analysis**

   - SAST tools can quickly scan large codebases, providing an extensive review of the application's entire source code. They identify issues related to

     - **Input Validation**: Ensuring user inputs are properly sanitized to prevent injection attacks.

     - **Data Handling**: Detecting improper handling of sensitive data, such as hardcoded credentials or plaintext passwords.

     - **Coding Best Practices**: Flagging deprecated functions or poor coding practices that may introduce vulnerabilities.

3. **Integration with Development Pipelines**
   - Modern SAST tools integrate seamlessly into CI/CD pipelines, allowing for automated scans during code commits or merges. This integration helps developers receive immediate feedback on potential vulnerabilities, making it easier to fix issues before they become deeply embedded.

Challenges

1. **False Positives**
   - SAST tools may generate a significant number of false positives, reporting issues that may not be actual vulnerabilities. This can overwhelm developers, requiring them to manually review each reported issue, which can be time-consuming and reduce productivity.

2. **Language and Framework Support**
   - Not all SAST tools support every programming language, framework, or library. This limitation can be a significant barrier in diverse environments with polyglot programming stacks, where different parts of an application may use different languages or frameworks.

3. **Scalability**
   - Scanning very large codebases or highly complex applications may slow down the CI/CD pipeline, especially if the SAST tool is not optimized for performance. Incremental scanning can mitigate this issue by analyzing only changed files.

Best Practices

- **Rule Customization**: Tailor SAST tools to the specific coding standards and security policies of the organization to reduce false positives and improve accuracy.

- **Developer Training**: Educate developers on common security issues and how to interpret SAST results, enabling them to effectively address vulnerabilities.

- **Regular Scanning**: Incorporate regular, automated scans into the development cycle to maintain a continuous assessment of code quality and security.

Dynamic Application Security Testing (DAST)

DAST is a black-box testing method that analyzes a running application by simulating external attacks to identify vulnerabilities. Unlike SAST, which inspects code statically, DAST evaluates the application in its operational state, testing for flaws that may not be visible in the source code alone. Common targets include **injection flaws, authentication weaknesses, session management issues**, and **insecure configurations**.

Key Features of DAST

- **Behavioral Analysis**: DAST tools interact with the application as an external user would, looking for vulnerabilities that manifest during execution.

- **No Source Code Access Needed**: Since it is a black-box technique, DAST does not require access to the source code, making it suitable for testing third-party applications or those developed by external vendors.

Benefits

1. **Real-World Simulation**
   - DAST mimics how an attacker would interact with the application, providing insights into potential exploit paths. This real-world approach helps uncover issues related to input validation, session handling, and data exposure.

2. **Broad Coverage**
   - DAST can detect runtime issues that are not visible in static code analysis, such as misconfigured servers, insecure APIs, or authentication flaws. It is particularly effective for identifying issues in web applications, where user interactions are dynamic and complex.

3. **Compliance and Risk Management**
   - Many regulatory standards, such as **PCI DSS**, **HIPAA**, and **GDPR**, require regular security testing of applications. DAST helps organizations meet these compliance requirements by providing evidence of thorough security assessments.

Challenges

1. **Performance Impact**
   - Running DAST on a live application can impact its performance, potentially slowing down response times or causing temporary service disruptions. This can be a significant concern for high-traffic or mission-critical applications.

2. **Complex Configuration**

   - Configuring DAST tools to accurately simulate attack scenarios without generating false positives or negatives can be challenging. It requires a deep understanding of the application's functionality and business logic to ensure that tests are both comprehensive and accurate.

3. **Remediation Complexity**

   - DAST often uncovers issues that are deeply embedded in the application's architecture or logic, making them harder to fix. Addressing these vulnerabilities may require significant changes to the codebase or underlying infrastructure, particularly if the issues involve core functionalities.

Best Practices

- **Comprehensive Testing Strategy**: Combine DAST with SAST and other security testing methods (e.g., penetration testing, software composition analysis) to provide a holistic view of the application's security posture.

- **Regular Scans**: Schedule DAST scans during non-peak hours or on a staging environment to minimize the impact on live application performance.

- **Custom Attack Profiles**: Configure DAST tools with specific attack profiles tailored to the application's architecture, ensuring that tests are relevant and focused on high-risk areas.

Integrating SAST and DAST in the SDLC

Combining SAST and DAST offers a powerful approach to application security testing:

- **Shift-Left Security (SAST Focus)**: Integrate SAST early in the SDLC to identify and resolve vulnerabilities during the coding phase, reducing the cost and complexity of fixes.

- **Shift-Right Security (DAST Focus)**: Employ DAST in the later stages of the SDLC, including the staging and production phases, to validate the application's behavior under real-world attack conditions.

- **CI/CD Integration**: Automate both SAST and DAST within the CI/CD pipeline, enabling continuous security assessments as part of the development process.

- **Feedback Loops**: Establish a feedback loop between the results of SAST and DAST, using the insights gained from runtime testing (DAST) to refine static analysis (SAST) rules and vice versa.

By implementing a comprehensive application security testing strategy that includes both SAST and DAST, organizations can better protect their applications from vulnerabilities, enhance their security posture, and ensure compliance with industry standards.

CHAPTER 6   ENDPOINT AND APPLICATION SECURITY

Mobile Device Security: Bring Your Own Device (BYOD) Policies

The BYOD approach allows employees to use their personal devices for work purposes. This trend is driven by the desire for flexibility, as employees prefer using familiar devices that are often more up-to-date than corporate-provided alternatives. However, BYOD introduces significant security challenges, as personal devices are less controlled and may not meet corporate security standards.

Security Considerations

1. **Device Security**

    - **Minimum Security Standards**: Organizations should require all personal devices that access corporate resources to meet specific security criteria. This includes

        - **Encryption**: Ensuring all data stored on the device is encrypted, preventing unauthorized access in case of loss or theft.

        - **Password Protection**: Enforcing strong, complex passwords or biometric authentication (e.g., fingerprint or facial recognition).

        - **Software Updates**: Mandating that devices run the latest operating system and security patches to reduce vulnerabilities.

2. **Data Protection**

    - **Containerization**: This technique separates personal and corporate data on the device, creating a secure, encrypted environment for business applications. It prevents unauthorized access to corporate data while maintaining user privacy.

    - **Remote Wipe Capability**: Allows IT administrators to remotely erase corporate data if the device is lost, stolen, or if the employee leaves the organization. This capability helps protect sensitive information from unauthorized access.

3. **Access Control**

    - **Multi-Factor Authentication (MFA)**: Enforces the use of multiple authentication methods (e.g., password + biometric verification) to add an extra layer of security when accessing corporate resources.

    - **Conditional Access Policies**: Implements rules that restrict access based on device compliance, location, or user role, ensuring only trusted devices can access sensitive data.

Challenges

1. **User Privacy**

    - Employees may be concerned about their privacy, as BYOD policies often require installing software that can monitor device usage, location, and apps. Balancing the need for security with respect for user privacy is a delicate issue that can affect employee satisfaction and compliance.

2. **Device Diversity**

    - BYOD environments include a wide range of devices with different operating systems (e.g., iOS, Android), hardware configurations, and software versions. Managing security across this diverse landscape is complex, requiring versatile tools and policies.

3. **Compliance**

    - Regulatory requirements such as **GDPR**, **HIPAA**, and **PCI DSS** mandate strict data protection measures. Ensuring BYOD practices align with these regulations often requires additional controls and oversight, such as data encryption and secure access protocols.

Best Practices

- **Employee Training**: Educate employees on security best practices, potential risks, and their role in protecting corporate data.

- **Clear BYOD Policy**: Develop a well-defined BYOD policy outlining acceptable use, security requirements, and consequences for non-compliance.

- **Regular Audits**: Conduct periodic audits of BYOD devices to ensure compliance with security standards and identify potential risks.

CHAPTER 6   ENDPOINT AND APPLICATION SECURITY

Mobile Device Management (MDM) Solutions

MDM solutions provide centralized control over mobile devices used within an organization. This technology allows IT administrators to enforce security policies, manage apps, and protect corporate data on both company-owned and personal devices used for work purposes.

Key Features

1. **Device Enrollment**

    - Automates the process of enrolling devices into the MDM system, ensuring each device is properly configured with necessary security settings, such as encryption and app restrictions, upon first connection to the corporate network.

2. **Policy Enforcement**

    - MDM tools enforce security policies across all managed devices, including

        - **Password Policies**: Require strong passwords or biometric authentication.

        - **Encryption Enforcement**: Ensure all sensitive data is encrypted on the device.

        - **App Management**: Restrict the installation of unauthorized or risky applications and manage permissions for installed apps.

3. **Remote Management**

    - Provides capabilities for remotely locking, wiping, or updating devices. This feature is critical for securing data if a device is lost or stolen, allowing administrators to erase corporate data remotely.

Benefits

1. **Improved Security**
   - MDM ensures that all devices meet security standards, reducing the risk of unauthorized access, malware infections, and data breaches.

2. **Compliance**
   - MDM solutions include compliance monitoring features, such as device encryption checks and real-time reporting, helping organizations meet regulatory requirements.

3. **User Productivity**
   - By enabling secure access to corporate resources (e.g., email, cloud storage), MDM solutions enhance user productivity without compromising security.

Challenges

1. **Cost**
   - Implementing MDM can be costly, especially for large organizations with a diverse array of devices. It often involves licensing fees, infrastructure costs, and ongoing maintenance.

2. **User Experience**
   - Strict security policies enforced by MDM solutions may impact the user experience, potentially leading to resistance from employees who may find certain restrictions inconvenient.

3. **Complexity**
   - Managing various devices with different configurations, operating systems, and usage patterns requires dedicated IT resources and expertise, making MDM implementation complex.

Best Practices

- **Regular Policy Updates**: Continuously update security policies to adapt to evolving threats and changes in regulatory requirements.

- **User Onboarding**: Provide clear guidance during the enrollment process to ensure users understand the security policies and the importance of compliance.

- **Monitoring and Reporting**: Use MDM analytics to monitor device compliance and generate reports for audits and risk assessments.

Mobile Threat Defense (MTD)

MTD solutions provide advanced threat detection, prevention, and response for mobile devices. They complement MDM solutions by offering additional layers of protection against sophisticated threats such as malware, phishing attacks, and network-based exploits.

Key Features

1. **Threat Detection**
   - Utilizes machine learning, behavioral analysis, and threat intelligence to detect a wide range of threats, including malware, phishing attempts, and suspicious app behaviors.

CHAPTER 6   ENDPOINT AND APPLICATION SECURITY

2. **Network Security**
   - Monitors network traffic to detect and block malicious activities like man-in-the-middle (MITM) attacks, rogue Wi-Fi networks, and DNS hijacking.

3. **App Security**
   - Analyzes installed apps for vulnerabilities, excessive permissions, and risky behaviors that could compromise device security.

4. **Integration with MDM**
   - MTD can be integrated with MDM systems to provide a comprehensive security framework, enabling automated responses to detected threats (e.g., quarantine devices, restrict access).

Benefits

1. **Enhanced Protection**
   - Provides robust defense against advanced mobile threats that may bypass traditional security measures, safeguarding sensitive corporate data.

2. **Real-Time Response**
   - MTD solutions can automatically respond to detected threats, such as isolating infected devices or blocking malicious network traffic, reducing the risk of data breaches.

3. **Compliance**
   - MTD helps organizations meet regulatory requirements by offering advanced security features that protect sensitive data on mobile devices.

Challenges

1. **Resource Intensive**
   - MTD deployment can be resource-heavy, requiring significant IT resources for setup, management, and continuous monitoring.

2. **User Resistance**
   - Some users may view MTD solutions as intrusive, impacting device performance and privacy, which can lead to resistance.

3. **Evolving Threat Landscape**
   - The rapidly changing nature of mobile threats requires MTD solutions to be continuously updated, demanding regular fine-tuning and updates.

Best Practices

- **Regular Threat Intelligence Updates**: Ensure MTD solutions are frequently updated with the latest threat intelligence to stay ahead of new threats.
- **User Education**: Train users on the importance of mobile security and the role of MTD in protecting sensitive data.

- **Comprehensive Security Strategy**: Combine MTD with MDM and other security measures for a layered defense approach.

By implementing a combination of BYOD policies, MDM solutions, and MTD capabilities, organizations can effectively safeguard their mobile devices against a wide range of threats, ensuring secure access to corporate data and maintaining regulatory compliance.

CHAPTER 7

Cryptography and Public Key Infrastructure

Cryptography is essential to information security, providing the mechanisms to secure data confidentiality, integrity, authentication, and non-repudiation. This chapter provides a thorough examination of cryptographic principles, algorithms, and Public Key Infrastructure (PKI) concepts to support both Security+ certification requirements and practical security applications.

Fundamentals of Cryptography: Symmetric vs. Asymmetric Encryption

Understanding the difference between symmetric and asymmetric encryption is crucial to grasping how cryptographic systems function, their unique strengths, and where each is best applied.

CHAPTER 7   CRYPTOGRAPHY AND PUBLIC KEY INFRASTRUCTURE

Symmetric Encryption

Symmetric encryption, also known as secret-key encryption, uses a single key for both encryption and decryption. Because both parties share the same key, it is faster and more efficient for large volumes of data.

- **Key Management**: The key distribution problem is central to symmetric encryption, as both the sender and receiver must have the same key while keeping it secret. Secure key exchange is critical because, if the key is exposed, the security of all data encrypted with it is compromised.

- **Performance**: Symmetric encryption is computationally efficient and ideal for encrypting large datasets quickly. For example, it is commonly used in securing database files, file transfers, and network communications.

- **Common Algorithms**

  - **AES (Advanced Encryption Standard)**

    - **Key Sizes**: AES supports 128, 192, and 256-bit key sizes, with 256-bit providing the highest level of security.

    - **Security**: AES is considered very secure, with widespread adoption across applications like Wi-Fi security (WPA2/WPA3), file encryption, and virtual private networks (VPNs).

- **Modes of Operation**
  - **ECB (Electronic Codebook)**: Basic encryption mode but vulnerable to pattern recognition.
  - **CBC (Cipher Block Chaining)**: Improves security by adding an initialization vector, creating unique ciphertext even for identical plaintext blocks.
  - **GCM (Galois/Counter Mode)**: Provides both encryption and authentication, ensuring data confidentiality and integrity, and is often used in SSL/TLS protocols.
- **DES (Data Encryption Standard)**
  - **Key Size**: DES uses a 56-bit key but is considered insecure against modern brute-force attacks.
  - **Triple DES (3DES)**: Increases security by applying DES encryption three times with different keys. It is often disallowed on newer systems and largely considered to be a legacy implementation for systems post 2023.

Asymmetric Encryption

Overview: Asymmetric encryption, or public-key encryption, uses a key pair—a public key for encryption and a private key for decryption. This setup eliminates the need for secure key exchange and enables features like digital signatures.

- **Key Distribution**: Unlike symmetric encryption, asymmetric encryption does not require a shared key. Instead, the public key can be freely distributed, while the private key remains confidential, simplifying secure communication.

- **Performance**: Asymmetric encryption is computationally intensive and generally slower, making it more suitable for smaller data encryption, such as secure symmetric key exchange or digital signature generation.

- **Common Algorithms**
  - **RSA (Rivest-Shamir-Adleman)**
    - **Key Sizes**: RSA typically employs 2048 or 4096-bit keys, with larger keys offering greater security.
    - **Applications**: RSA is widely used for digital signatures, SSL/TLS certificates, and data encryption.
    - **Security Considerations**: RSA relies on the difficulty of factoring large prime numbers, making it secure against current computational capabilities. However, advancements in quantum computing could potentially threaten RSA's security in the future.
  - **ECC (Elliptic Curve Cryptography)**
    - **Key Sizes**: ECC provides equivalent security to RSA with much smaller key sizes (e.g., a 256-bit ECC key offers security similar to a 3072-bit RSA key).

- **Efficiency**: ECC is more efficient in terms of processing power and storage, making it ideal for resource-constrained environments like mobile devices and IoT.

- **Applications**: ECC is used in secure communications, ECDSA (Elliptic Curve Digital Signature Algorithm), and SSL/TLS, offering high-performance cryptographic solutions.

Hashing: Ensuring Data Integrity

Hashing algorithms produce fixed-size output from variable-length input, offering data integrity assurance. A hash value, or digest, is unique to the input data, making it suitable for verifying data integrity without revealing the original content.

- **MD5 (Message Digest 5)**
  - **Key Characteristics**: Produces a 128-bit hash value but is now considered insecure due to vulnerabilities like collision attacks.
  - **Usage Consideration**: Not recommended for security purposes but still used for basic file integrity checks.
- **SHA (Secure Hash Algorithm)**
  - **SHA-1**: Generates a 160-bit hash value. While once popular, SHA-1 is now deprecated due to susceptibility to collision attacks.

- **SHA-2**: An improvement over SHA-1, SHA-2 includes variations like SHA-256 and SHA-512, offering stronger security. SHA-2 is widely used in digital certificates, SSL/TLS, and file integrity checks.

- **SHA-3**: The newest SHA variant, designed to improve security further with a different cryptographic foundation. While adoption is still growing, SHA-3 offers an alternative in environments requiring additional security.

Digital Signatures: Authenticating Data and Ensuring Non-repudiation

Digital signatures leverage asymmetric encryption to authenticate the origin of data and ensure non-repudiation.

- **Process**: A digital signature is created by hashing the data and encrypting the hash with the sender's private key. The recipient can then verify the hash by decrypting it with the sender's public key.

- **Applications**: Digital signatures are critical for verifying software authenticity, securing emails, and providing legal assurance in digital transactions.

- **Common Protocols and Standards**
    - **Digital Signature Algorithm (DSA)**: A US government standard for digital signatures, providing authentication and non-repudiation.
    - **ECDSA**: The elliptic curve variant of DSA, offering high security with shorter key lengths, suitable for mobile devices and embedded systems.

CHAPTER 7   CRYPTOGRAPHY AND PUBLIC KEY INFRASTRUCTURE

Public Key Infrastructure (PKI): Enabling Trust in Digital Communication

PKI is an essential framework for managing digital certificates and public-key encryption, allowing organizations to establish trusted identities and secure communications.

- **Components of PKI**

    - **Certificate Authority (CA)**: Issues and revokes digital certificates, serving as a trusted entity that verifies identities.

    - **Registration Authority (RA)**: Acts as an intermediary between users and the CA, verifying user identities before certificate issuance.

    - **Certificates**: Digital documents that associate a public key with an identity. X.509 is the standard format for certificates used in SSL/TLS and other applications.

    - **Certificate Revocation List (CRL)**: A list of certificates that have been revoked by the CA before expiration, providing a way to check if a certificate is still trusted.

- **PKI Applications**

    - **SSL/TLS**: Encrypts data between web servers and clients, ensuring secure online transactions and data protection.

    - **Email Security**: Secures email content and attachments through encryption and digital signatures, protecting against unauthorized access and tampering.

- **Code Signing**: Ensures the authenticity and integrity of software code, preventing malware and other malicious code alterations.

Cryptographic Protocols and Applications

Cryptographic protocols are widely used to secure communication channels, ensure data integrity, and authenticate users.

- **SSL/TLS (Secure Sockets Layer/Transport Layer Security)**: Encrypts data in transit between clients and servers, securing web browsing, online transactions, and other internet communications.

- **IPsec (Internet Protocol Security)**: A suite of protocols that encrypt and authenticate IP packets, commonly used in VPNs to secure data between remote users and corporate networks.

- **PGP/GPG (Pretty Good Privacy/GNU Privacy Guard)**: Encrypts and digitally signs emails and files, widely used for secure communication.

Cryptography Considerations for the Security+ Exam

For the Security+ exam, it is crucial to understand both the theory and practical applications of cryptography:

- **Key Management**: Understand the importance of secure key exchange, storage, and rotation policies.

- **Algorithm Selection**: Be familiar with the strengths and weaknesses of different cryptographic algorithms and know when to apply symmetric vs. asymmetric encryption.

- **Certificate Life Cycle**: Recognize the process of certificate issuance, validation, and revocation within a PKI system.

- **Security of Protocols**: Understand how cryptographic protocols like SSL/TLS and IPsec secure data in transit and know the security implications of outdated protocols.

- **Impact of Quantum Computing**: Be aware of emerging threats posed by quantum computing, which could impact asymmetric encryption methods in the future, prompting a potential shift to quantum-resistant algorithms.

In summary, cryptography and PKI form the backbone of secure digital communications. This chapter equips readers with foundational and advanced concepts, preparing them for real-world scenarios and Security+ exam success.

Blockchain: Beyond Cryptocurrency

Blockchain technology, originally designed to underpin cryptocurrencies like Bitcoin, has evolved into a versatile solution that extends far beyond digital currency. At its core, blockchain is a **distributed ledger technology (DLT)** characterized by its secure, transparent, and immutable record-keeping. Its applications have expanded into various industries, providing enhanced security, traceability, and operational efficiency.

CHAPTER 7   CRYPTOGRAPHY AND PUBLIC KEY INFRASTRUCTURE

Applications Beyond Cryptocurrency

1. **Identity Management:** Blockchain offers a revolutionary approach to identity management, addressing challenges related to privacy, security, and control.

    - **Decentralized Identity**

        - Traditional identity systems rely on central authorities, such as governments or corporations, to verify and store user data. In contrast, **decentralized identity** systems powered by blockchain allow users to maintain control over their digital identities. This reduces the risk of centralized data breaches and gives individuals ownership of their personal information.

    - **Authentication and Verification**

        - Blockchain's tamper-proof and cryptographic nature makes it ideal for **secure identity verification**. It enables a reliable method for authenticating identities without requiring a centralized authority, significantly reducing the likelihood of identity fraud.

    - **Self-Sovereign Identity**

        - **Self-sovereign identity** systems empower users to manage their own identities, selectively sharing information with service providers. This model enhances privacy and security by minimizing the amount of personal data exposed during transactions. For example, a user might prove their age without revealing their exact birthdate.

2. **Supply Chain Security**: Blockchain is transforming supply chain management by offering increased transparency, traceability, and automation through smart contracts.

    - **Transparency and Traceability**

        - With blockchain, every transaction is recorded on an immutable ledger, making it easy to trace the **origin and movement of products** through the supply chain. This is especially useful in industries like **pharmaceuticals** and **food**, where verifying the authenticity and provenance of products is critical. For instance, a blockchain-based system can track a batch of medications from the manufacturer to the end consumer, ensuring that no counterfeit products enter the supply chain.

    - **Smart Contracts**

        - **Smart contracts** are self-executing contracts with predefined rules coded into them. Once the conditions are met, the contract automatically executes the agreed-upon actions, such as releasing payment or updating shipment status. This automation reduces the need for intermediaries, decreases transaction times, and enhances the efficiency of supply chain operations.

Elliptic Curve Cryptography (ECC)

Elliptic Curve Cryptography (ECC) is a type of public key cryptography based on the mathematical properties of elliptic curves. ECC has gained popularity due to its efficiency and strong security, making it a preferred choice for secure communications, especially in environments with limited processing power.

Advantages of ECC

1. **Efficiency and Performance**
   - One of the key advantages of ECC is its **smaller key size**. ECC can provide the same level of security as other cryptographic algorithms, such as RSA, but with much smaller keys. For example, a 256-bit key in ECC offers a comparable level of security to a 3072-bit RSA key. This results in faster computation, reduced processing overhead, and lower power consumption, making ECC an ideal solution for **mobile devices**, **IoT**, and **embedded systems**.
   - The smaller key sizes and reduced computational requirements also mean ECC can be used effectively in **bandwidth-constrained** environments, allowing secure communications with minimal impact on network performance.

2. **Security and Resilience**

    - ECC is considered secure against most known cryptographic attacks. Its resilience lies in the difficulty of solving the **Elliptic Curve Discrete Logarithm Problem (ECDLP)**, which forms the basis of its cryptographic strength.

    - ECC is widely used in **digital signature algorithms** such as **ECDSA (Elliptic Curve Digital Signature Algorithm)**. ECDSA provides robust data integrity and authentication, which is crucial for secure communications, especially in sensitive applications like financial transactions and secure messaging.

    - However, like other forms of encryption, ECC faces potential risks from future developments in **quantum computing**. Quantum computers could potentially solve ECDLP more efficiently than classical computers, making current ECC-based systems vulnerable. Research into **quantum-resistant cryptographic algorithms** is ongoing to address this potential threat.

Conclusion

Blockchain and ECC have become pivotal technologies in enhancing security and transparency across various industries. Blockchain's application beyond cryptocurrency, particularly in **identity management** and **supply chain security**, showcases its potential to transform traditional systems by enabling decentralized, tamper-proof record-keeping and automated processes. On the other hand, ECC's **efficiency** and **security** make it a cornerstone of modern cryptography, particularly for resource-constrained environments.

As both technologies continue to evolve, their integration with emerging fields such as **IoT**, **5G**, and **cloud computing** is likely to drive further innovation and provide robust solutions for enhancing data security and operational efficiency in the digital age.

Hashing

Hashing is a process that transforms input data of any size into a fixed-size string of characters, typically a sequence of numbers and letters. The resulting output, known as a **hash** or **digest**, acts as a digital "fingerprint" for the original data. Hash functions play a critical role in ensuring data integrity and are widely used in various security applications.

Key Properties of Hash Functions

1. **Deterministic**
   - A hash function is **deterministic**, meaning that the same input will always produce the same hash output. This consistency allows systems to reliably compare data by comparing their hashes rather than the original data itself.

2. **Collision Resistance**
   - **Collision resistance** ensures it is extremely unlikely for two different inputs to produce the same hash output. A collision occurs when two distinct pieces of data yield the same hash, potentially compromising data integrity. Modern cryptographic hash functions are designed to minimize the risk of such collisions.

3. **Pre-image Resistance**

    - **Pre-image resistance** makes it computationally infeasible to reverse-engineer the original input from its hash output. This property is essential for securing sensitive information, as it prevents attackers from retrieving the original data based solely on its hash.

Common Hash Functions

- **SHA-256 (Secure Hash Algorithm 256-bit)**

    - Part of the **SHA-2** family, SHA-256 is widely used in applications requiring secure hashing, such as **blockchain** transactions, **digital certificates**, and **password hashing**. It produces a 256-bit (32-byte) hash, providing a high level of security against collision and pre-image attacks.

- **MD5 (Message Digest Algorithm 5)**

    - Once a popular choice for checksums and integrity checks, **MD5** is now considered **insecure** due to its vulnerability to collision attacks. While it still appears in legacy systems, MD5 should be avoided in modern applications requiring cryptographic security.

CHAPTER 7   CRYPTOGRAPHY AND PUBLIC KEY INFRASTRUCTURE

Applications of Hashing

- **Data Integrity**
  - Hashing is crucial for verifying **data integrity**. For example, file integrity checks often use hash functions to ensure files have not been altered. Users can compare the hash of a downloaded file to a known good hash provided by the source to verify its authenticity.

- **Password Storage**
  - Instead of storing plaintext passwords, secure systems store **hashed and salted** passwords. **Salting** involves adding random data (a salt) to the password before hashing, which helps prevent **rainbow table attacks**—a method used by attackers to crack hashes using precomputed tables.

Digital Signatures

Digital signatures use asymmetric cryptography to authenticate a message, verify data integrity, and prevent repudiation. They provide a way to ensure that a message or document has been sent by the claimed sender and has not been tampered with during transmission.

Process of Digital Signature

1. **Hashing**
   - The sender first hashes the original document using a cryptographic hash function (e.g., SHA-256). This step produces a fixed-size hash that represents the content of the document.

2. **Signing**
   - The sender then **encrypts** the hash using their **private key**, creating the digital signature. This process ensures that only the sender, who owns the private key, could have generated the signature.

3. **Verification**
   - The recipient uses the sender's **public key** to decrypt the digital signature, obtaining the original hash. They then hash the received document separately. If the computed hash matches the decrypted hash, the recipient can be confident that the document is authentic and unaltered.

Applications of Digital Signatures

- **Email Security**
  - Digital signatures are commonly used in **email encryption** protocols such as **S/MIME** and **PGP** to verify that emails are genuine, unaltered, and sent by the claimed sender. This helps prevent email spoofing and phishing attacks.

CHAPTER 7   CRYPTOGRAPHY AND PUBLIC KEY INFRASTRUCTURE

- **Software Distribution**
    - When software developers distribute their applications, they often sign the software with a digital signature. This allows users to verify that the software has not been tampered with since its release, ensuring its authenticity and integrity. For example, many operating systems use digital signatures to verify updates and executable files before installation.

Summary

Hashing and **digital signatures** are foundational components of modern cybersecurity. Hash functions provide a means to verify data integrity through unique, fixed-size outputs. Despite their deterministic nature, strong hash functions like **SHA-256** offer collision and pre-image resistance, making them reliable for verifying data and storing sensitive information like passwords. On the other hand, digital signatures leverage the strengths of asymmetric encryption to authenticate senders, validate data integrity, and prevent repudiation. These technologies are widely employed in email security, software distribution, and other applications where data authenticity is paramount.

By understanding and implementing these cryptographic methods, organizations can bolster their security posture, safeguard sensitive information, and maintain trust in digital communications.

Certificates

Certificates are digital documents that bind a public key to a specific identity, such as an individual or an organization. These are fundamental in establishing trust and enabling secure communications over the internet. In protocols like **SSL/TLS**, certificates are used to authenticate and encrypt data between parties, ensuring data integrity and confidentiality.

X.509 Certificates

- **Structure**: X.509 certificates are a standard format for public key certificates. They include
    - The certificate holder's name (subject)
    - The public key associated with the holder
    - Information about the issuer (Certificate Authority)
    - The digital signature of the issuer, which verifies the authenticity of the certificate
- **Certificate Authorities (CAs)**: CAs are trusted entities that issue certificates. They verify the identity of the applicant before issuing the certificate, establishing trust.

Types of Certificates

- **SSL/TLS Certificates**: Used to secure web communications by enabling HTTPS, they encrypt data between the client (browser) and server, ensuring data privacy.
- **Code Signing Certificates**: Used by software developers to sign applications, confirming that the code has not been altered or corrupted after being signed.

- **Email Encryption Certificates (S/MIME):** Secure email communications, allowing the sender to encrypt emails so only the intended recipient can decrypt and read them.

SSL/TLS (Secure Sockets Layer/Transport Layer Security)

SSL/TLS are protocols designed to provide secure communication over a network. TLS is the modern successor to SSL, offering enhanced security features.

- **SSL vs. TLS**
  - **SSL** was the original protocol for securing data but has been deprecated due to various vulnerabilities.
  - **TLS** improved upon SSL with stronger encryption algorithms and better security practices. TLS 1.3 is the current standard, offering enhanced performance and security features.
- **Key Exchange Algorithms**
  - **Diffie-Hellman (DH):** Enables two parties to establish a shared secret over an unsecured channel. However, DH alone does not provide authentication.
  - **Elliptic Curve Diffie-Hellman (ECDH):** A variant of DH using elliptic curve cryptography, offering similar security with smaller key sizes, which improves efficiency.

- **Certificates in SSL/TLS**
  - **Role of Certificates**: Authenticate the server (and sometimes the client), assuring users they are connecting to a trusted service.
  - **Certificate Chain**: A hierarchical chain of trust starting from a root CA, followed by intermediate CAs, and ending with the server's certificate. This chain validates the authenticity of the certificate.

HTTPS (Hypertext Transfer Protocol Secure)

HTTPS is the secure version of HTTP, combining it with SSL/TLS to encrypt data between a web browser and a server.

- **Importance of HTTPS**
  - **Privacy**: Encrypts data to prevent eavesdropping and unauthorized access.
  - **Integrity**: Ensures that the data sent between the browser and server is not tampered with.
  - **Security**: Helps protect against man-in-the-middle attacks by verifying the server's identity with a certificate.
- **Implementation**: Websites obtain SSL/TLS certificates from a CA to enable HTTPS. Modern browsers mark sites without HTTPS as "Not Secure," emphasizing its importance in protecting user data.

IPsec (Internet Protocol Security)

IPsec is a suite of protocols that secure IP communications by authenticating and encrypting each IP packet in a data stream. It is commonly used in VPNs and network security.

- **Components of IPsec**
  - **Authentication Header (AH):** Provides data integrity and authenticity for IP packets but does not encrypt the data, ensuring it has not been altered during transit.
  - **Encapsulating Security Payload (ESP):** Encrypts the payload of IP packets, offering confidentiality, data integrity, and authentication.
- **Modes of Operation**
  - **Transport Mode:** Encrypts only the data portion (payload) of the IP packet, leaving the IP header unchanged. It is typically used for end-to-end communication between hosts.
  - **Tunnel Mode:** Encrypts the entire IP packet (both header and payload), encapsulating it in a new IP header. This mode is ideal for site-to-site VPNs, where secure communication between networks is required.

Key Takeaways

- **Certificates** play a vital role in establishing trust and securing communications, especially in SSL/TLS.
- **SSL/TLS protocols** have evolved to **TLS**, which is now the standard for secure communications on the internet.

CHAPTER 7   CRYPTOGRAPHY AND PUBLIC KEY INFRASTRUCTURE

- **HTTPS** relies on SSL/TLS certificates to secure web traffic, protecting user data from various threats.
- **IPsec** secures IP traffic by providing authentication and encryption, making it a cornerstone of VPN technology.

These components are fundamental for maintaining security in network communications, preventing data breaches, and ensuring user privacy.

Key Management and the Cryptographic Life Cycle

Key management is a fundamental part of cryptographic systems, encompassing the creation, handling, distribution, storage, rotation, and eventual destruction of cryptographic keys. The effectiveness of any encryption solution relies heavily on robust key management practices. Without proper management, even the most sophisticated encryption algorithms can become vulnerable to attacks.

Phases of the Cryptographic Life Cycle

The life cycle of cryptographic keys includes four main stages:

1. **Key Generation**
2. **Key Distribution**
3. **Key Rotation**
4. **Key Destruction**

CHAPTER 7   CRYPTOGRAPHY AND PUBLIC KEY INFRASTRUCTURE

1. Key Generation

Key generation is the initial step in the cryptographic life cycle. It involves creating secure, random cryptographic keys that are resistant to attacks.

- **Overview**
  - The strength of cryptographic systems starts with the **quality** and **randomness** of the keys. High-entropy keys ensure unpredictability, making them resistant to brute-force attacks.
  - Keys are typically generated using **Random Number Generators (RNGs)** or **Pseudorandom Number Generators (PRNGs)**:
    - **RNGs** use physical sources of randomness (e.g., system noise or thermal variations).
    - **PRNGs** rely on algorithms to simulate randomness, ideal for cryptographic applications where high-speed generation is required.
    - Standards like **FIPS 140-2** and **FIPS 140-3** outline the security requirements for cryptographic modules used by government agencies to ensure reliable key generation.
- **Key Length**
  - The **length** of a cryptographic key directly impacts its security. Longer keys provide more possible combinations, making brute-force attacks significantly more challenging.

CHAPTER 7   CRYPTOGRAPHY AND PUBLIC KEY INFRASTRUCTURE

- For symmetric encryption algorithms like **AES**, key lengths of **128 bits** (AES-128) and **256 bits** (AES-256) are common, with AES-256 offering enhanced security for high-value data.

- For asymmetric encryption methods like **RSA**, commonly used key lengths include **2048 bits** and **4096 bits**, with longer keys providing better resistance against future computational advancements.

2. Key Distribution

Key distribution is the process of securely delivering cryptographic keys to authorized parties while preventing unauthorized access. It is one of the most challenging aspects of key management, especially for symmetric encryption systems.

- **Overview**
    - In symmetric encryption, both parties use the same key for encryption and decryption, requiring a secure channel for key exchange.
    - In asymmetric encryption, a **public key** can be shared openly, while a **private key** is kept confidential, simplifying key distribution but requiring a reliable public-key infrastructure (PKI).

- **Methods of Key Distribution**
  - **Pre-shared Keys (PSKs)**
    - Used in simpler environments, such as home Wi-Fi networks, **PSKs** involve sharing a key in advance. However, distributing PSKs securely is a challenge, as sharing over insecure channels can expose the key to interception.
  - **Key Exchange Protocols**
    - **Diffie-Hellman (DH)**: Allows two parties to securely establish a shared secret key over a public channel without directly transmitting the key. It is commonly used in VPNs and TLS protocols.
    - **RSA**: Enables a sender to encrypt a symmetric session key using the recipient's public key, ensuring that only the intended recipient (with the corresponding private key) can decrypt it.
  - **Challenges**
    - **Man-in-the-Middle (MitM) Attacks**: During key distribution, an attacker might intercept or alter the key exchange. Mitigating this risk requires **authentication mechanisms** and secure channels, such as **TLS** or **IPsec**, to validate the identity of the communicating parties.

3. Key Rotation

Key rotation is the periodic replacement of cryptographic keys to reduce the risk of key compromise.

- **Overview**
    - The longer a key is in use, the greater the chance it may be exposed through attacks, errors, or vulnerabilities. Regularly rotating keys limits the window of opportunity for attackers.
    - **Automated key rotation** helps streamline this process in large systems, reducing manual handling errors and ensuring that keys are updated according to a schedule.

- **Reasons for Key Rotation**
    - **Compromise Risk**: If a key is compromised, an attacker can decrypt all data encrypted with that key. Regular rotation minimizes the potential damage by reducing the lifespan of any single key.
    - **Compliance Requirements**: Regulations like **PCI DSS** and **HIPAA** mandate key rotation at specific intervals to maintain security standards and protect sensitive data.

- **Best Practices for Rotation**
    - **Key Versioning**: Assigning version numbers to keys helps keep track of different key iterations throughout their life cycle. This practice aids in transitioning smoothly from old keys to new ones and ensures that legacy data encrypted with older keys remains accessible.

4. Key Destruction

Key destruction involves securely erasing cryptographic keys when they are no longer needed, ensuring they cannot be recovered and misused.

- **Overview**
    - Proper key destruction is critical to maintaining the confidentiality of previously encrypted data. Retaining old keys increases the risk of unauthorized decryption, especially if the keys are exposed during decommissioning or system upgrades.

- **Methods for Key Destruction**
    - **Overwriting**: Digital keys stored on devices are securely erased by overwriting the data multiple times, making it irrecoverable.
    - **Physical Destruction**: For hardware storing keys, such as **Hardware Security Modules (HSMs)**, physical destruction methods like **shredding** or **degaussing** ensure the keys cannot be retrieved.

- **Importance**
    - Secure key destruction is essential when devices are decommissioned, systems are upgraded, or cryptographic algorithms are retired. Failure to securely destroy old keys can result in unauthorized access to encrypted data long after the original encryption.

Summary

Effective **key management** is vital for maintaining the security of cryptographic systems. It encompasses the entire life cycle of a cryptographic key, from **generation** and **distribution** to **rotation** and **destruction**. By adhering to best practices and employing robust methods like **automated key rotation**, **secure key exchange protocols**, and **physical destruction of hardware**, organizations can mitigate risks and protect sensitive data from unauthorized access.

Key management is not just a technical requirement but also a compliance necessity. Regulatory standards often mandate specific key management practices to safeguard data, making it a critical component of an organization's overall security strategy. With advancements in quantum computing on the horizon, organizations must continue to evolve their key management practices to stay ahead of emerging threats and maintain the integrity of their cryptographic systems.

Real-World Applications of Cryptography in Security

Cryptography is at the heart of modern digital security, playing a pivotal role in protecting data, communications, and systems across various industries. Its real-world applications span from securing online transactions to protecting sensitive corporate data, ensuring privacy and integrity in a connected world. Let's dive into some of the most common uses of cryptography that safeguard everyday digital interactions and services.

CHAPTER 7   CRYPTOGRAPHY AND PUBLIC KEY INFRASTRUCTURE

Securing Online Transactions

One of the most visible applications of cryptography is in securing online transactions, especially in e-commerce and banking. When you make an online purchase or access your bank account, cryptographic protocols like **SSL/TLS** are in action, encrypting the data exchanged between your browser and the server. This encryption prevents attackers from intercepting and stealing sensitive information such as credit card numbers, login credentials, and personal details. Digital certificates and public key infrastructure (PKI) are also used to authenticate websites, ensuring that users connect to legitimate, trusted services. Without these cryptographic protections, users would be at significant risk of phishing, data breaches, and financial fraud.

Cryptocurrencies and Blockchain

Cryptography is the foundation of blockchain technology and cryptocurrencies like Bitcoin and Ethereum. In these systems, cryptographic hashing algorithms (e.g., SHA-256) are used to secure the integrity of transaction data, making it virtually impossible to alter records once they are added to the blockchain. Public and private keys are also central to cryptocurrency wallets, enabling users to securely send and receive digital assets. The private key acts as a digital signature, verifying the authenticity of transactions without revealing the user's identity. This decentralized approach to currency relies heavily on cryptographic principles to provide security, privacy, and immutability, fundamentally changing how financial transactions and data are managed.

Digital Signatures and Authentication

Digital signatures are another widespread application of cryptography, ensuring the authenticity and integrity of digital messages, documents, and software. When you receive an email with a digital signature or

CHAPTER 7 CRYPTOGRAPHY AND PUBLIC KEY INFRASTRUCTURE

download a software update, cryptographic algorithms verify that the content has not been altered and that it comes from a trusted source. This is especially important in scenarios such as software distribution, where tampered files could introduce malware into a user's system. Public key infrastructure (PKI) supports this process, allowing individuals and organizations to sign documents digitally, providing a higher level of trust in electronic communications and transactions. As businesses increasingly move toward digital solutions, cryptography plays an essential role in maintaining secure and reliable interactions.

IoT Security

The rapid growth of the Internet of Things (IoT) has introduced new security challenges, as millions of interconnected devices communicate over networks. Cryptography helps protect data exchanged between IoT devices, ensuring that sensitive information, such as health data from wearables or control signals in smart homes, remains confidential. Techniques like **end-to-end encryption** and **mutual authentication** are employed to secure these communications. For example, TLS can be used to encrypt data sent from a smart thermostat to a cloud server, preventing unauthorized parties from intercepting or manipulating the data. Additionally, cryptographic methods like digital signatures ensure the authenticity of firmware updates, safeguarding devices from malicious software injections.

These examples illustrate the critical role cryptography plays in securing a wide array of applications. From protecting personal data and financial transactions to enabling the safe operation of emerging technologies, cryptographic techniques are integral to building trust in our digital landscape.

VPNs (Virtual Private Networks)

VPNs, or Virtual Private Networks, are tools that create secure, encrypted tunnels for data transmission between devices over the internet. By encrypting the data, VPNs protect against eavesdropping, man-in-the-middle attacks, and data tampering. This technology is widely used in both corporate environments for secure remote access and by individuals seeking privacy protection. VPNs ensure that sensitive information, such as login credentials or financial data, remains safe when transmitted over public networks like Wi-Fi.

Types of VPNs

Remote Access VPNs

Remote Access VPNs are designed for individual users to securely connect to a private network from remote locations. This is particularly useful for remote employees who need to access corporate resources securely, even when using public Wi-Fi. By encrypting the connection, Remote Access VPNs ensure that sensitive data cannot be intercepted by unauthorized parties.

Site-to-Site VPNs

Site-to-Site VPNs connect entire networks, such as linking a company's headquarters with its branch offices. This type of VPN is often used as a cost-effective alternative to leased lines, providing secure communication between different geographical locations. It allows multiple users across different sites to share resources securely as if they were part of the same local network.

Encryption Protocols

IPsec (Internet Protocol Security)

IPsec is a suite of protocols that secures IP communications by encrypting each IP packet in a data stream. It provides confidentiality, integrity, and authentication, making it a popular choice for securing VPN traffic. IPsec can be used in both Remote Access and Site-to-Site VPNs.

SSL/TLS (Secure Sockets Layer/Transport Layer Security)

SSL/TLS protocols are commonly used for securing web-based VPNs, particularly in Remote Access setups. These protocols encrypt data between the client and server, protecting it from interception. SSL/TLS-based VPNs are often preferred for their ease of use and ability to bypass firewalls that may block IPsec traffic.

Secure Email

Secure email technologies focus on protecting the confidentiality, integrity, and authenticity of email communications. Email encryption is crucial because, without it, emails can be easily intercepted and read by attackers. This is especially important for emails containing sensitive information, such as personal data, financial details, or confidential business communications.

Encryption Protocol Examples

PGP (Pretty Good Privacy)

PGP uses asymmetric encryption to secure email messages. The sender encrypts the email using the recipient's public key, ensuring that only the recipient, who possesses the corresponding private key, can decrypt it. PGP also provides digital signatures to verify the sender's identity and ensure the message has not been altered during transmission.

S/MIME (Secure/Multipurpose Internet Mail Extensions)

S/MIME is a widely adopted protocol that provides email encryption and digital signatures using digital certificates. It ensures that only the intended recipient can read the email and verifies the sender's identity, preventing spoofing and tampering. S/MIME is commonly used in enterprise environments to protect sensitive communications.

Disk Encryption

Disk encryption is a security measure that protects data stored on physical drives by converting it into unreadable ciphertext. This prevents unauthorized access, even if the device is lost or stolen. Disk encryption is crucial for safeguarding sensitive data on laptops, external drives, and corporate servers, ensuring compliance with data protection regulations.

Encryption Tools

BitLocker

BitLocker is a disk encryption feature built into Windows that uses the AES encryption algorithm to secure the entire drive, including the operating system. It integrates with Trusted Platform Modules (TPMs) for enhanced security, checking the integrity of the system before unlocking the drive. BitLocker is widely used in enterprises to protect data on endpoints and ensure regulatory compliance.

VeraCrypt

VeraCrypt is an open source encryption software that offers both full disk and partition encryption. It supports multiple encryption algorithms, such as AES, Serpent, and Twofish, allowing users to customize their security settings. VeraCrypt is popular among users seeking a flexible, transparent alternative to proprietary encryption tools.

CHAPTER 7 CRYPTOGRAPHY AND PUBLIC KEY INFRASTRUCTURE

Encryption Methods

Full Disk Encryption (FDE)

Full Disk Encryption encrypts the entire disk, including system files, applications, and user data. This method ensures that all data on the disk is protected, making it unreadable without the correct decryption key. FDE is commonly used in enterprise settings to meet data protection requirements and secure devices from unauthorized access.

File/Folder Encryption

This method encrypts specific files or folders rather than the entire disk, giving users more granular control over what data is protected. It is a useful approach when only certain sensitive files need to be secured, allowing the rest of the system to operate without the overhead of full disk encryption. This method is often used for encrypting individual documents, spreadsheets, or sensitive folders containing confidential information.

In summary, VPNs, secure email, and disk encryption are key components of a robust cybersecurity strategy, each addressing specific needs for data protection. They help maintain the confidentiality, integrity, and availability of information, whether it is being transmitted over the internet, communicated via email, or stored on a device.

Quantum Cryptography

Quantum cryptography explores methods to counteract the unique risks posed by quantum computing to traditional cryptographic systems. With the arrival of quantum computing, many of today's encryption protocols, such as RSA and ECC, are vulnerable because quantum computers can solve complex mathematical problems exponentially faster than classical computers. This creates an urgent need for encryption mechanisms that are "quantum-resistant" or can withstand the computational power of quantum systems. Current research and development efforts aim to establish quantum-resistant cryptographic protocols, which are grouped under **post-quantum cryptography**.

Post-Quantum Cryptography: Current Threats

Quantum computing poses specific challenges to current encryption models. For instance, algorithms like **RSA** rely on the difficulty of integer factorization, and **ECC** (Elliptic Curve Cryptography) relies on solving discrete logarithmic problems. Both of these are "hard" for classical computers, which means they take too long to solve for brute-force attacks to be feasible. However, **quantum computers could efficiently break these protocols** using algorithms like Shor's algorithm, designed to solve both integer factorization and discrete logarithmic problems in polynomial time. This rapid solving capability would make previously secure systems, such as banking, e-commerce, and encrypted communication, vulnerable to quantum-powered attacks.

Preparing for the Quantum Era

Organizations, governments, and standards bodies are now working on quantum-resistant solutions through several key areas of focus.

Research: Significant research is underway to create encryption protocols that quantum computers cannot easily break. Examples include **lattice-based cryptography**, which relies on solving complex lattice problems, and **hash-based cryptography**, which builds on secure hash functions. These protocols offer promising resistance to quantum attacks and are often more efficient in computational performance than traditional cryptography.

Standards Development: Organizations like **NIST** (National Institute of Standards and Technology) are spearheading the development of post-quantum standards to ensure consistent and effective security measures.

NIST is in the final stages of selecting and standardizing a set of post-quantum algorithms, anticipated to replace or complement RSA, ECC, and similar protocols widely used today.

Migration Strategies: Transitioning to post-quantum cryptographic infrastructure is a complex and resource-intensive process. Organizations are advised to develop migration plans to introduce quantum-resistant algorithms into their systems gradually. This often involves **hybrid cryptographic systems**, which combine classical and post-quantum algorithms, allowing for smoother transitions and enhanced security in the interim.

Example

For instance, banking systems using RSA for secure communications must prepare to switch to quantum-safe algorithms, such as **CRYSTALS-Kyber** (a lattice-based algorithm shortlisted by NIST) to ensure customer data remains secure even if quantum computing becomes mainstream.

Quantum Key Distribution (QKD)

Quantum Key Distribution (QKD) provides a highly secure method for key exchange by using the fundamental properties of quantum mechanics. Unlike traditional key exchange protocols that rely on complex mathematical problems for security, QKD uses principles of quantum physics, making it inherently resistant to eavesdropping. With QKD, any attempt to intercept or measure the quantum bits (or "qubits") during transmission will disturb their quantum state. This disturbance acts as an alert, immediately revealing the presence of an eavesdropper.

Security in Quantum Key Distribution

The security of QKD relies on two quantum properties: **superposition** and **entanglement**. Superposition enables qubits to exist in multiple states simultaneously, while entanglement connects qubits so that a change in one instantly affects the other, even over vast distances. The most common QKD protocol, **BB84**, uses these properties to encode and share keys between two parties, typically referred to as Alice and Bob. Any eavesdropper (Eve) trying to intercept the key will be detected due to the quantum state changes caused by her intrusion.

Limitations and Practical Challenges

While QKD holds significant promise, practical limitations impact its deployment. For example, QKD is highly **sensitive to distance**; reliable QKD connections are currently limited to a few hundred kilometers. Specialized **hardware, such as photon transmitters and receivers**, is also required, which restricts QKD's widespread application due to high implementation costs and the need for dedicated infrastructure. Nonetheless, progress is being made to overcome these limitations, and QKD systems are already in limited use in government and high-security sectors in countries like China and Switzerland.

Example

In a real-world scenario, banks and financial institutions might use QKD over short-range fiber optic connections to securely transfer sensitive financial data. In this context, QKD provides added assurance that no one is intercepting or tampering with the communication channel.

Real-World Applications and Future Prospects

Quantum cryptography is anticipated to play a pivotal role in fields where data sensitivity and security are paramount. Here are some key applications and future implications:

- **Government Communications**: Many governments are investing in QKD for secure communications, particularly for diplomatic and military use. China, for instance, has already launched a quantum communications satellite, **Micius**, which enables QKD-based data exchange between ground stations.

- **Financial Services**: With substantial financial transactions requiring high security, banks are exploring QKD and post-quantum cryptographic methods to future-proof their encryption standards, especially as cybercrime grows more sophisticated.

- **Healthcare and Legal Sectors**: Industries handling sensitive data, like healthcare and law, can benefit from QKD to ensure the privacy of patient records and sensitive documents.

Future Outlook

As quantum computing technology advances, the need for quantum-resistant and quantum-based cryptographic solutions will only increase. The primary challenge will be **scalability**, as quantum cryptographic protocols require specialized infrastructure and are limited by distance. However, with continuous advancements in fiber optics, satellite QKD, and hybrid cryptographic models, the vision for a quantum-secure future is becoming more achievable.

Quantum cryptography, through protocols like QKD and post-quantum cryptographic algorithms, offers transformative potential in data security, promising robust solutions to counter the risks introduced by quantum computing's growth. As organizations worldwide begin adopting these next-generation cryptographic standards, industries that manage highly sensitive data will be at the forefront of quantum-secure technology deployment, setting a new standard for digital security in the quantum era.

CHAPTER 8

Security Operations and Incident Response

A Security Operations Center (SOC) is the centralized team or facility within an organization responsible for continuously monitoring, detecting, analyzing, and responding to cybersecurity incidents. SOCs serve as the frontline defense against cyber threats, integrating people, processes, and technology to safeguard the organization's assets. They play a vital role in identifying potential vulnerabilities, mitigating security risks, and minimizing damage from attacks.

The SOC is typically structured into various roles and tiers, each responsible for different tasks to ensure a comprehensive approach to security operations. These roles range from analysts at different experience levels to dedicated incident responders and proactive threat hunters. Together, these roles work cohesively to protect the organization from emerging threats and support the broader goals of the information security program.

CHAPTER 8   SECURITY OPERATIONS AND INCIDENT RESPONSE

Roles and Responsibilities

SOC analysts are divided into tiers based on their expertise and responsibilities. Each level serves a distinct function to ensure comprehensive coverage of potential threats:

- **Tier 1 Analysts**

    Tier 1 analysts are the first line of defense and primarily focus on **monitoring and triaging alerts**. They respond to potential security incidents as they occur, assessing the nature of alerts and escalating issues that require further investigation. These analysts often use Security Information and Event Management (SIEM) tools to filter through volumes of logs and pinpoint suspicious activity. The efficiency of Tier 1 analysts in handling routine alerts and recognizing true positives from false positives is critical in reducing response times.

- **Tier 2 Analysts**

    When incidents are escalated, Tier 2 analysts perform **in-depth investigations and analyses**. They handle more complex incidents by conducting root cause analysis, studying patterns of suspicious activity, and initiating containment and remediation efforts. These analysts often have more advanced technical skills and experience in handling varied threat scenarios, enabling them to coordinate initial response strategies and manage incidents with a greater degree of sophistication.

- **Tier 3 Analysts**

    Often referred to as threat hunters, Tier 3 analysts proactively search for cyber threats that might bypass traditional detection methods. They use **threat**

intelligence, behavioral analysis, and advanced threat-hunting tools to identify hidden or advanced threats. Unlike other SOC analysts who react to alerts, threat hunters seek out potential issues before they can escalate, adding a proactive element to the SOC's capabilities. Their efforts often lead to improvements in threat detection and reveal vulnerabilities that may otherwise remain undetected.

- Threat hunters may operate individually as a separate entity that is separated from the normal tiered SOC hierarchy.

Incident Responders

Incident responders focus on managing active security incidents. Their responsibilities include identifying the scope and nature of attacks, containing threats, eradicating malicious actors from systems, and restoring normal operations. These responders typically work closely with other SOC members and business units to manage incidents efficiently:

- **Role**: Incident responders are responsible for executing the incident response plan, working to **contain, eradicate, and recover** from security incidents.

- **Responsibilities**: They develop response procedures, manage communication during incidents, and coordinate with IT teams and other stakeholders to ensure a unified response. After incidents, responders document the process, conduct debriefs, and analyze what went well and what could be improved. It is common for the Incident Responders to coordinate directly with the organization's legal, compliance, or public relation departments.

CHAPTER 8   SECURITY OPERATIONS AND INCIDENT RESPONSE

Threat Hunters

Distinct from reactive SOC roles, threat hunters work proactively to **identify cyber threats before they can cause harm**. They use tools and techniques such as anomaly detection, behavioral analysis, and leveraging threat intelligence to identify and neutralize threats:

- **Role**: Threat hunters actively investigate potential threats using **proactive analysis**, rather than waiting for alerts.
- **Responsibilities**: They analyze behavior patterns, scrutinize data sources, and work to improve overall SOC visibility into hard-to-detect threats, ensuring the organization stays one step ahead of attackers.

The Incident Response Process

The incident response process is a structured approach for handling and resolving security incidents to mitigate the impact on the organization. This process is divided into several key phases.

Preparation

Preparation is a critical phase in incident response, focusing on building and maintaining the capability to respond effectively. This includes establishing policies, developing an incident response plan, forming an incident response team, and ensuring that tools and training are in place.

- **Incident Response Team:** Designating a team with clearly defined roles ensures a coordinated response to incidents.

- **Training and Awareness**: Regular training helps personnel understand their roles and ensures readiness to handle incidents.

- **Tools and Technologies**: Necessary tools like SIEM, Endpoint Detection and Response (EDR), and forensic tools must be in place to facilitate swift detection and investigation.

Detection and Analysis

This phase involves identifying and verifying potential security incidents. Detection and analysis require continuous monitoring and a thorough approach to analyzing suspicious activity:

- **Monitoring**: SOCs continuously monitor networks, systems, and endpoints for anomalies.

- **Alerting**: Automated tools like SIEMs trigger alerts when predefined criteria are met.

- **Analysis**: Analysts assess the incident's nature and scope by conducting log analysis, forensics, and consulting threat intelligence sources. This process helps determine the appropriate response.

Containment

Containment limits the impact of a security incident. This phase includes both short-term and long-term strategies to prevent the incident from spreading further:

- **Short-Term Containment**: Actions taken immediately, such as isolating affected systems to stop the attack's spread.

- **Long-Term Containment**: Implementing measures like network segmentation or patching vulnerabilities to keep systems operational while addressing the incident's root cause.

Eradication

During eradication, the focus shifts to removing the root cause of the incident:

- **Malware Removal**: Complete removal of any malicious code found on systems.

- **Vulnerability Mitigation**: Closing security gaps that were exploited in the attack to prevent recurrence.

- **Verification**: Running scans and tests to ensure all malicious elements have been removed.

Recovery

The recovery phase involves restoring and validating system functionality after the incident has been resolved. This process ensures that systems return to a secure operational state:

- **System Restoration**: Bringing affected systems back online, often using backups.

- **Validation**: Verifying that all systems are functioning correctly and securely.

- **Monitoring**: Continued monitoring of previously affected systems to detect any signs of remaining or new threats.

Post-incident Activities

Following the containment and eradication of an incident, the SOC conducts a post-incident review to assess the response and identify improvements:

- **Lessons Learned**: Reviewing the incident to understand what strategies worked well and identifying areas for improvement.

- **Incident Reporting**: Documenting the incident, including causes, impact, and response actions, and sharing this report with stakeholders.

Through these structured processes and roles, SOCs and their incident response capabilities are critical to maintaining an organization's cybersecurity posture. As cyber threats become increasingly sophisticated, an effective SOC can detect, contain, and resolve incidents quickly to minimize damage and ensure the security of sensitive data and systems.

Threat Hunting
Proactive vs. Reactive Security

In cybersecurity, there are two fundamental approaches to threat management: proactive and reactive security. Each plays a critical role, but threat hunting is inherently proactive, meaning it aims to find and neutralize threats before they materialize into active incidents.

- **Proactive Security (Threat Hunting)**

  Proactive security is about **actively searching for threats** rather than waiting for an alert or signs of an incident to emerge. The goal is to get ahead of potential attacks by investigating indicators that may signal early-stage threats.

  - **Objective**: Threat hunting seeks to detect threats that may be evading automated systems by analyzing patterns and behaviors that don't necessarily trigger alerts but could indicate malicious intent.

  - **Methods**: Threat hunters utilize a combination of **behavioral analysis, threat intelligence, and indicators of compromise (IOCs)** to uncover possible threats. This might involve looking for unusual login patterns, studying network traffic, or investigating anomalies that could signify malicious activity.

- **Reactive Security**

  In contrast to proactive hunting, reactive security focuses on **responding to threats** once they are detected, often through automated alerts.

  - **Objective**: Reactive security involves responding to confirmed incidents after they've been detected by security systems.

  - **Methods**: This approach depends on **alerts from tools** like Security Information and Event Management (SIEM), Endpoint Detection and Response (EDR), and other automated security mechanisms. Alerts prompt investigation and response to contain and resolve the threat.

CHAPTER 8 SECURITY OPERATIONS AND INCIDENT RESPONSE

The Role of Threat Hunting in Modern SOCs

In today's cybersecurity landscape, threat hunting is crucial within Security Operations Centers (SOCs) as it adds an essential layer to existing security operations:

- **Enhancing Security Posture**

    Threat hunting provides an additional, proactive layer of defense by identifying threats that may not trigger automated alerts. This strengthens the SOC's overall security capabilities and allows the team to respond to potential threats more effectively.

- **Reducing Dwell Time**

    A primary goal of threat hunting is to **reduce dwell time**—the amount of time an undetected threat remains in the network. By reducing this window, SOCs minimize the potential damage and data loss that a threat could cause if it were allowed to persist undetected.

Forensics and Evidence Handling

In incident response and security operations, forensics and proper evidence handling are essential for investigating incidents and ensuring legal admissibility of evidence.

CHAPTER 8   SECURITY OPERATIONS AND INCIDENT RESPONSE

Chain of Custody

The chain of custody refers to the rigorous documentation process required to maintain the integrity of evidence. It is crucial for tracking the handling, transfer, and analysis of evidence, ensuring it remains tamper-free and can be used in legal proceedings.

- **Overview**

    The chain of custody tracks **who handles evidence, when it was accessed, and why**. It serves as a record for every point of contact with the evidence from the time of collection to its presentation in court.

- **Importance**

    - **Legal Considerations**: An unbroken chain of custody is essential for evidence to be legally admissible in court. Without proper documentation, there is a risk that the evidence could be discredited.

    - **Integrity of Evidence**: Documenting each transfer and access point helps ensure that the evidence remains unaltered. Proper handling procedures reduce the likelihood of tampering or accidental changes that could affect the investigation's outcome.

- **Maintenance**

    - **Documentation**: Every individual who interacts with the evidence must document the **date, time, purpose, and their identification details**. This documentation creates a comprehensive record that verifies the evidence's authenticity.

- **Secure Storage**: Evidence should be kept in **secure, controlled-access storage** areas, ensuring it is only accessible to authorized personnel. This control mitigates the risk of unauthorized handling and maintains the evidence's integrity.

Backup Strategies

Backing up data is critical for ensuring the availability and integrity of information in the event of a disaster, system failure, or cyberattack. Different backup methods offer varying levels of convenience, storage efficiency, and ease of restoration, making it essential to choose the right approach for your organization's needs.

Full Backup

A full backup is the most comprehensive form of data backup, as it involves creating a complete copy of all files and data within the system.

- **Overview**

  A full backup captures everything within the system, providing a **complete snapshot** of the organization's data at a specific point in time. This type of backup is often performed initially and serves as a foundational point for other backup strategies.

- **Pros**
  - **Simplifies Restoration**: Since all data is stored in one place, restoring from a full backup is straightforward, making it faster and easier to return to normal operations after a data loss event.

- **Reliability**: A full backup is self-contained, so it's less prone to restoration errors compared to other methods.
- **Cons**
  - **Time-Consuming**: A full backup requires a significant amount of time to complete, especially for large datasets.
  - **High Storage Requirements**: Because it stores an entire copy of all data, a full backup consumes substantial storage space, which may increase costs and complexity.

Incremental Backup

An incremental backup is a more storage-efficient approach that only backs up data that has changed since the last backup, whether that last backup was full or incremental.

- **Overview**

  In an incremental backup strategy, the system saves **only the data that has been modified** since the most recent backup. This incremental approach results in a series of small backups that track daily changes.
- **Pros**
  - **Faster Backup Process**: Since incremental backups only capture modified data, they are quicker to perform than full backups.

- **Reduced Storage Requirements**: Incremental backups require significantly less storage space because they save only the changes made since the last backup.

- **Cons**

  - **Longer Restoration Time**: To restore a system, incremental backups require the last full backup and all subsequent incremental backups. This can be time-intensive, as the system must sequentially apply each incremental backup.

  - **Complexity in Management**: Since multiple backups must be managed, the process can become complex, and missing any backup can disrupt the restoration process.

Differential Backup

A differential backup strikes a balance between full and incremental backups by backing up all data that has changed since the last full backup.

- **Overview**

  Unlike incremental backups, which track changes since the last backup of any type, differential backups **track changes since the last full backup**. As a result, each differential backup grows in size until the next full backup is completed.

- **Pros**
  - **Simplified Restoration**: Restoration from a differential backup only requires the last full backup and the most recent differential backup, making it easier to manage than incremental backups.
  - **Moderate Storage Needs**: Differential backups require less storage than full backups but more than incremental backups, offering a balance between storage efficiency and recovery speed.
- **Cons**
  - **Increasing Backup Size**: Each differential backup captures all changes since the last full back up, so they grow larger over time, which can impact storage efficiency.
  - **Longer Backup Time**: As the volume of data increases, differential backups take progressively longer to complete, making them less ideal for rapid, repeated backups.

Choosing the Right Backup Strategy

The ideal backup strategy depends on several factors, including the organization's data volume, recovery time objectives (RTOs), and available storage capacity. A **combination of full, incremental, and differential backups** is often employed to balance storage efficiency, backup speed, and recovery time. Regularly testing the restoration process for each backup type is also essential to ensure data recovery when needed.

Log Analysis

Log analysis is a foundational process in detecting and investigating security incidents. Logs generated by systems, applications, and networks contain valuable data that, when properly analyzed, can reveal signs of malicious activity and help with incident investigation.

- **Overview**

    Log analysis involves examining data from various logs to **identify patterns** or **anomalies** that may indicate a security incident. This process helps security teams trace the origins, methods, and scope of potential threats.

- **Techniques**

    - **Pattern Matching**: Involves searching logs for specific patterns, such as keywords, IP addresses, or timestamps, that are known indicators of potential threats.

    - **Anomaly Detection**: Identifies deviations from normal behavior. For example, a spike in login attempts may suggest a brute-force attack, while unusual login times could point to account compromise.

CHAPTER 8   SECURITY OPERATIONS AND INCIDENT RESPONSE

Network Traffic Analysis

Network traffic analysis is crucial for detecting malicious activities that may not be evident from log analysis alone. By inspecting data packets and flows, security teams can identify anomalies and potential attacks on the network.

- **Overview**

  Network traffic analysis focuses on **capturing and examining data** traveling across the network, allowing analysts to spot potential threats that are attempting to bypass standard defenses.

- **Methods**

  - **Packet Analysis**: Inspecting individual data packets to detect suspicious content or unusual protocols that may indicate malicious intent.

  - **Flow Analysis**: Analyzing traffic patterns over time to identify unusual activity, such as sudden increases in outbound traffic that may indicate data exfiltration.

Security Information and Event Management (SIEM) Tools

SIEM tools are essential in modern security operations, combining real-time monitoring, correlation, and alerting capabilities to detect and respond to security threats efficiently.

- **Features**

  - **Real-Time Monitoring**: Provides continuous visibility across network and system events, ensuring timely detection of potential threats.

  - **Correlation**: SIEM tools correlate events from multiple sources (e.g., firewalls, antivirus logs) to identify complex threats that may not be apparent in isolation.

  - **Alerting**: Automated alerts notify analysts of potential threats as they occur, allowing for swift action to mitigate risks.

- **Use Cases**

  - **Threat Detection**: SIEM tools aggregate data across the environment to detect security incidents in real time, enhancing the SOC's response capabilities.

  - **Compliance Reporting**: SIEMs simplify regulatory compliance by automating the collection, analysis, and reporting of security data to meet standards like GDPR and HIPAA.

  - **Incident Response**: By centralizing logging and analysis, SIEMs enable rapid investigation and coordination in incident response efforts.

Advanced SIEM Capabilities

Advanced SIEM tools use more sophisticated analytics and automation to enhance threat detection, compliance, and incident response processes.

- **Threat Detection**
  - **Advanced Analytics**: Machine learning, behavioral analysis, and threat intelligence integration help SIEMs detect advanced threats.
  - **Anomaly Detection**: SIEMs identify deviations from baseline behavior, which may signify stealthy or persistent threats.
- **Compliance**
  - **Automated Compliance Reporting**: Many SIEMs have built-in templates and automation for regulatory compliance reporting, helping organizations stay up-to-date with evolving requirements.
- **Incident Response**
  - **Automated Response**: Some SIEMs have automated actions for specific alerts, such as isolating compromised devices or locking accounts, to minimize damage from active threats.

Security Orchestration and Automated Response (SOAR) Tools

SOAR tools extend the capabilities of SIEMs by automating response workflows, coordinating across tools, and enhancing the efficiency of security operations centers (SOCs).

CHAPTER 8   SECURITY OPERATIONS AND INCIDENT RESPONSE

- **Overview**

  SOAR platforms **integrate with SIEMs and other security tools** to provide a centralized response platform, where tasks can be automated to reduce manual workload, streamline incident handling, and improve response times.

- **Enhancing Incident Response with Automation**

  - **Playbooks**: SOAR playbooks define automated response actions for specific incidents, reducing human error and improving response consistency.

  - **Integration with SIEM**: By connecting with SIEM tools, SOAR platforms trigger automatic responses to alerts, enhancing response speed and efficiency.

  - **Case Management**: SOAR tools provide features for tracking incidents from detection to resolution, enabling SOC teams to document actions and improve future incident response efforts.

Together, these tools and methods in security operations help SOC teams monitor, detect, analyze, and respond to threats more effectively, creating a more resilient security posture.

CHAPTER 9

Governance, Risk, and Compliance

Risk management is a vital component of organizational governance that focuses on identifying, evaluating, and mitigating potential risks to safeguard assets, ensure compliance, and maintain operational continuity. This chapter dives into the core processes of risk assessments and risk mitigation. Together, these processes form the backbone of effective risk management, helping organizations proactively address potential threats and minimize their impact.

Risk Assessments

Risk assessments are structured processes aimed at systematically identifying, evaluating, and prioritizing risks associated with an organization's assets. By conducting thorough risk assessments, organizations can develop targeted strategies to address vulnerabilities and minimize exposure to potential threats.

CHAPTER 9   GOVERNANCE, RISK, AND COMPLIANCE

Key Components of Risk Assessments

1. **Asset Identification**

    The first step in any risk assessment is to identify and catalog all critical assets that need protection. These assets can be tangible, like physical hardware, or intangible, like data and intellectual property. Understanding the value and importance of each asset helps in determining the level of protection required.

    - **Data:** Includes sensitive customer information, proprietary data, financial records, and other crucial datasets that must be protected from unauthorized access.

    - **Hardware:** Comprises servers, workstations, network devices, and any other physical infrastructure that supports organizational operations.

    - **Software:** Encompasses applications, operating systems, and services that are integral to business processes.

    - **Intellectual Property:** Covers patents, trademarks, proprietary methodologies, and trade secrets that give the organization a competitive edge.

2. **Threat Assessment**

    Once assets are identified, the next step is to assess potential threats that could exploit vulnerabilities. Threats can be external or internal, and understanding these risks helps organizations prepare appropriate defenses.

- **Cyberattacks**: Includes threats like malware, phishing attacks, ransomware, and distributed denial-of-service (DDoS) attacks, which can compromise data integrity and availability.

- **Natural Disasters**: Such as earthquakes, floods, and fires, which can cause physical damage to assets and disrupt operations.

- **Insider Threats**: Actions by current or former employees, contractors, or business associates who may intentionally or unintentionally cause harm through unauthorized access or misuse of resources.

    i. **This often will include**

    1. **Data Theft**: This is the most common target of malicious insider threats. It could be targeted toward selling to competitors, similar to corporate espionage, or to further personal gain.

    2. **Sabotage**: There are various methods for sabotage, whether physical, environmental, system, etc. The commonality here is that it is a direct and malicious action taken against the organization.

    3. **Privilege Abuse: Unlike the other** two instances, this is not necessarily always of malicious intent. There are plenty of cases where an individual exploits privilege abuse and/or scope creep out of laziness. It is common that an individual will see a more direct route than the known and proven standard procedure.

3. **Vulnerability Assessment**

   This process involves identifying weaknesses within systems, processes, and policies that could be exploited by identified threats. Recognizing these gaps is crucial for developing targeted risk mitigation strategies.

   - **Technical Vulnerabilities**: These include outdated or unpatched software, misconfigured systems, and insecure network configurations that could be exploited by cyber attackers.

   - **Operational Weaknesses**: Includes inadequate staff training, lack of clear security policies, and insufficient incident response planning, which may leave the organization vulnerable to threats.

4. **Impact Analysis**

   Impact analysis estimates the potential consequences of a risk event on the organization. Understanding the extent of the damage a risk could cause helps prioritize mitigation efforts.

   - **Financial Impact**: Assesses potential revenue losses, costs related to incident recovery, legal fees, and potential fines due to non-compliance.

   - **Operational Impact**: Evaluates the disruption to critical services or production processes, which can affect business continuity.

   - **Reputational Impact**: Considers the potential damage to the organization's brand image and customer trust, which could have long-term effects on business performance.

5. **Risk Likelihood**

   Determining the likelihood of a risk occurring is essential for effective risk prioritization. This involves analyzing historical data, industry trends, threat intelligence, and the current threat landscape to gauge the probability of a threat successfully exploiting a vulnerability.

6. **Risk Rating**

   The final step in the risk assessment process involves combining the impact and likelihood assessments to prioritize risks based on their severity. This is often visualized using a risk matrix, which classifies risks into categories such as low, medium, and high. By assigning a risk rating, organizations can prioritize their response efforts, focusing on high-risk areas that require immediate attention.

Summary

Risk assessments are the cornerstone of a robust risk management strategy. By systematically identifying assets, assessing potential threats, evaluating vulnerabilities, and analyzing the impact and likelihood of risks, organizations can develop a clear picture of their risk landscape. This process enables them to make informed decisions on how to allocate resources effectively, implement appropriate security controls, and prioritize risk mitigation efforts to protect their most valuable assets.

Risk Mitigation

Risk mitigation involves implementing controls and strategies to reduce the impact or likelihood of identified risks. The goal is to create a balanced approach that protects organizational assets without incurring excessive costs.

Strategies

1. **Risk Avoidance**
   - Taking steps to eliminate the risk entirely, often by discontinuing the risky activity. For example, if a business operation poses a high risk, the organization may decide to stop that operation altogether.

2. **Risk Reduction**
   - Implementing controls to minimize the impact or likelihood of risks. This includes
     - **Technical Controls**: Firewalls, intrusion detection systems, and encryption.
     - **Administrative Controls**: Policies, procedures, and employee training to foster a security-aware culture.

3. **Risk Transfer**
   - Shifting the risk to a third party, typically through insurance or outsourcing certain functions. For example, organizations may purchase cyber insurance to cover potential losses from data breaches.

CHAPTER 9   GOVERNANCE, RISK, AND COMPLIANCE

4. **Risk Acceptance**
   - Acknowledging the risk and deciding to accept it without additional controls. This approach is usually taken when the cost of mitigation exceeds the potential impact of the risk, allowing organizations to allocate resources more efficiently.

By thoroughly understanding risk assessments and implementing effective risk mitigation strategies, organizations can enhance their overall security posture, ensuring resilience in the face of threats while complying with governance and regulatory requirements. This chapter provides a framework for managing risks effectively, facilitating informed decision-making, and prioritizing resources for the most significant risks facing the organization.

Risk Management Frameworks

Risk management frameworks provide structured methodologies for organizations to identify, assess, and manage risks effectively. Two prominent frameworks are the **NIST Risk Management Framework (RMF)** and **ISO/IEC 27001**. Each framework offers unique guidelines and standards to enhance information security and risk management practices.

NIST Risk Management Framework (RMF)

The NIST RMF is a structured approach to managing risk, offering comprehensive guidelines for categorizing information systems, selecting security controls, and monitoring their effectiveness. It emphasizes a continuous cycle of risk management to ensure that security measures adapt to evolving threats.

CHAPTER 9   GOVERNANCE, RISK, AND COMPLIANCE

Steps

1. **Categorize Systems**
   - Determine the criticality and sensitivity of the information system based on its potential impact on the organization. This involves assessing the confidentiality, integrity, and availability (CIA) of the data processed by the system.

2. **Select Controls**
   - Choose appropriate security controls from the NIST SP 800-53 catalog. This catalog provides a comprehensive set of security controls that organizations can tailor to their specific needs and risk profiles.

3. **Implement Controls**
   - Apply the selected controls within the system environment. This step includes integrating the controls into the organization's operations and ensuring they are operationally effective.

4. **Assess Controls**
   - Evaluate the effectiveness of the implemented controls through testing and review. This assessment helps identify any gaps or weaknesses in the security measures.

5. **Authorize Systems**
   - Approve the system to operate based on the risk assessment and control implementation. This step involves a formal acceptance of the residual risk associated with the system.

CHAPTER 9   GOVERNANCE, RISK, AND COMPLIANCE

6. **Monitor Controls**

    - Continuously monitor the system's security controls for effectiveness and changes in risk. This ongoing assessment ensures that the controls remain effective over time and adapt to new threats.

ISO/IEC 27001

ISO/IEC 27001 is an international standard for managing information security risks. It focuses on establishing, implementing, maintaining, and improving an Information Security Management System (ISMS) to safeguard sensitive information.

Key Elements

1. **Context of the Organization**

    - Understand the internal and external factors that affect information security. This includes identifying stakeholders, regulatory requirements, and the organization's risk appetite.

2. **Leadership**

    - Ensure top management's commitment to information security. This element emphasizes the importance of leadership in establishing roles, responsibilities, and accountability for information security.

3. **Planning**

    - Identify risks and opportunities related to information security. Set objectives and develop plans to achieve these objectives, ensuring that they align with the organization's overall strategy.

CHAPTER 9 GOVERNANCE, RISK, AND COMPLIANCE

4. **Support**

    - Provide the necessary resources, competence, awareness, and communication for effective information security management. This includes training staff and ensuring they understand their roles in maintaining security.

5. **Operation**

    - Implement the ISMS and associated security controls effectively. This operational aspect involves executing the plans developed during the planning phase.

6. **Performance Evaluation**

    - Monitor, measure, analyze, and evaluate the performance of the ISMS. This evaluation helps determine the effectiveness of the information security measures in place.

7. **Improvement**

    - Focus on the continuous improvement of the ISMS based on performance evaluations, audits, and changes in the organizational context. This iterative process ensures that the ISMS evolves to meet new challenges and threats.

By leveraging frameworks like the **NIST RMF** and **ISO/IEC 27001**, organizations can establish robust risk management practices that not only protect their assets but also ensure compliance with regulatory requirements. These frameworks provide a systematic approach to managing risks, enabling organizations to respond effectively to the ever-changing landscape of threats.

Compliance Standards: GDPR, HIPAA, PCI-DSS

Compliance standards are regulations designed to protect sensitive data and ensure privacy, particularly in industries that handle personal, financial, or healthcare information. Organizations must adhere to these standards to safeguard data, mitigate the risk of breaches, and avoid significant legal and financial penalties. Let's look at three of the most impactful compliance standards: **GDPR (General Data Protection Regulation)**, **HIPAA (Health Insurance Portability and Accountability Act)**, and **PCI-DSS (Payment Card Industry Data Security Standard)**.

General Data Protection Regulation (GDPR)

The **GDPR** is a comprehensive data protection regulation enacted by the European Union in 2018. It was designed to give individuals more control over their personal data and to standardize data privacy laws across Europe. GDPR applies to any organization that processes the personal data of EU citizens, regardless of the organization's location.

Key aspects of GDPR include

- **Data Subject Rights**: GDPR grants individuals several rights regarding their data, including the right to access, correct, delete, and restrict the processing of their data. Organizations must provide transparency in how they collect, use, and store personal data.

- **Data Protection Principles**: GDPR enforces principles such as data minimization (only collecting data necessary for the intended purpose), accuracy, integrity, and confidentiality. Organizations must implement appropriate technical and organizational measures to protect personal data from unauthorized access or breaches.

- **Data Breach Notifications**: Under GDPR, organizations must notify affected individuals and the relevant data protection authority of a data breach within 72 hours if the breach is likely to result in a risk to individual rights and freedoms.

- **Fines and Penalties**: GDPR imposes strict fines for non-compliance, with penalties reaching up to €20 million or 4% of the organization's global annual revenue, whichever is higher. This has made GDPR compliance a critical focus for organizations handling EU citizen data.

Health Insurance Portability and Accountability Act (HIPAA)

HIPAA is a US federal law enacted in 1996 to protect sensitive patient health information from being disclosed without the patient's consent or knowledge. HIPAA sets the standard for how healthcare providers, insurers, and related entities handle protected health information (PHI).

Key components of HIPAA include

- **Privacy Rule**: The HIPAA Privacy Rule establishes national standards to protect individuals' medical records and personal health information. It gives patients' rights over their health information, including the right to obtain a copy of their health records and request corrections.

- **Security Rule**: The Security Rule specifies administrative, physical, and technical safeguards that covered entities must implement to protect electronic protected health information (ePHI). This includes measures like access controls, encryption, and regular security assessments.

- **Breach Notification Rule**: HIPAA requires covered entities to notify affected individuals, the Department of Health and Human Services (HHS), and, in some cases, the media when a breach of unsecured PHI occurs. The notification must be made without unreasonable delay and no later than 60 days after the breach is discovered.

- **Enforcement and Penalties**: The HHS Office for Civil Rights (OCR) enforces HIPAA compliance. Penalties for violations can be severe, ranging from $100 to $50,000 per violation, with a maximum annual penalty of $1.5 million for repeated violations.

Payment Card Industry Data Security Standard (PCI-DSS)

PCI-DSS is a set of security standards designed to ensure that all companies that accept, process, store, or transmit credit card information maintain a secure environment. Developed by the Payment Card Industry Security Standards Council (PCI SSC), PCI-DSS aims to protect cardholder data and reduce credit card fraud.

CHAPTER 9   GOVERNANCE, RISK, AND COMPLIANCE

Key requirements of PCI-DSS include

- **Build and Maintain a Secure Network**: Organizations must install and maintain a firewall configuration to protect cardholder data. This also includes using strong passwords and regularly updating security settings to prevent unauthorized access.

- **Protect Cardholder Data**: PCI-DSS mandates the encryption of cardholder data transmitted across open, public networks and requires storing sensitive information securely. Organizations must ensure that data is only accessible to authorized personnel.

- **Maintain a Vulnerability Management Program**: Organizations must regularly update anti-virus software, perform security scans, and apply patches to protect against malware and other vulnerabilities.

- **Implement Strong Access Control Measures**: Access to cardholder data should be limited based on the need to know. This includes assigning unique IDs to each person with computer access and restricting physical access to cardholder data.

- **Regularly Monitor and Test Networks**: Organizations must track and monitor all access to network resources and cardholder data. Regular security testing, including vulnerability scans and penetration tests, is also required to identify and mitigate potential security issues.

- **Compliance and Penalties**: Non-compliance with PCI-DSS can result in hefty fines, increased transaction fees, and even the loss of the ability to process credit card payments. Penalties are determined by the payment brands (Visa, MasterCard, etc.) and can vary based on the severity and duration of the non-compliance.

The Importance of Compliance

Adhering to these compliance standards is critical for protecting sensitive data and maintaining customer trust. Non-compliance can lead to severe financial penalties, reputational damage, and even legal action. By implementing robust security measures and adhering to these regulations, organizations can better safeguard their data, reduce the risk of breaches, and demonstrate their commitment to data protection and privacy.

Global vs. Regional Compliance

In today's interconnected world, organizations must comply with a complex landscape of data protection regulations and standards that vary by country and region. These compliance frameworks are designed to ensure the security, privacy, and confidentiality of sensitive data, and they can differ significantly in scope and requirements. The distinction between **global compliance** and **regional compliance** is crucial for organizations that operate across borders, as they must navigate these regulations to maintain legal and operational standards.

Global Compliance

Global compliance refers to the standards and regulations that apply to organizations on an international level. These frameworks set universal principles for data protection and privacy, and their requirements are designed to be applicable across multiple jurisdictions.

CHAPTER 9   GOVERNANCE, RISK, AND COMPLIANCE

The **General Data Protection Regulation (GDPR)** is one of the most prominent examples of global compliance. Enacted by the European Union (EU), GDPR sets a high bar for data privacy and protection, with strict rules about how organizations must handle personal data of EU citizens. GDPR applies not only to companies based in the EU but also to organizations worldwide that process the data of EU residents. As such, global compliance standards like GDPR are crucial for businesses involved in international trade, e-commerce, and data exchange, as they ensure that personal information is handled with care and accountability, regardless of geographical boundaries.

Regional Compliance

Regional compliance refers to regulations and standards that apply within a specific geographic area or country. These laws are typically designed to address unique legal, cultural, or economic concerns within the region they govern. Regional compliance requirements can vary widely, and they may be more focused on particular types of data or industries compared to global standards.

For instance, in the **United States**, **HIPAA (Health Insurance Portability and Accountability Act)** governs the protection of healthcare information, and **PCI-DSS (Payment Card Industry Data Security Standard)** regulates the security of payment card transactions. Similarly, other regions like the Asia-Pacific or Latin America may have their own local laws that are tailored to their specific needs and priorities. Regional compliance frameworks often have unique requirements, such as specific encryption standards, breach notification procedures, or the handling of certain types of data (e.g., financial records or medical information).

CHAPTER 9   GOVERNANCE, RISK, AND COMPLIANCE

Overlaps Between Global and Regional Compliance

While global and regional compliance requirements can differ, there are notable overlaps. Many of the fundamental principles of data protection are shared between the two, including

- **Data Protection**: Both global and regional regulations often require organizations to implement strong data protection measures, including encryption, access controls, and secure storage of sensitive information.

- **Breach Notification**: Most compliance standards—whether global or regional—demand that organizations notify affected individuals and authorities in the event of a data breach. For example, GDPR mandates breach notification within 72 hours, and similar requirements exist under HIPAA and other regional laws.

- **Personal Information Handling**: The secure handling of personally identifiable information (PII) or sensitive personal data is a key element of both global and regional standards. This includes ensuring that data is used for legitimate purposes, protecting it from unauthorized access, and obtaining consent where necessary.

Despite these commonalities, the specifics of these requirements can differ. For instance, GDPR has strict consent and data portability provisions that may not be explicitly covered in regional laws like HIPAA, which focuses more on healthcare-related data.

CHAPTER 9   GOVERNANCE, RISK, AND COMPLIANCE

Challenges of Global and Regional Compliance

For organizations operating across multiple regions, navigating global and regional compliance can be challenging. Some of the key challenges include

- **Differing Requirements**: Different regions may have different thresholds for data protection, breach notification timelines, and consent management. An organization may need to reconcile these differences to ensure they meet the most stringent requirements applicable to each region.

- **Conflicting Regulations**: In some cases, global and regional standards may conflict. For example, a global regulation like GDPR may mandate the transfer of data outside the EU under strict conditions, while certain regional laws may prohibit or restrict such transfers. This can create compliance challenges for companies with international operations.

- **Cost and Resource Allocation**: Maintaining compliance with multiple regional and global standards requires significant investment in resources, including legal counsel, compliance officers, and technical infrastructure. Organizations must ensure that they are allocating adequate resources to meet the complex demands of compliance without overburdening their operations.

- **Ongoing Monitoring**: Compliance is not a one-time task but an ongoing process. Organizations need to continuously monitor changes in local and international laws to ensure that their practices remain compliant over time.

CHAPTER 9   GOVERNANCE, RISK, AND COMPLIANCE

Navigating Global and Regional Compliance

To successfully navigate the complexities of global and regional compliance, organizations must take a proactive approach. This includes

- **Conducting a Thorough Risk Assessment**: Organizations should assess the regions they operate in and the types of data they handle to understand the compliance requirements that apply to their business activities.

- **Implementing a Comprehensive Compliance Framework**: Establishing a unified compliance framework that accounts for both global and regional standards can help organizations streamline their efforts. This framework should include robust data protection practices, breach response plans, and regular audits to ensure adherence to all relevant regulations.

- **Leveraging Technology**: Tools like automated compliance management software, data encryption technologies, and data loss prevention systems can help organizations maintain compliance with global and regional standards.

- **Staying Informed**: Given that compliance standards can change over time, organizations must keep abreast of updates to global and regional regulations to ensure continued compliance and avoid penalties.

In conclusion, while global and regional compliance standards may have similarities, the differences in their scope, requirements, and enforcement can present challenges for multinational organizations. Understanding and effectively navigating these regulations is essential for businesses to safeguard sensitive data, maintain customer trust, and avoid costly penalties. By staying informed and adopting best practices, organizations can ensure they meet their compliance obligations across multiple jurisdictions.

Security Policies, Procedures, and Best Practices

Establishing strong security policies and procedures is essential for organizations to protect sensitive information, ensure compliance, and mitigate risks. These policies not only guide the organization's security efforts but also help maintain a consistent approach to managing security across various teams and departments. Developing effective security policies involves a comprehensive, well-coordinated effort that aligns with business objectives, involves key stakeholders, and remains adaptable to evolving security needs.

Policy Development and Enforcement

The foundation of any strong security program is a set of clearly defined policies that provide guidance on how to protect organizational assets and data. Effective security policies are not one-size-fits-all; they must be tailored to the specific needs, goals, and regulatory requirements of the organization.

1. **Alignment with Business Objectives**: Security policies must align with the organization's broader goals, including compliance requirements and the protection of critical business functions. They should directly support business continuity, risk management, and the overall strategic vision of the company.

2. **Stakeholder Involvement**: It is essential to involve key stakeholders from across the organization when developing security policies. This includes representatives from legal, human resources, IT, and management, ensuring that all relevant perspectives and expertise are considered. Involvement from these departments also helps in gaining organizational buy-in, making it more likely that employees will adhere to the policies.

3. **Clarity and Accessibility**: Security policies should be written in clear, understandable language. Jargon should be avoided where possible, and the policies should be concise yet comprehensive. Ensuring accessibility is also crucial; these policies should be easy to find and accessible to all employees at any time. A well-communicated policy will foster an environment where security is prioritized by all staff.

4. **Regular Review and Updates**: The security landscape is dynamic, with new threats and technological advancements constantly reshaping the environment. Therefore, policies must be regularly reviewed and updated to reflect any changes in these areas. Additionally, any changes in business operations, such as new product launches or shifts in business models, may require policy adjustments to maintain relevance and effectiveness.

CHAPTER 9   GOVERNANCE, RISK, AND COMPLIANCE

5. **Policy Enforcement**: Having robust policies in place is only effective if they are enforced consistently. Mechanisms such as regular monitoring, auditing, and disciplinary actions for non-compliance should be implemented. Enforcement should be carried out in a way that is fair, transparent, and proportionate to the severity of the violation.

Key Security Policies

Several key security policies are critical for any organization to ensure a comprehensive and secure framework. These policies serve as guidelines for users and administrators to follow and set clear expectations for behavior across the company.

1. **Acceptable Use Policy (AUP)**: This policy defines what constitutes acceptable and unacceptable behavior when using organizational resources, such as the internet, email, and social media. By setting clear guidelines, the AUP helps prevent misuse of resources, limits liability, and reduces the risk of cyber threats, such as phishing or data leakage through personal accounts.

2. **Access Control Policy**: This policy establishes rules for managing access to sensitive systems, networks, and data based on user roles and responsibilities. It outlines the processes for granting, reviewing, and revoking access to ensure that only authorized individuals can access specific resources. Access control is fundamental for preventing unauthorized access, ensuring that employees only have access to the information necessary for their job functions.

3. **Data Classification Policy**: The data classification policy defines how data should be categorized based on its sensitivity and importance. It provides guidelines for handling and protecting data at various levels, ensuring that highly sensitive information, such as financial records or personal health data, is given the highest level of protection. This policy also dictates how data should be stored, transmitted, and disposed of securely.

4. **Incident Response Policy**: In the event of a security breach or data incident, an incident response policy provides a clear, step-by-step process for detecting, responding to, and recovering from the event. The policy outlines roles and responsibilities, communication procedures, and the use of incident management tools. This ensures that all staff understand their responsibilities during an incident and can act quickly to mitigate damage, restore systems, and comply with regulatory requirements.

5. **Password Policy**: Passwords are one of the most common methods for securing systems and data, so a robust password policy is essential. This policy sets requirements for password complexity, and management to ensure that passwords are strong and effective in preventing unauthorized access. It may also include requirements for multi-factor authentication (MFA) as an additional layer of protection.

CHAPTER 9   GOVERNANCE, RISK, AND COMPLIANCE

Procedures and Best Practices

While policies set the guidelines, procedures provide the specific steps necessary to implement and enforce those policies effectively. In addition, best practices are important for ensuring that security practices are adhered to across the organization, creating a culture of security awareness.

1. **Procedure Development**: To ensure consistency in the application of security policies, detailed procedures should be developed for each policy. These procedures outline step-by-step actions to take in a specific situation, such as setting up new user accounts, handling security incidents, or reviewing access rights. Procedures should be standardized, documented, and regularly tested to ensure they are practical and effective in real-world scenarios.

2. **Best Practices**

    - **Least Privilege**: A fundamental principle in access management, least privilege dictates that users should be granted only the minimum level of access necessary to perform their job duties. This minimizes the risk of accidental or malicious data exposure or modification.

    - **Separation of Duties**: By dividing responsibilities among different individuals, separation of duties helps reduce the risk of fraud, errors, and misuse of resources. This principle ensures that no single individual has enough access or control to carry out critical processes on their own, such as approving payments and authorizing transfers.

- **Change Management**: The process of managing changes to systems, applications, and networks should be carefully controlled to minimize the risk of introducing vulnerabilities. A structured change management process includes assessing the potential risks, testing changes in a controlled environment, and obtaining approval before implementing the change into production. This helps to ensure that all changes align with the organization's security posture and are thoroughly evaluated for potential impact.

By developing well-structured security policies, implementing clear procedures, and following best practices, organizations can create a security framework that minimizes risks and ensures compliance. Regular policy reviews, stakeholder involvement, and effective enforcement mechanisms ensure that security is not just a theoretical concept but a key operational priority. With a comprehensive approach to security policy, procedures, and best practices, organizations can safeguard their data and systems while fostering a culture of awareness and compliance across all departments.

Data Loss Prevention Techniques and Tools

Data Loss Prevention (DLP) is a crucial component in modern cybersecurity strategies, focusing on detecting and preventing the unauthorized transfer or exposure of sensitive data. By implementing DLP solutions, organizations can safeguard their confidential information from being leaked, stolen, or misused, whether due to insider threats or external cyberattacks. The goal of DLP is to maintain the integrity and confidentiality of sensitive data, ensuring that it is only accessed and shared by authorized users under appropriate conditions.

CHAPTER 9   GOVERNANCE, RISK, AND COMPLIANCE

DLP Implementation

Data Loss Prevention solutions are designed to monitor, detect, and block potential data breaches or unauthorized data transfers outside an organization's network. DLP solutions can be implemented in various ways, addressing the full spectrum of data—whether it's in motion, at rest, or in use. The aim is to mitigate risks while ensuring compliance with legal and regulatory requirements related to data protection.

Types of DLP

1. **Network-Based DLP**

    Network-based DLP solutions focus on monitoring and controlling data as it moves across an organization's network. These tools analyze traffic for signs of sensitive data being transferred via email, web uploads, file-sharing services, or other network channels. They can block or alert administrators when unauthorized data transfers are detected, helping to prevent potential breaches before data leaves the organization. This type of DLP is particularly valuable for protecting data in transit.

2. **Endpoint-Based DLP**

    Endpoint-based DLP solutions focus on protecting data on user devices such as laptops, desktops, and mobile devices. These tools monitor files and communications on these devices, ensuring that sensitive data is not inadvertently or maliciously accessed, copied, or transmitted. Endpoint DLP can prevent the use of USB drives or external storage devices, block the copying of sensitive data, and ensure that files are not uploaded to unauthorized cloud storage platforms. It provides comprehensive protection for data at rest and in use.

3. **Cloud-Based DLP**

    As more businesses move to cloud services, cloud-based DLP tools have become critical for securing data stored in cloud environments. These solutions extend DLP functionality to cloud storage, Software-as-a-Service (SaaS) applications, and other cloud-based platforms. Cloud DLP allows organizations to monitor and protect sensitive data that resides outside the traditional corporate network, ensuring that files stored in cloud environments remain secure and comply with internal policies and regulatory standards.

DLP Techniques

Content Inspection: One of the most powerful techniques in DLP is content inspection, which involves analyzing the actual content of files and communications to detect sensitive information. This can include personally identifiable information (PII) like Social Security numbers or credit card details, as well as proprietary data such as trade secrets, intellectual property, or client data. Content inspection tools scan emails, documents, and web traffic in real time to identify this sensitive information and block or alert on suspicious activities.

Contextual Analysis: Contextual analysis is another key DLP technique, which involves evaluating the context surrounding a data transfer. This includes examining factors such as the user's identity, their behavior, the device being used, and the destination of the data. For instance, if a user who typically works in HR suddenly tries to transfer a large amount of sensitive financial data to an external cloud storage account, the DLP system might flag this activity as a risk. By analyzing patterns and anomalies, contextual analysis helps to identify potentially unauthorized or risky behavior.

Policy Enforcement: DLP solutions operate based on predefined policies that outline acceptable and unacceptable actions related to sensitive data. These policies specify what constitutes unauthorized activity, such as sending confidential data via email, uploading it to unauthorized cloud storage, or copying it to a removable USB drive. The system automatically enforces these policies by blocking or restricting these actions, ensuring that users adhere to data protection requirements without manual intervention.

Encryption: Encryption is a foundational DLP technique that adds an additional layer of security for sensitive data. Even if a data breach occurs or unauthorized access is gained, encryption ensures that the data remains unreadable without the proper decryption key. DLP solutions can automatically encrypt sensitive files or data being transferred, protecting it during storage or while in transit across networks. Encryption can be applied to individual files, entire volumes, or even network traffic to secure data in all stages of its lifecycle.

Data Classification

Effective data classification is vital for the success of any DLP strategy. Data should be categorized based on its sensitivity and importance so that DLP policies can be tailored accordingly. By classifying data into categories such as public, internal, confidential, and highly confidential, organizations can ensure that appropriate protections are applied to different types of information. This helps to reduce the risk of over-protecting low-risk data while focusing the organization's resources on securing its most valuable assets.

User Training

User behavior plays a crucial role in the effectiveness of a DLP program. To ensure that DLP policies are followed, organizations must educate employees about the importance of data protection and how to comply with the security policies in place. Regular training sessions on data handling best practices, recognizing phishing attempts, and reporting suspicious activities can help mitigate human error and insider threats, ensuring that employees understand their role in maintaining data security.

Regular Audits

Regular audits of DLP systems and policies are necessary to ensure they remain effective and compliant with changing regulations. Auditing tools allow organizations to review the logs and actions taken by DLP systems, ensuring that sensitive data is being properly protected and that policies are being enforced correctly. Regular audits also help identify areas where policies may need updating due to shifts in technology, business practices, or regulatory requirements.

Conclusion

Data Loss Prevention techniques and tools are essential for any organization seeking to protect its sensitive information from unauthorized access, disclosure, or loss. By implementing a combination of network-based, endpoint-based, and cloud-based DLP solutions, organizations can ensure comprehensive data protection. Employing techniques such as content inspection, contextual analysis, policy enforcement, and encryption further strengthens the security posture. However, to be effective, DLP programs must also incorporate best practices like data classification, user training, and regular audits.

Together, these measures form a robust defense against the ever-evolving threat landscape, ensuring that sensitive data remains secure and compliant with regulations.

Business Impact Analysis and Third-Party Risk Management

A Business Impact Analysis (BIA) is a critical process that helps organizations identify and evaluate the potential effects of disruptions to their essential business operations. These disruptions can stem from a variety of sources, including cyberattacks, natural disasters, system failures, or human errors. The BIA is a fundamental component of business continuity and disaster recovery planning, providing insights into which operations are most critical to the organization's survival. By understanding these impacts, businesses can develop strategies to minimize downtime and ensure continuity in the face of adversity.

Steps in Conducting a BIA

1. **Identify Critical Business Functions**

   The first step in a BIA is to pinpoint which functions are vital to the organization's day-to-day operations and long-term success. This may include key processes such as financial operations, customer service, IT infrastructure, and supply chain management. Identifying these functions ensures that the organization can focus resources on protecting them from potential disruptions.

2. **Impact Assessment**

   Once critical functions are identified, the next step is to assess the potential impact of disruptions to these functions. This includes evaluating the financial, operational, and reputational consequences of downtime. For example, the loss of access to financial systems may have immediate financial consequences, while a prolonged disruption in customer service could damage the organization's reputation.

3. **Recovery Time Objectives (RTO)**

   The RTO defines the maximum acceptable downtime for each critical function before significant impacts occur. It sets a clear benchmark for recovery priorities, helping organizations determine how quickly they must restore operations to avoid substantial damage. Setting realistic RTOs is essential for making informed decisions about resource allocation and response strategies.

4. **Resource Requirements**

   To recover critical business functions, organizations must identify the necessary resources, such as personnel, technology, and physical infrastructure. This ensures that the organization is prepared to mobilize the right resources when needed and avoid delays in the recovery process.

5. **Dependency Analysis**

    Businesses often rely on external parties, such as vendors, service providers, and partners, for key services or products. A thorough dependency analysis helps to identify these external relationships and assess how a disruption to these parties might affect business operations. Understanding these dependencies allows organizations to plan for potential disruptions beyond their direct control, ensuring a more comprehensive business continuity plan.

Third-Party Risk Management

Third-party risk management involves assessing and mitigating risks associated with external entities, such as vendors, contractors, service providers, and partners. These third parties may have access to sensitive data, critical infrastructure, or other business resources, creating potential vulnerabilities that need to be managed. As businesses increasingly rely on third-party services, the risk of breaches, service interruptions, or non-compliance escalates. Effective third-party risk management ensures that these relationships do not introduce undue risk to the organization.

Key Considerations in Third-Party Risk Management

1. **Third-Party Selection**

    When selecting third parties, organizations should evaluate potential partners based on their security posture, adherence to industry regulations, and

CHAPTER 9 GOVERNANCE, RISK, AND COMPLIANCE

ability to meet contractual obligations. This includes reviewing the third party's history of security incidents, their compliance with relevant laws (such as GDPR, HIPAA, or PCI-DSS), and their overall reliability in terms of service delivery.

2. **Risk Assessments**

   Regular risk assessments are essential to identify any emerging risks associated with third-party relationships. These assessments should cover security vulnerabilities, potential compliance gaps, and other operational risks that could affect the organization. Regular assessments help ensure that the third party continues to meet the organization's security and compliance standards over time.

3. **Contractual Agreements**

   Contracts with third parties should explicitly outline security requirements, including data protection measures, confidentiality obligations, and the right to audit third-party systems and processes. These agreements should also define the actions to be taken in the event of a security breach, ensuring that there are clear responsibilities for both parties in mitigating and responding to risks.

4. **Continuous Monitoring**

   Third-party risk management does not end once a contract is signed. Continuous monitoring is necessary to track third-party activities, including security performance, compliance with contractual obligations, and incident reporting. Regular audits,

CHAPTER 9   GOVERNANCE, RISK, AND COMPLIANCE

security reviews, and assessments of third-party activities ensure that organizations stay informed about potential risks and can take corrective actions promptly.

Privacy Impact Analysis (PIA) and Data Protection Impact Assessments (DPIA)

A Privacy Impact Analysis (PIA) is a process that organizations use to evaluate how their data collection, processing, and storage practices impact the privacy of individuals. This analysis helps to ensure that personal data is handled in compliance with privacy laws such as the GDPR, CCPA, and other data protection regulations. By identifying privacy risks early in the data handling process, PIAs enable organizations to take corrective measures before any harm is done. The analysis typically involves mapping out data flows, assessing how personal data is used, stored, and shared, and determining the legal basis for processing. It also includes identifying any risks of data breaches, unauthorized access, or misuse, and proposing mitigation strategies such as encryption, anonymization, or limiting data collection to only what is necessary.

In the context of the GDPR, a Data Protection Impact Assessment (DPIA) is a more specific form of PIA required for processing activities that may pose a high risk to individuals' rights and freedoms. DPIAs are mandatory for activities like large-scale data processing or using new technologies that could impact privacy. A DPIA involves a detailed analysis of the proposed data processing, including its necessity and proportionality, the risks to individual rights, and measures to address those risks. It also requires consultation with data protection authorities when high risks cannot be mitigated adequately. Both PIAs and DPIAs are essential tools for ensuring transparency, accountability, and compliance with privacy laws while helping organizations protect sensitive personal data from misuse.

CHAPTER 9 GOVERNANCE, RISK, AND COMPLIANCE

Privacy Impact Analysis (PIA)

A Privacy Impact Analysis (PIA) is a process used by organizations to assess how their data processing activities affect the privacy of individuals' personal data. The PIA is crucial for ensuring compliance with privacy regulations such as the GDPR (General Data Protection Regulation) and CCPA (California Consumer Privacy Act), which require organizations to assess privacy risks before initiating certain types of data processing. A PIA helps organizations identify potential privacy risks early, allowing them to implement safeguards and minimize the likelihood of data breaches or privacy violations.

Components of a PIA

1. **Data Collection**

    A key step in the PIA process is understanding what personal data the organization collects, how it is used, and for what purposes. This involves reviewing data collection methods, the types of personal data being collected (such as names, addresses, or financial information), and the systems in which it is stored.

2. **Data Sharing**

    Organizations need to identify with whom they share personal data, including any third parties, and the conditions under which this data is shared. This could include partners, service providers, or government agencies. It is essential to ensure that data sharing complies with privacy laws and that adequate safeguards are in place to protect the data.

3. **Legal Compliance**

    Organizations must ensure that their data processing activities comply with applicable privacy laws and regulations, including GDPR, CCPA, and other local regulations. The PIA process involves reviewing how data is handled to ensure that the collection, processing, and sharing of personal data adhere to these laws.

4. **Privacy Risks**

    Identifying privacy risks is a critical component of the PIA process. This includes evaluating potential threats such as unauthorized access, data breaches, and misuse of personal data. Assessing these risks enables organizations to implement appropriate mitigation measures.

5. **Mitigation Measures**

    After identifying privacy risks, organizations must recommend actions to mitigate or eliminate these risks. This could involve data minimization (collecting only the data necessary for a specific purpose), anonymization techniques, or enhanced security controls to protect sensitive data.

6. **Stakeholder Involvement**

    It is important to engage stakeholders such as data protection officers, legal teams, and IT professionals in the PIA process. Their expertise ensures that all potential privacy risks are thoroughly evaluated and that the appropriate measures are put in place to mitigate them.

Data Protection Impact Assessments (DPIA)

A Data Protection Impact Assessment (DPIA) is a specific type of PIA required under the GDPR for processing activities that may result in a high risk to individuals' privacy. DPIAs are designed to assess and mitigate privacy risks related to high-risk data processing activities, such as large-scale data collection, profiling, or the use of new technologies.

Key Elements of a DPIA

1. **Processing Description**

    The DPIA must document a detailed description of the data processing activity, including the nature, scope, context, and purpose of the processing. This ensures that all aspects of the processing are well understood and can be assessed for potential privacy risks.

2. **Risk Assessment**

    A core component of the DPIA is assessing the likelihood and severity of risks to individuals' rights and freedoms. This involves evaluating how the processing activity could impact individuals' privacy and whether there are any vulnerabilities that could lead to a breach or misuse of personal data.

3. **Mitigation Strategies**

    The DPIA should propose strategies to address identified risks, such as implementing technical safeguards (e.g., encryption), organizational measures (e.g., access controls), and policies (e.g., staff training) to reduce the risks to acceptable levels.

4. **Consultation**

    In cases where the DPIA identifies high risks that cannot be mitigated, the organization may be required to consult with data protection authorities. This step ensures that the organization has adequately addressed potential privacy concerns before proceeding with the processing activity.

5. **Documentation**

    Thorough documentation of the DPIA process is essential for demonstrating compliance with the GDPR. This includes records of the assessment, decisions made, and the mitigation measures taken. The documentation serves as evidence that the organization has conducted a proper risk assessment and is committed to protecting individuals' privacy rights.

By effectively conducting Business Impact Analyses, Third-Party Risk Management, Privacy Impact Analyses, and Data Protection Impact Assessments, organizations can better protect sensitive data, comply with regulatory requirements, and minimize the risks posed by disruptions, third-party vulnerabilities, and privacy violations. These processes are integral to maintaining operational resilience, regulatory compliance, and consumer trust in an increasingly data-driven world.

Legal and Ethical Considerations in Cybersecurity

In today's digital world, organizations must navigate a complex variety of laws, regulations, and ethical standards to ensure their cybersecurity practices are compliant and responsible. These legal and regulatory frameworks vary significantly across jurisdictions, requiring organizations to stay informed about local and international requirements. Key areas of compliance include data protection laws, such as the GDPR in Europe and HIPAA in the United States, which govern how personal data should be collected, stored, and protected. Organizations also need to follow industry-specific cybersecurity regulations, such as PCI-DSS for payment processing, to mitigate the risks of breaches that can affect both customers and businesses. A particular challenge is managing cross-border data transfers, which require careful attention to international laws governing data movement, such as the EU-US Privacy Shield framework. Additionally, organizations must ensure they are prepared to report cybersecurity incidents promptly in accordance with legal obligations, including data breaches and other critical events.

Navigating legal challenges becomes even more complex when operating across multiple jurisdictions. Different countries may have conflicting laws or vary in how strictly they enforce regulations. To navigate these complexities, organizations often engage legal counsel familiar with the regulatory landscape in each jurisdiction where they operate. Where possible, they aim to harmonize cybersecurity policies across regions to streamline compliance efforts. However, some aspects may require localization of policies and procedures to comply with specific local laws, while maintaining alignment with global standards.

Beyond legal compliance, ethical considerations play a significant role in cybersecurity. Organizations must consider the potential impact of their practices on individuals' privacy and rights, ensuring transparency about how data is collected and used. Ethical cybersecurity practices prioritize fairness, ensuring that security measures do not disproportionately harm certain groups or violate rights. Accountability is another crucial ethical principle; organizations are responsible for their cybersecurity actions and must ensure that stakeholders, including customers and employees, are protected and informed.

CHAPTER 9   GOVERNANCE, RISK, AND COMPLIANCE

Third-Party Auditing

Third-party audits are essential for verifying that an organization's cybersecurity practices align with relevant standards and regulations, providing an independent assessment of security measures. Preparing for these audits involves clearly defining the audit scope, ensuring that all necessary systems, processes, and security controls are included. It's crucial that organizations maintain comprehensive and up-to-date documentation, policies, and procedures to make the audit process smoother. Pre-audit reviews should also be conducted internally to identify and resolve any gaps in compliance or security practices before external auditors get involved. During the audit itself, close collaboration between the organization and auditors is key to ensuring transparency and efficiency.

Best practices for third-party audits include selecting reputable auditors with the appropriate industry expertise, scheduling audits regularly to maintain compliance, and involving stakeholders in the process. This approach not only ensures that the organization remains compliant with security standards but also helps to continuously improve security practices. Maintaining detailed records of audit activities and follow-up actions is critical, as it demonstrates both the organization's commitment to cybersecurity and its preparedness for future audits. Regular auditing, alongside corrective measures based on audit findings, fosters an ongoing cycle of improvement, ensuring that security controls evolve in response to emerging risks and regulatory changes.

CHAPTER 10

Final Review and Exam Preparation

To start off this chapter, we are going to review the eight domains covered by the Security+ exam. Each of these topics are thoroughly covered throughout the book, but the intent of this chapter is to provide a quick summary of topics to expect on the examination. I would recommend making flashcards, or other preferred study materials, in order to thoroughly cover these domains. This chapter is **NOT** intended to suffice to pass the exam, and the remainder of the book is important in your success of obtaining the Security+ certification.

Domain 1: Threats, Attacks, and Vulnerabilities

The **Threats, Attacks, and Vulnerabilities** domain focuses on identifying, understanding, and mitigating the various cyber threats that organizations face today. Cybersecurity professionals must have a deep understanding of the different types of threats, including malicious software (malware), various attack methods, the adversaries behind these attacks, and the common vulnerabilities that can be exploited. This knowledge is fundamental to developing effective defenses, as it allows professionals to recognize, prevent, and respond to attacks.

CHAPTER 10   FINAL REVIEW AND EXAM PREPARATION

Effective defense requires not only understanding the types of malicious activities that can occur but also being able to anticipate potential vulnerabilities in systems, applications, and networks that could be exploited. This domain covers various attack vectors, the tactics and techniques used by adversaries, and the types of malware commonly used to compromise systems. With this knowledge, professionals can implement appropriate mitigation strategies and controls to safeguard against these evolving threats.

Understanding **threat actors** is crucial for developing proactive defense strategies. This includes identifying motivations behind attacks, ranging from financial gain to political or social causes, and how different adversaries might employ specific methods to achieve their goals. Additionally, it is critical to recognize how attacks can be delivered through different **attack vectors**, such as emails, websites, networks, and social engineering techniques. Finally, recognizing **vulnerabilities** within these vectors is vital to preventing exploitation.

Malware Types

- **Viruses**
    - Viruses are a type of malware that attaches itself to a legitimate program or file and spreads when that file or program is executed. A virus typically replicates, infecting other files, systems, or networks. It can cause system failures, data loss, and corruption. Viruses often require user interaction (like opening an infected email attachment) to spread.

- **Worms**
  - Worms are a form of self-replicating malware that spreads autonomously across networks without user intervention. Unlike viruses, worms do not attach themselves to a host file or program; they exploit network vulnerabilities to propagate. Worms can cause significant harm by consuming network resources, slowing down or disabling systems, and spreading rapidly through interconnected systems.

- **Trojans**
  - Trojans are a type of malware disguised as legitimate software. Once executed, they provide unauthorized access to a system, enabling attackers to steal data, install additional malicious software, or gain remote control of the system. Trojans often rely on social engineering tactics to trick users into installing them.

- **Ransomware**
  - Ransomware encrypts a victim's files, making them inaccessible until the victim pays a ransom for the decryption key. This form of malware has grown in prominence, with attackers demanding payment in cryptocurrencies to avoid detection. Ransomware attacks can cripple organizations, especially if critical data is encrypted, leading to significant financial losses and operational disruptions.

- **Spyware/Adware**
  - **Spyware** monitors user activity without their knowledge, often capturing sensitive information like passwords or financial data, while **adware** bombards users with unwanted advertisements. Both can be used to collect personal data or track behavior for financial gain, undermining privacy and system security.

Types of Attacks

- **Denial of Service (DoS) and Distributed Denial of Service (DDoS)**
  - A DoS attack aims to make a system or network resource unavailable by overwhelming it with traffic or requests. A **DDoS** attack uses multiple systems to launch a coordinated attack, amplifying the scale and impact. These attacks can disable websites, applications, or even entire networks, leading to downtime and loss of service.

- **Phishing and Spear-Phishing**
  - **Phishing** attacks involve sending fraudulent communications, typically via email, that appear to come from a trustworthy source. The goal is to trick recipients into revealing sensitive information, such as login credentials or financial details. **Spear-phishing** is a targeted form of phishing that customizes the message for a specific individual or organization, often using personal details to increase the likelihood of success.

- **Man-in-the-Middle (MitM) Attacks**
  - A MitM attack occurs when an attacker intercepts and potentially alters the communication between two parties without their knowledge. This can lead to the theft of sensitive information, such as login credentials or financial transactions, or even the insertion of malicious data. MitM attacks are common in insecure networks, especially wireless ones.

- **SQL Injection**
  - SQL injection is a code injection attack that allows attackers to manipulate SQL queries executed by a database. By inserting malicious SQL statements into input fields (such as login forms), attackers can retrieve, modify, or delete data stored in the database, compromising the confidentiality and integrity of the system.

- **Cross-Site Scripting (XSS)**
  - XSS involves injecting malicious scripts into web applications that are then executed by a user's browser. This can lead to the theft of session cookies, account hijacking, or redirection to malicious websites. XSS vulnerabilities are often found in poorly secured web applications that fail to properly sanitize user inputs.

CHAPTER 10   FINAL REVIEW AND EXAM PREPARATION

Threat Actors

- **Hacktivists**
  - Hacktivists are individuals or groups who use cyberattacks to promote political, social, or environmental causes. Their attacks are typically aimed at making a statement or drawing attention to an issue, such as defacing websites or disrupting services. While their motives may be ideological, the impact of their attacks can still be significant.

- **Nation-State Actors**
  - Nation-state actors are state-sponsored or state-affiliated groups conducting cyberattacks to advance political or military objectives. These actors have significant resources, advanced techniques, and access to critical infrastructure, enabling them to launch highly sophisticated and persistent attacks. Nation-state cyberattacks can target everything from government systems to private sector organizations, with the aim of espionage, sabotage, or influence.

- **Insider Threats**
  - Insider threats refer to individuals within an organization (e.g., employees, contractors) who misuse their access to systems or data for malicious purposes. These threats can be intentional, such as a disgruntled employee stealing sensitive data, or unintentional, like an employee falling for a phishing attack. Insider threats are particularly difficult to detect, as the perpetrators have legitimate access to systems.

- **Cybercriminals and Organized Crime**
  - Cybercriminals are individuals or groups who use digital means to engage in illegal activities, often for financial gain. Organized cybercrime groups may operate on a large scale, conducting attacks such as ransomware campaigns, data theft, or financial fraud. These actors typically operate in a manner similar to traditional organized crime, with networks that facilitate illicit activity.

Attack Vectors

- **Email and Phishing**
  - Email is one of the most common vectors for delivering malicious content, such as phishing emails or attachments containing malware. Cybercriminals often use email to impersonate legitimate sources, tricking users into clicking on malicious links or downloading infected files.

- **Web Applications**
  - Web applications, especially those with poor security practices, are frequent targets for cyberattacks. Vulnerabilities such as SQL injection, cross-site scripting (XSS), and insufficient input validation can be exploited to gain unauthorized access to systems or steal sensitive data.

- **Networks and Wireless Networks**
  - Unsecured networks, including public Wi-Fi and poorly configured private networks, are ripe for exploitation. Attackers can use tools to eavesdrop on communications, intercept data, or execute MitM attacks. Wireless networks are particularly vulnerable to attacks if proper encryption (e.g., WPA3) is not implemented.
- **Social Engineering**
  - Social engineering exploits human psychology rather than technical vulnerabilities. Attackers may manipulate individuals into revealing confidential information, bypassing security controls, or performing actions that compromise system security. Phishing, pretexting, and baiting are all common social engineering tactics.

Summary

Domain 1, **Threats, Attacks, and Vulnerabilities**, is crucial for understanding the landscape of cyber threats and the tactics employed by cyber adversaries. By recognizing the different types of **malware**, such as viruses, worms, trojans, and ransomware, professionals can take proactive measures to defend against these malicious programs. Understanding **attack methods** like DoS/DDoS, phishing, and SQL injection equips security professionals to implement the necessary defenses, from firewalls and IDS to web application security controls. Additionally, knowledge of the various **threat actors**, including cybercriminals, insider threats, and nation-state actors, helps organizations anticipate and mitigate specific types of attacks based on the threat's origin and motive.

Moreover, familiarity with **attack vectors**, such as email phishing, web applications, and social engineering, allows professionals to deploy layered defenses across the system, focusing on areas that are more prone to exploitation. By mastering these concepts, security practitioners can significantly reduce the risk of successful attacks, enhancing their organization's ability to respond to threats effectively.

Domain 2: Technologies and Tools

The **Technologies and Tools** domain focuses on the essential security devices, protocols, and design principles that organizations use to safeguard their networks, systems, and data. Cybersecurity professionals must understand how various security technologies work, their configuration, and how they contribute to the overall security posture of an organization. This domain emphasizes practical, hands-on knowledge of security tools, including **firewalls**, **intrusion detection and prevention systems**, **virtual private networks (VPNs)**, **proxies**, and secure **network protocols**.

In addition to tools and protocols, this domain also highlights the importance of **secure network design**. A well-structured and secure network is vital for minimizing vulnerabilities and defending against external and internal threats. This includes implementing **defense in depth** strategies, designing **demilitarized zones (DMZs)**, and applying **network segmentation** to isolate sensitive data and systems.

A strong grasp of these technologies and design principles is critical for defending against a wide range of threats, from malware and unauthorized access to denial-of-service attacks. Properly configuring and deploying these tools enables organizations to create layered defenses that work together to detect, prevent, and mitigate attacks while ensuring secure communication and access for legitimate users.

CHAPTER 10   FINAL REVIEW AND EXAM PREPARATION

Network Security Devices

- **Firewalls**
  - Firewalls are one of the foundational security devices used to monitor and control network traffic. They enforce security policies by filtering traffic based on rules related to IP addresses, ports, protocols, and content. Firewalls can be hardware-based (physical devices) or software-based (installed on servers or endpoints) and can function at different layers of the network stack. Key types include **packet-filtering firewalls**, **stateful inspection firewalls**, and **next-generation firewalls (NGFW)**, the latter of which provide additional features like deep packet inspection (DPI) and intrusion prevention.

- **Intrusion Detection Systems (IDS) and Intrusion Prevention Systems (IPS)**
  - **IDS** are used to monitor network traffic for signs of suspicious activity or known attack patterns, generating alerts for further analysis. They are typically **passive** systems, meaning they do not block traffic but notify administrators of potential security incidents.
  - **IPS**, on the other hand, is an active system that not only detects but also **prevents** attacks by blocking malicious traffic in real time. An IPS can be deployed in line with network traffic, making it more proactive than an IDS, which only monitors and alerts.

- It is worth noting that IDS and IPS can and often should be utilized in tandem. The configuration of each can supplement one another to provide a broader level of security.

- **VPNs (Virtual Private Networks)**
  - VPNs are crucial for securing remote access to an organization's internal network. They use encryption to create a secure, private tunnel over a public network (like the internet), protecting sensitive data from interception. VPNs can be configured to provide access to specific network segments or systems, ensuring that remote workers or branch offices can securely access corporate resources. Key protocols used for VPNs include **IPsec**, **SSL/TLS**, and **PPTP**.

- **Proxies**
  - A **proxy** acts as an intermediary server between a client and a destination server. Proxies are commonly used to filter web traffic, cache data for faster access, hide internal IP addresses from the external network, and provide anonymity to users. A **web proxy** can filter and control access to websites, ensuring users only access authorized resources. Proxy servers can also be employed for content filtering, load balancing, and bypassing geo-restrictions.

CHAPTER 10   FINAL REVIEW AND EXAM PREPARATION

Secure Protocols

- **SSL/TLS (Secure Sockets Layer/Transport Layer Security)**
  - SSL and its successor **TLS** are cryptographic protocols designed to secure communications over networks. They are most commonly used to encrypt web traffic, ensuring confidentiality and data integrity between clients and servers. SSL/TLS work by encrypting the data being transmitted, thus protecting it from eavesdropping and tampering. Today, **TLS** is widely used, while SSL has been deprecated due to vulnerabilities.

- **HTTPS (Hypertext Transfer Protocol Secure)**
  - HTTPS is an extension of HTTP that uses **SSL/TLS** encryption to secure communication between web browsers and web servers. When a website uses HTTPS, it ensures that any data exchanged between the user's browser and the website is encrypted and cannot be easily intercepted by malicious actors. This is crucial for protecting sensitive transactions, such as online banking, e-commerce, or login credentials.

- **IPsec (Internet Protocol Security)**
  - IPsec is a suite of protocols used to secure Internet Protocol (IP) communications by encrypting and authenticating IP packets. It operates at the network layer and is often used in **VPNs** to protect data transmitted between two devices, such as

remote workers accessing an internal network or two branch offices communicating securely. IPsec supports both **transport mode**, which encrypts only the payload of the IP packet, and **tunnel mode**, which encrypts the entire IP packet.

Secure Network Design

- **Defense in Depth**
  - **Defense in depth** is a multi-layered security approach that aims to protect systems by employing multiple defenses at different levels. This strategy assumes that no single security measure can protect against all threats, so combining different techniques—such as firewalls, IDS/IPS, antivirus software, encryption, and access controls—provides a more comprehensive security posture. The idea is that even if one layer is breached, additional layers will still provide protection.
- **DMZs (Demilitarized Zones)**
  - A **DMZ** is a network segment that acts as a buffer zone between an organization's internal network and external networks (e.g., the internet). The DMZ hosts publicly accessible services, such as web servers, mail servers, or DNS servers, while isolating these services from the internal network. By placing public-facing resources in the DMZ, an organization can protect its internal network from attacks that target these services, as they are exposed to the internet. This helps minimize risk and containment of breaches.

CHAPTER 10   FINAL REVIEW AND EXAM PREPARATION

- **Network Segmentation**
  - **Network segmentation** is the practice of dividing a network into smaller, isolated segments to improve security. Each segment can have its own set of security controls, policies, and access restrictions. This reduces the potential attack surface by limiting access to sensitive resources and makes it more difficult for attackers to move laterally within the network. For example, an organization may segment its network to isolate finance systems from general employee systems, ensuring that only authorized users can access critical data.

Summary

Domain 2, **Technologies and Tools**, emphasizes the critical tools, technologies, and best practices that cybersecurity professionals need to secure networks, systems, and data. Understanding the role and functionality of network security devices such as **firewalls**, **IDS/IPS**, **VPNs**, and **proxies** is fundamental for setting up a secure network infrastructure. These tools work together to detect, block, and prevent attacks while ensuring secure communications. Additionally, the proper use of **secure protocols** such as **SSL/TLS**, **HTTPS**, and **IPsec** ensures that sensitive data is protected during transmission.

A secure network design is just as important as the tools used to protect it. **Defense in depth** and **network segmentation** are essential strategies for mitigating risk, while **DMZs** help isolate publicly accessible services from the internal network. By combining these tools and practices, organizations can build robust defenses that minimize vulnerabilities and ensure the confidentiality, integrity, and availability of their systems and data.

Through this domain, cybersecurity professionals gain the knowledge needed to configure, deploy, and manage the tools that are essential for building and maintaining a secure network environment, responding effectively to cyber threats, and ensuring that communication remains secure and confidential.

Domain 3: Architecture and Design

In today's rapidly evolving digital landscape, security cannot be an afterthought; it must be an integral part of the entire system architecture and design process. The **Architecture and Design** domain of the Security+ exam focuses on ensuring that security is embedded into the foundation of systems, networks, and applications, rather than merely being layered on top as an afterthought. This domain provides insights into the principles, methodologies, and best practices that help in building secure infrastructures from the ground up, ensuring their resilience against a variety of cyber threats.

Security professionals must understand how to balance the need for secure designs with the operational demands of performance, scalability, and availability. They must also recognize that security is not a one-size-fits-all solution; it requires a customized approach based on the type of system, the data being handled, and the threat landscape. This domain covers the application of core security principles throughout the system lifecycle, from planning and design to implementation and maintenance.

The concept of **Defense in Depth** plays a pivotal role in the architecture and design of secure systems. This strategy advocates for multiple layers of security controls at different stages, ensuring that even if one layer is compromised, others still provide protection. The domain also highlights the importance of implementing security best practices like **least privilege**, **network segmentation**, and **failover and redundancy** to mitigate risks associated with system vulnerabilities, data breaches, and system failures.

A major component of this domain is understanding the **cloud security** models and the security responsibilities shared between cloud providers and consumers. As organizations increasingly migrate to cloud environments, security professionals must be adept at designing secure cloud architectures, managing identity and access, ensuring data protection, and implementing compliance frameworks within the cloud.

Another critical area addressed in this domain is **high availability** and **redundancy**—key design elements that ensure systems remain operational during failures or attacks. Security architects must also understand the importance of **patch management** and **secure coding practices** as part of the software development life cycle (SDLC) to prevent common vulnerabilities and ensure software remains secure over time.

By mastering these principles, professionals can ensure that security is embedded in the system architecture and design, significantly reducing the risk of successful cyberattacks and minimizing the impact of potential security breaches.

Key Concepts

- **Defense in Depth**
    - This multi-layered security approach ensures that multiple security measures are put in place at various points in the system. For example, securing networks with firewalls, securing systems with access controls, and ensuring data encryption are all layers that work together to protect an organization's critical assets.

- **Secure System Design**
  - Secure system design integrates security throughout the entire lifecycle of a system. This includes adopting secure coding practices to prevent vulnerabilities like SQL injection or buffer overflows, using encryption to protect sensitive data both at rest and in transit, and implementing regular patching schedules to address known vulnerabilities in software.

- **Patch Management**
  - Timely patching is crucial to keeping systems secure. Vulnerabilities in both operating systems and applications can be exploited by attackers, and patch management ensures that systems remain up-to-date with the latest security fixes, thus mitigating potential security risks.

- **Least Privilege**
  - This principle ensures that users, applications, and systems are given only the minimum level of access necessary to perform their functions. By limiting the scope of access, organizations can reduce the potential for unauthorized access and mitigate the damage caused by insider threats.

- **Cloud Security**
  - As more organizations transition to the cloud, understanding the nuances of cloud security becomes increasingly important. The shared responsibility model dictates that security in the cloud is a joint effort between the cloud service

provider and the customer. The provider is responsible for securing the cloud infrastructure, while the customer is responsible for securing their data and applications within the cloud.

- **High Availability and Redundancy**
  - Ensuring that systems are always available and resilient to failure is vital. Redundancy involves having backup systems, such as duplicate servers or data storage devices, so that if one fails, another takes its place seamlessly. High availability architectures are designed to minimize downtime and ensure business continuity, even during failures.

- **Network Segmentation**
  - This strategy involves dividing a network into smaller, isolated segments to enhance security. By doing so, organizations can control traffic flow between different segments and reduce the impact of a potential breach in one area of the network. Segmentation also helps in minimizing lateral movement by attackers within the network.

- **Secure Software Development Life Cycle (SDLC)**
  - Security should be integrated into the SDLC from the very beginning. By incorporating security testing, code reviews, and vulnerability scanning during the development phases, developers can prevent common software vulnerabilities, such as buffer overflows and cross-site scripting (XSS), before they become security risks.

- **Risk Management and Compliance**
  - The architecture and design of systems must consider not just security threats, but also compliance with regulations and industry standards such as GDPR, HIPAA, or PCI-DSS. Compliance frameworks guide organizations in designing systems that not only meet security objectives but also adhere to legal and regulatory requirements.
- **Zero Trust Architecture**
  - In the Zero Trust model, trust is never assumed based on network location. Every access request—whether internal or external—must be authenticated and authorized before being allowed. This architecture focuses on identity verification, strict access control policies, and continuous monitoring to mitigate the risks associated with insider threats and external attacks.

Summary

Domain 3, **Architecture and Design**, is fundamental for anyone aspiring to be proficient in system security. Security professionals must understand how to design and implement secure systems, networks, and applications from the ground up. This involves applying key principles like **Defense in Depth, least privilege**, and **high availability**, as well as integrating security throughout the **system development life cycle**. With increasing reliance on cloud technologies, knowledge of **cloud security** and the **shared responsibility model** is essential. Furthermore, understanding the need for **patch management, secure coding practices**, and **compliance standards** ensures that systems remain secure, scalable, and resilient.

CHAPTER 10   FINAL REVIEW AND EXAM PREPARATION

By mastering the topics in this domain, professionals will be better equipped to secure an organization's infrastructure, protect its data, and mitigate risks posed by both internal and external threats. Whether working in traditional on-premises environments or managing cloud-based infrastructures, securing the architecture and design of systems is key to safeguarding against modern cyber threats.

Domain 4: Identity and Access Management (IAM)

The **Identity and Access Management (IAM)** domain is crucial in ensuring the proper management of user identities, authentication processes, and access controls. It is designed to ensure that only authorized users can access specific systems, applications, and data, and that these users are appropriately authenticated and granted the appropriate level of access. IAM plays a key role in both security and compliance by managing who can access what resources, when, and under what conditions.

This domain covers a variety of concepts, including the implementation of **authentication mechanisms**, the application of various **access control models**, and the integration of technologies that support **identity federation** and **single sign-on (SSO)** capabilities. The use of effective IAM practices reduces the risks associated with unauthorized access and ensures that sensitive data is only accessible to those who need it.

In today's increasingly complex and distributed IT environments, it is essential for organizations to implement strong identity management systems that are flexible, scalable, and able to adapt to new technologies, such as cloud computing and mobile devices. Additionally, as organizations move toward more centralized management of user credentials and permissions, technologies like **MFA (Multi-Factor Authentication)** and **SSO** become even more critical in improving security while also enhancing user convenience.

CHAPTER 10   FINAL REVIEW AND EXAM PREPARATION

Authentication Mechanisms

- **Password-Based Authentication**
  - **Password-based authentication** remains one of the most common methods of verifying a user's identity. This traditional approach relies on users creating a secret password that they must remember and input to access systems or services. While password-based authentication is simple to implement, it is prone to weaknesses such as poor password hygiene (weak or reused passwords) and susceptibility to attacks like **brute force** and **dictionary attacks**. Organizations must enforce strong password policies to mitigate these risks, including **password complexity** and **account lockout mechanisms**.

- **Biometrics**
  - **Biometric authentication** leverages unique physical characteristics—such as **fingerprints**, **iris scans**, **facial recognition**, or **voice patterns**—to verify a user's identity. Biometrics offer a higher level of security compared to passwords since they are harder to replicate or steal. This form of authentication is becoming more widespread in smartphones, laptops, and high-security systems. However, the primary concern with biometrics is privacy and the potential for biometric data to be compromised or misused, as well as issues with accuracy and user consent.

- **Multi-factor Authentication (MFA)**
    - **Multi-factor authentication (MFA)** adds layers of security by requiring users to provide multiple forms of verification before granting access. MFA typically combines at least two of the following:
        - **Something you know** (e.g., a password or PIN)
        - **Something you have** (e.g., a smart card, token, or phone app generating a one-time password)
        - **Something you are** (e.g., biometric data such as fingerprints or facial recognition)
    - MFA significantly reduces the risk of unauthorized access because it is far more difficult for attackers to compromise multiple factors. Common implementations of MFA include **TOTP (Time-based One-Time Passwords)**, SMS codes, or authentication apps like **Google Authenticator** or **Authy**.
- **Smart Cards and Tokens**
    - **Smart cards** and **tokens** are physical devices used to enhance authentication. A **smart card** contains embedded microchips that store encrypted credentials, which must be paired with a PIN or password for authentication. **Hardware tokens** generate time-sensitive one-time passwords or act as key fobs to provide physical authentication. Both smart cards and tokens are typically used in combination with other authentication methods (e.g., passwords or biometrics) to create a more secure and reliable form of access control.

Access Control Models

- **Role-Based Access Control (RBAC)**
  - **Role-Based Access Control (RBAC)** assigns permissions based on a user's role within an organization. In this model, roles are defined based on job functions (e.g., administrator, manager, or employee), and users are assigned to one or more roles. Permissions to access resources are granted to the roles rather than individual users, making it easier to manage access across a large organization. The primary advantage of RBAC is its simplicity and scalability, as it ensures that users can only access resources necessary for their role and helps prevent privilege creep (where users accumulate unnecessary permissions over time).

- **Discretionary Access Control (DAC)**
  - **Discretionary Access Control (DAC)** is a more flexible and user-centric access control model, where resource owners have control over who can access their resources. The owner of an object (e.g., a file, database, or application) has the discretion to grant or deny access to others. This model is more common in environments where users need the ability to manage their own access to certain resources, but it can lead to security risks if not carefully managed. One potential downside is the possibility of users inadvertently granting excessive access to others.

- **Mandatory Access Control (MAC)**
  - **Mandatory Access Control (MAC)** is a more rigid access control model, where access decisions are based on predefined security policies that cannot be changed by users. In this model, access is determined by labels assigned to resources (e.g., **classification levels** such as confidential or top-secret) and the security clearances of the users. MAC is often used in highly regulated environments where access control needs to be tightly enforced. A key advantage of MAC is that it ensures access controls cannot be bypassed by users, making it suitable for sensitive data.

Identity Federation and Single Sign-On (SSO)

- **Identity Federation**
  - **Identity Federation** allows different organizations or domains to share identity information, enabling users to access resources across multiple organizations with a single identity. Federation eliminates the need for users to create and manage separate credentials for each organization or domain. Federation standards, such as **SAML (Security Assertion Markup Language)** and **OAuth**, enable secure and seamless sharing of identity data. For example, a user who logs in to their corporate network can use the same credentials to access partner organizations' systems or services without needing to reauthenticate.

CHAPTER 10   FINAL REVIEW AND EXAM PREPARATION

- **Single Sign-On (SSO)**
  - **Single Sign-On (SSO)** allows users to authenticate once and gain access to multiple applications or services without having to log in again for each one. SSO improves the user experience by reducing the need for multiple logins, while also enhancing security by centralizing authentication. In an SSO environment, once a user logs in, an identity provider issues a token or credential that can be used across all linked applications. This reduces the risk of password fatigue and simplifies the management of user credentials across multiple systems. Technologies such as **OAuth**, **OpenID Connect**, and **SAML** are commonly used to implement SSO in web and enterprise applications.

Summary

Domain 4, **Identity and Access Management (IAM)**, emphasizes the critical importance of managing user identities, authentication, and access controls to secure systems, applications, and data. Through robust **authentication mechanisms** such as passwords, biometrics, and **multi-factor authentication (MFA)**, organizations can strengthen their security posture by ensuring that only authorized individuals can access sensitive resources.

Implementing appropriate **access control models**, including **Role-Based Access Control (RBAC)**, **Discretionary Access Control (DAC)**, and **Mandatory Access Control (MAC)**, enables organizations to enforce least-privilege access policies and reduce the risks associated with unauthorized or excessive access. These models ensure that users are granted only the necessary permissions for their roles, thereby limiting the potential impact of breaches or malicious insider actions.

CHAPTER 10　FINAL REVIEW AND EXAM PREPARATION

In today's interconnected world, technologies like **identity federation** and **Single Sign-On (SSO)** enable users to authenticate once and gain access to multiple resources across various systems, improving both security and user experience. As organizations continue to expand their digital environments, IAM will play an increasingly important role in protecting user identities, managing access, and ensuring that sensitive information remains secure.

Domain 5: Risk Management

Risk **management** is an essential part of maintaining the security and continuity of an organization's operations. It involves identifying, assessing, and mitigating security risks to protect critical assets, ensuring business resilience and complying with relevant regulations. Effective risk management ensures that organizations understand potential threats, allocate resources to address risks appropriately, and take steps to minimize the impact of those risks.

In cybersecurity, risk management is a continuous process of identifying potential risks, evaluating their impact, and taking actions to mitigate or manage them. Organizations must balance security measures with business goals, aligning resources to both protect against threats and support organizational growth. Risk management activities also help organizations comply with industry regulations and standards to safeguard data and avoid legal consequences.

The key concepts in this domain revolve around risk assessment and analysis, business continuity planning, and regulatory compliance. Effective risk management involves using both **qualitative** and **quantitative** methods to assess risk, applying strategies for **risk treatment**, and ensuring the organization is prepared to handle disruptions through **Business Impact Analysis (BIA)**.

Risk Assessment and Analysis

- **Qualitative vs. Quantitative Methods**
  - **Qualitative risk assessment** involves evaluating risks based on subjective criteria, often using descriptions or categories to assess the likelihood and impact of potential threats. This method is useful when precise numerical data is not available but provides a more general view of the risks.
    - For example, an organization might assess a risk as "high," "medium," or "low" based on expert opinions or past experiences, without using specific numbers.
  - **Quantitative risk assessment**, on the other hand, uses numerical data to assess risk. It involves assigning specific values to the likelihood of a risk and the potential impact of that risk. Quantitative assessments are more data-driven and provide a clearer picture of risk by calculating potential financial losses, the probability of an event, or other measurable factors.
    - For example, a quantitative risk analysis might calculate the potential cost of a data breach based on the number of records affected and the per-record cost of the breach.
- **Risk Matrix**
  - A **risk matrix** is a tool used to visually represent the likelihood and impact of identified risks. This tool is often used in risk assessments to help

prioritize risks based on their potential severity. It typically categorizes risks on a grid where one axis represents the likelihood (probability) of a risk occurring, and the other axis represents the potential impact (consequences) of the risk.

- o Risks are usually assigned a rating based on this matrix (e.g., low, medium, or high), which helps organizations focus on the most critical risks first.
- o Example: A **high likelihood** event with **high impact** would be classified as a priority risk that needs immediate attention.

- **Risk Treatment**
  - **Risk treatment** refers to the strategies used to manage identified risks. It involves deciding how to address risks based on their priority, the organization's risk appetite, and available resources. There are several key approaches to risk treatment:
    - o **Mitigation**: Taking steps to reduce the likelihood or impact of the risk, such as implementing security controls, policies, or training.
    - o **Avoidance**: Changing business processes or practices to avoid the risk altogether (e.g., discontinuing a risky project).
    - o **Transfer**: Shifting the risk to another party, such as purchasing insurance or outsourcing a risky process.

- **Acceptance**: Acknowledging the risk and choosing not to take any action because the risk is considered acceptable, typically due to low likelihood or minimal impact.

Business Impact Analysis (BIA)

- **Identifying Critical Business Functions**
  - A **Business Impact Analysis (BIA)** is a process that helps organizations identify their most critical business functions, systems, and processes and understand the potential impacts of a disruption. The BIA helps prioritize recovery efforts by identifying which operations are essential for business continuity and which systems would be most disruptive if unavailable.
    - For example, in a financial institution, core banking services might be deemed critical, while non-essential services such as marketing systems might be lower in priority for recovery.
- **Recovery Time Objective (RTO)**
  - The **Recovery Time Objective (RTO)** is the target time within which a business function or system must be restored after a disruption to prevent significant harm to the organization. The RTO helps to determine the urgency and priority of recovery efforts.

- For instance, if the RTO for an e-commerce platform is 4 hours, it means the business expects that platform to be fully operational within that timeframe to avoid unacceptable losses in revenue.

- **Recovery Point Objective (RPO)**
  - The **Recovery Point Objective (RPO)** is the maximum amount of data loss an organization is willing to tolerate in terms of time. RPO defines the point in time to which data must be recovered after a disruption.
    - For example, if an organization has an RPO of 1 hour, it means the organization is willing to accept the loss of no more than 1 hours' worth of data. This is a critical factor in determining backup frequencies and data recovery strategies.

Compliance and Regulatory Standards

- **HIPAA (Health Insurance Portability and Accountability Act)**
  - **HIPAA** is a US federal law that mandates data privacy and security protections for health information. It is especially relevant to organizations in the healthcare sector, ensuring that personal health information (PHI) is protected from unauthorized access and breaches. Compliance with HIPAA is essential for avoiding penalties and ensuring the confidentiality, integrity, and availability of healthcare data.

CHAPTER 10 FINAL REVIEW AND EXAM PREPARATION

- **GDPR (General Data Protection Regulation)**
  - The **General Data Protection Regulation (GDPR)** is a European Union regulation that governs how personal data is collected, stored, processed, and protected. GDPR applies to all organizations that handle the personal data of EU citizens, regardless of the organization's location. It establishes strict requirements for data protection, consent, and privacy, and non-compliance can result in significant fines. GDPR emphasizes the principles of data protection by design and by default, as well as individuals' rights over their data.
- **PCI-DSS (Payment Card Industry Data Security Standard)**
  - **PCI-DSS** is a set of security standards designed to protect cardholder data and secure payment card transactions. It is applicable to any organization that handles, processes, or stores credit card information. PCI-DSS outlines requirements for securing networks, systems, and data, and compliance is necessary to prevent fraud and protect customer data.

Summary

Domain 5, **Risk Management**, is a fundamental component of an organization's security framework. It involves assessing potential risks, understanding their impact, and implementing strategies to mitigate, avoid, or transfer risks. Through **qualitative** and **quantitative risk** assessments, organizations can identify vulnerabilities and prioritize actions accordingly. The **risk matrix** serves as a key tool for visually categorizing risks based on their likelihood and impact.

Business Impact Analysis (BIA) helps organizations determine the criticality of their functions and set objectives for **Recovery Time (RTO)** and **Recovery Point (RPO)** to ensure that essential business operations can resume quickly after a disruption. Lastly, compliance with regulations like **HIPAA**, **GDPR**, and **PCI-DSS** ensures that organizations meet legal requirements for protecting sensitive data and minimizing security risks.

By following effective risk management practices, organizations can protect their assets, comply with industry regulations, and maintain the continuity of their operations in the face of security threats or incidents.

Domain 6: Cryptography and PKI

Cryptography plays a crucial role in protecting data by ensuring confidentiality, integrity, and authenticity. It involves using encryption and decryption methods to secure information both at rest and in transit. Cryptographic systems use mathematical algorithms to transform readable data into unreadable ciphertext, which can only be returned to its original form using a decryption key. Cryptography underpins a variety of security mechanisms that ensure privacy, protect data, and verify identities.

The concepts in this domain cover various cryptographic algorithms, the infrastructure that supports cryptography (known as **Public Key Infrastructure (PKI)**), and the encryption protocols used to secure communications over networks.

CHAPTER 10   FINAL REVIEW AND EXAM PREPARATION

Cryptographic Algorithms

- **Symmetric Encryption**

  - **Symmetric encryption** algorithms use the **same key** for both **encryption** and **decryption**. The primary advantage of symmetric encryption is its speed and efficiency, making it ideal for encrypting large amounts of data. However, both the sender and receiver must securely exchange the secret key before they can use the system.

    o A commonly used symmetric encryption algorithm is **AES (Advanced Encryption Standard)**. AES is widely used for encrypting sensitive data because of its strength and speed.

    o **Challenges**: The main challenge with symmetric encryption is the secure distribution of the encryption key. If the key is intercepted, the security of the encrypted data is compromised.

- **Asymmetric Encryption**

  - **Asymmetric encryption**, also known as **public key encryption**, uses two different keys for encryption and decryption: a **public key** and a **private key**. The **public key** is used to encrypt data, and only the corresponding **private key** can decrypt it.

    o **RSA** (Rivest-Shamir-Adleman) is one of the most commonly used asymmetric encryption algorithms. It enables secure key exchange and is widely used for digital signatures and secure communications.

- The key advantage of asymmetric encryption is that the public key can be shared openly, and only the owner of the corresponding private key can decrypt the message. This makes key distribution much simpler compared to symmetric encryption.
- **Challenges**: Asymmetric encryption tends to be slower than symmetric encryption, so it's often used for smaller amounts of data, such as encrypting the symmetric key for data encryption.

- **Hashing**
  - **Hashing** is a **one-way function** that converts input data (like a message or a file) into a fixed-length string of characters, which is typically a **hash value** or **hash digest**. This hash value is unique to the original data, and even small changes to the data will result in a completely different hash value.
    - Common hashing algorithms include **SHA (Secure Hash Algorithm)**, particularly **SHA-256** and **SHA-3**, which are used for verifying data integrity.
    - Hashing is often used for **digital signatures** and **message authentication codes (MACs)** to verify that data has not been altered. Since hashing is one-way, it cannot be used to recover the original data from the hash.

- Challenges: While hashing is efficient for ensuring data integrity, it does not provide confidentiality. The hash does not "encrypt" the data; it only provides a unique representation.

Public Key Infrastructure (PKI)

- **Digital Certificates and Signatures**
    - A **Digital Certificate** is an electronic document used to prove the ownership of a public key. It includes the public key, information about the key owner, and the digital signature of a trusted certificate authority (CA) that verifies the authenticity of the certificate.
        - **Digital signatures** are used to verify the identity of the sender and ensure that the message has not been tampered with. A digital signature is created by encrypting a hash of the message with the sender's private key. The recipient can verify the signature by decrypting it with the sender's public key and comparing the hash value.
        - Digital certificates and signatures are essential for establishing trust in many online transactions, such as in **SSL/TLS** communications and **email encryption**.

- **Key Management**
  - **Key management** refers to the processes and procedures for handling cryptographic keys, including **key generation**, **distribution**, **storage**, and **rotation**.
    - Keys must be securely generated, often using random number generators, and distributed through secure channels. **Key storage** requires safe environments such as hardware security modules (HSMs) or trusted platforms that protect keys from unauthorized access.
    - **Key rotation** is the practice of periodically changing cryptographic keys to reduce the risk of a key being compromised over time. This is an essential part of maintaining a secure cryptographic system.

Encryption Protocols

- **SSL/TLS (Secure Sockets Layer/Transport Layer Security)**
  - **SSL** and **TLS** are cryptographic protocols used to secure data transmitted over networks, especially the internet. TLS is the successor to SSL and provides a more secure and efficient encryption mechanism. These protocols are most commonly seen in **HTTPS** (Hypertext Transfer Protocol Secure), which is used to secure communications between web browsers and servers.

CHAPTER 10   FINAL REVIEW AND EXAM PREPARATION

- o **SSL/TLS** ensures **data confidentiality**, **integrity**, and **authenticity** by encrypting the data in transit, preventing unauthorized parties from intercepting or altering the data.
- o **Challenges**: While SSL has been deprecated in favor of TLS, it is still important to recognize legacy systems that may still be using SSL. Proper configuration of SSL/TLS, including the use of strong ciphers and up-to-date certificates, is critical to avoid vulnerabilities.

- **IPsec (Internet Protocol Security)**

- **IPsec** is a suite of protocols used to secure **IP communications** by encrypting and authenticating each IP packet in a communication session. It is commonly used to secure **Virtual Private Networks (VPNs)**, providing a secure tunnel for transmitting data over the internet.

    - o IPsec can operate in two modes:
        - **Transport Mode**: Encrypts only the payload (data) of the IP packet.
        - **Tunnel Mode**: Encrypts the entire IP packet, adding a new header to the packet for routing.
    - o **IPsec** helps ensure the confidentiality and integrity of transmitted data, making it a vital tool in securing remote communications and protecting data during transmission.

CHAPTER 10   FINAL REVIEW AND EXAM PREPARATION

Summary

Domain 6, **Cryptography and PKI**, provides the foundational concepts and tools for securing data through encryption, decryption, and key management. The use of **symmetric** and **asymmetric encryption** allows organizations to protect sensitive data both at rest and during transmission, while **hashing** provides data integrity by ensuring that information is not tampered with.

Public Key Infrastructure (PKI) supports the use of **digital certificates** and **digital signatures**, which authenticate identities and verify the integrity of communications. The management of cryptographic keys, from their generation to their secure storage and rotation, is critical to maintaining a robust cryptographic system.

Lastly, encryption protocols like **SSL/TLS** and **IPsec** secure data transmissions, ensuring confidentiality, integrity, and authenticity in network communications. Mastery of these concepts is essential for securing digital communications and protecting sensitive information from unauthorized access or modification.

Domain 7: Security Assessment and Testing

Security assessment and testing are critical activities that help ensure the effectiveness of security controls and identify vulnerabilities within an organization's infrastructure. The goal is to proactively discover weaknesses before malicious actors can exploit them. This domain focuses on methods for testing and evaluating the security posture of systems, networks, and applications, as well as monitoring and auditing mechanisms that help detect and respond to security incidents.

By performing regular security assessments, organizations can identify gaps in their defenses, assess the impact of vulnerabilities, and verify that their security controls are functioning as intended.

Security Testing

- **Penetration Testing**
    - **Penetration testing** (often referred to as **ethical hacking**) is a **simulated attack** on an organization's systems, networks, or applications to identify vulnerabilities that could be exploited by malicious attackers. This process typically involves attempting to bypass security controls and exploiting weaknesses to assess the potential damage of a real-world attack.
        - Penetration tests can focus on different aspects, such as web applications, network security, or social engineering.
        - The testing process often includes the following steps:
            - **Reconnaissance**: Gathering information about the target system.
            - **Vulnerability scanning**: Identifying known vulnerabilities.
            - **Exploitation**: Attempting to exploit identified weaknesses.
            - **Post-exploitation**: Evaluating the potential damage and determining what additional risks arise from successful exploitation.
        - The results of penetration testing help organizations understand how an attacker might break into their systems and what defenses need to be strengthened.

- **Challenges**: Penetration testing should be performed regularly to keep up with evolving security threats, but it requires experienced professionals to conduct effectively.

- **Vulnerability Scanning**
  - **Vulnerability scanning** is the process of using automated tools to detect known vulnerabilities in an organization's systems, networks, or software applications. These scanners check for weaknesses such as outdated software, missing patches, or improperly configured security settings.
    - The tools perform scans by comparing the target system against a database of known vulnerabilities, such as the **Common Vulnerabilities and Exposures (CVE)** list.
    - Vulnerability scans are usually performed on a regular basis to identify issues early and help prioritize remediation efforts based on risk.
    - **Challenges**: While automated tools are effective for identifying known vulnerabilities, they may miss newer or zero-day vulnerabilities. Additionally, they can sometimes generate false positives, requiring further investigation to confirm the findings.

Auditing and Monitoring

- **Log Management**
    - **Log management** involves the collection, aggregation, and analysis of logs from various sources within an organization's infrastructure, such as servers, workstations, network devices, and applications. Logs provide an audit trail of activities and can be invaluable for detecting and investigating security incidents.
        - By regularly reviewing logs, organizations can identify signs of **anomalies** or **malicious activity**, such as unauthorized access attempts, failed logins, or unusual network traffic.
        - Log management practices include
            - **Log Aggregation**: Collecting logs from multiple sources into a centralized location.
            - **Log Analysis**: Identifying patterns and anomalies that may indicate a security breach.
            - **Log Retention**: Storing logs for a period of time to ensure compliance with regulations and support forensic investigations.
        - **Challenges**: Logs can generate a large volume of data, making it difficult to monitor them manually. Therefore, automation tools are often used to filter and analyze logs for relevant security events.

CHAPTER 10   FINAL REVIEW AND EXAM PREPARATION

- **Security Information and Event Management (SIEM)**
  - **SIEM** systems provide real-time analysis of security alerts generated by various hardware and software components in the IT environment. These tools combine **security information** (log data) and **event management** (alerts about security incidents) to provide organizations with comprehensive visibility into their security posture.
    - SIEM systems aggregate and analyze logs from various sources, detect anomalies, and generate alerts about potential security incidents.
    - Key functions of SIEM include
      - **Real-Time Monitoring**: Continuously analyzing network and system activity to identify potential security threats.
      - **Event Correlation**: Combining data from multiple sources to detect patterns indicative of malicious activity.
      - **Alerting**: Sending alerts to security personnel when suspicious activity is detected.
      - **Reporting**: Generating detailed reports to comply with security standards and regulations.
    - SIEM systems help organizations respond quickly to potential security incidents by providing actionable intelligence in a centralized dashboard.

- **Challenges**: SIEM implementation can be complex and costly, and organizations must ensure they have the necessary personnel and processes to respond to alerts. Additionally, SIEM systems can produce a large number of false positives, which may lead to alert fatigue.

Summary

Domain 7, **Security Assessment and Testing**, emphasizes the importance of proactive security measures to assess the effectiveness of security controls and identify vulnerabilities. **Penetration testing** provides a hands-on approach to simulate attacks and evaluate the resilience of systems against potential threats. **Vulnerability scanning**, on the other hand, offers automated detection of known vulnerabilities, helping to quickly identify weaknesses before they are exploited.

Auditing and monitoring are also critical components of an organization's security strategy. **Log management** enables the collection and analysis of system logs to detect suspicious activity, while **SIEM systems** provide real-time monitoring and analysis to respond quickly to security threats. By integrating these practices into a continuous security framework, organizations can ensure that they maintain robust defenses against evolving cyber threats.

Domain 8: Security Operations and Incident Response

Security Operations and Incident Response is a crucial domain that focuses on the operational aspects of maintaining a secure environment. It encompasses the planning and execution of security incident management, business continuity, and disaster recovery efforts. Ensuring a prompt and effective response to security incidents, coupled with robust continuity plans, is vital for minimizing the impact of attacks or disasters on the organization's operations.

Effective **incident response** allows organizations to detect, contain, and recover from security incidents in an orderly, efficient manner. At the same time, well-established **business continuity** and **disaster recovery** plans ensure that critical systems and data can be restored and operations continue with minimal downtime after an event.

Incident Response

- **Incident Response Plan (IRP)**
    - An **Incident Response Plan (IRP)** is a **documented process** that outlines the steps an organization will take to identify, contain, and mitigate the effects of a security incident. The goal is to respond to security events in a coordinated manner to minimize damage and recover as quickly as possible.
        - The plan typically includes
            - **Preparation**: Identifying assets, creating a response team, and defining roles and responsibilities.
            - **Detection and Analysis**: Identifying potential incidents and analyzing their scope and impact.
            - **Containment**: Implementing measures to limit the spread and impact of the incident.

- **Eradication**: Removing the cause of the incident from the environment (e.g., malware removal).

- **Recovery**: Restoring affected systems and services to normal operation.

- **Lessons Learned**: Analyzing the response and identifying improvements for future incidents.

    o An effective IRP helps organizations **respond quickly** and **reduce recovery time**, as well as ensure proper documentation for compliance purposes.

- **Forensics**

  - **Forensics** is the process of investigating and analyzing data after a security incident has occurred to determine the **cause**, **impact**, and **extent** of the breach. Forensic analysis involves gathering evidence in a way that preserves its integrity, ensuring that it can be used for legal or regulatory purposes if needed.

    o Key steps in forensic investigations include

    - **Data Collection**: Securely gathering logs, files, and other artifacts from affected systems.

    - **Data Analysis**: Examining collected data to understand the timeline of events, the attack vectors used, and the methods employed by the attacker.

- **Reporting**: Documenting the findings and providing a detailed report that includes actions taken, impact assessment, and recommendations for preventing future incidents.
    - **Challenges**: Ensuring that the forensics process is performed **timely**, without compromising the **chain of custody**, and in a manner that complies with **legal requirements**.

Business Continuity and Disaster Recovery

- **BCP/DRP (Business Continuity Planning/Disaster Recovery Planning)**
    - **Business Continuity Planning (BCP)** and **Disaster Recovery Planning (DRP)** are two closely related processes that focus on maintaining or quickly restoring essential operations in the face of significant disruptions or disasters, such as cyberattacks, natural disasters, or hardware failures.
        - **Business Continuity Planning (BCP)** ensures that essential business functions can continue during and after an incident. It includes
            - Identifying critical operations and services that need to remain available.
            - Developing procedures and strategies to ensure business operations continue, even with limited resources.

- Communication plans for internal and external stakeholders during crises.
- **Disaster Recovery Planning (DRP)** focuses specifically on the restoration of **IT systems** and **data** after a disaster. This includes
  - **Recovery objectives**, such as the **Recovery Time Objective (RTO)** and **Recovery Point Objective (RPO)**.
  - Ensuring that backups are available and systems can be restored promptly.
  - Creating plans to re-establish critical systems, services, and applications.
- Together, BCP/DRP ensures that an organization can recover quickly from any major event and continue functioning with minimal disruption.

- **Backup Strategies**
  - **Backup strategies** are essential for ensuring the **availability** and **integrity** of critical data in the event of system failures or disasters. Proper backup strategies focus on ensuring that data can be quickly restored to minimize downtime and data loss.
    - Key considerations for effective backup strategies include
      - **Frequency**: How often backups are taken (e.g., daily, weekly) to ensure data is up-to-date.

- **Storage Location**: Where backups are stored, ensuring they are geographically separated from the primary data center to protect against local disasters (e.g., off-site or cloud-based backups).

- **Backup Types**
    - **Full backups**: A complete copy of all data.
    - **Incremental backups**: Only the data that has changed since the last backup.
    - **Differential backups**: All data changed since the last full backup.

- **Retention Period**: How long backup copies are kept to meet business and compliance requirements.

- **Testing**: Regularly testing backups to ensure they are complete and functional for recovery.

A **robust backup strategy** is essential for ensuring that an organization can quickly restore operations in the event of data loss or corruption.

Summary

Domain 8, **Security Operations and Incident Response**, emphasizes the importance of having a well-defined, actionable response plan for addressing security incidents and ensuring business continuity. An effective **Incident Response Plan (IRP)** provides a structured approach to handling security incidents, from detection to recovery. **Forensics** plays a key role in investigating the root cause and impact of incidents to inform future prevention measures.

CHAPTER 10   FINAL REVIEW AND EXAM PREPARATION

Business Continuity and Disaster Recovery are essential for minimizing the disruption caused by disasters or attacks. By having **BCP/DRP** plans in place, organizations can ensure that critical functions continue operating during a crisis and that systems and data are restored quickly. Additionally, **backup strategies** provide a critical safeguard for protecting data and ensuring its recoverability after a disaster.

Practice Questions and Exam Strategies
Domain 1: Threats, Attacks, and Vulnerabilities

Question 1: What type of malware disguises itself as legitimate software but delivers a malicious payload once installed?

- A) Worm
- B) Trojan
- C) Adware
- D) Ransomware

Correct Answer: B) Trojan

Question 2: Which attack involves tricking a user into providing sensitive information by pretending to be a trustworthy entity?

- A) Phishing
- B) Spoofing
- C) DDoS
- D) Brute Force

Correct Answer: A) Phishing

Question 3: What is a zero-day vulnerability?

A) A weakness that is fixed before discovery

B) A vulnerability discovered on the first day of an attack

C) A previously unknown vulnerability exploited by attackers

D) A vulnerability that only affects zero-rated applications

Correct Answer: C) A previously unknown vulnerability exploited by attackers

Question 4: Which type of attack exploits a vulnerability to execute code on a remote server?

A) SQL Injection

B) Man-in-the-Middle

C) Cross-Site Scripting (XSS)

D) Remote Code Execution

Correct Answer: D) Remote Code Execution

Question 5: Which tool is commonly used for network scanning to identify open ports and services?

A) Wireshark

B) Nmap

C) Metasploit

D) Nessus

Correct Answer: B) Nmap

CHAPTER 10   FINAL REVIEW AND EXAM PREPARATION

Domain 2: Architecture and Design

Question 6: What principle ensures that users only have the minimum level of access needed to perform their job functions?

- A) Least Privilege
- B) Defense in Depth
- C) Separation of Duties
- D) Need to Know

Correct Answer: A) Least Privilege

Question 7: Which type of firewall inspects both incoming and outgoing packets and monitors their state?

- A) Packet-filtering Firewall
- B) Stateless Firewall
- C) Stateful Firewall
- D) Proxy Firewall

Correct Answer: C) Stateful Firewall

Question 8: What is the primary purpose of a demilitarized zone (DMZ) in a network?

- A) To prevent DDoS attacks
- B) To provide a buffer zone between internal and external networks
- C) To host critical internal servers
- D) To encrypt data in transit

Correct Answer: B) To provide a buffer zone between internal and external networks

Question 9: Which cloud service model provides infrastructure components like virtual machines and storage?

A) SaaS

B) PaaS

C) IaaS

D) FaaS

Correct Answer: C) IaaS

Question 10: Which authentication method uses multiple pieces of evidence to verify a user's identity?

A) Single Sign-On (SSO)

B) Multi-Factor Authentication (MFA)

C) Kerberos

D) Role-Based Access Control (RBAC)

Correct Answer: B) Multi-Factor Authentication (MFA)

Domain 3: Implementation

Question 11: Which encryption protocol is commonly used to secure VPN connections?

A) PPTP

B) IPsec

C) FTP

D) Telnet

Correct Answer: B) IPsec

CHAPTER 10   FINAL REVIEW AND EXAM PREPARATION

Question 12: What type of encryption uses the same key for both encryption and decryption?

   A)   Asymmetric

   B)   Public Key

   C)   Symmetric

   D)   Hashing

Correct Answer: C) Symmetric

Question 13: Which port is used by HTTPS to secure web traffic?

   A)   80

   B)   21

   C)   443

   D)   110

Correct Answer: C) 443

Question 14: What is the function of a Certificate Authority (CA) in a Public Key Infrastructure (PKI)?

   A)   Encrypts emails

   B)   Issues digital certificates

   C)   Manages password policies

   D)   Creates private keys

Correct Answer: B) Issues digital certificates

Question 15: Which tool can be used to capture and analyze network traffic?

    A) Metasploit

    B) Nessus

    C) Wireshark

    D) Burp Suite

Correct Answer: C) Wireshark

Domain 4: Operations and Incident Response

Question 16: What is the first step in the incident response process?

    A) Containment

    B) Eradication

    C) Detection

    D) Preparation

Correct Answer: D) Preparation

Question 17: Which log type would you check to verify access attempts to a server?

    A) Firewall logs

    B) DNS logs

    C) Authentication logs

    D) Application logs

Correct Answer: C) Authentication logs

CHAPTER 10   FINAL REVIEW AND EXAM PREPARATION

Question 18: Which phase of incident response involves identifying the scope and impact of an incident?

A) Containment

B) Recovery

C) Eradication

D) Detection and Analysis

Correct Answer: D) Detection and Analysis

Question 19: What is the primary goal of the containment phase in incident response?

A) To eliminate the threat

B) To restore normal operations

C) To limit the damage and prevent spread

D) To notify stakeholders

Correct Answer: C) To limit the damage and prevent spread

Question 20: Which of the following is a common tool used for digital forensic analysis?

A) Nmap

B) Autopsy

C) Burp Suite

D) Wireshark

Correct Answer: B) Autopsy

CHAPTER 10   FINAL REVIEW AND EXAM PREPARATION

Question 21: What type of backup strategy involves copying only the data that has changed since the last full backup?

   A) Full backup

   B) Incremental backup

   C) Differential backup

   D) Snapshot backup

Correct Answer: B) Incremental backup

Domain 5: Governance, Risk, and Compliance

Question 22: What is the purpose of a business impact analysis (BIA)?

   A) To identify potential threats

   B) To determine the effect of disruptions on business operations

   C) To implement security controls

   D) To conduct a vulnerability assessment

Correct Answer: B) To determine the effect of disruptions on business operations

Question 23: Which framework is commonly used for IT governance and management?

   A) ISO 27001

   B) COBIT

   C) PCI DSS

   D) NIST SP 800-53

Correct Answer: B) COBIT

CHAPTER 10   FINAL REVIEW AND EXAM PREPARATION

Question 24: What is the main focus of the General Data Protection Regulation (GDPR)?

A)   Intellectual property protection

B)   Data privacy and protection for EU citizens

C)   Cybersecurity incident reporting

D)   Financial audit compliance

Correct Answer: B) Data privacy and protection for EU citizens

Question 25: Which document outlines the steps for responding to an information security incident?

A)   Disaster Recovery Plan

B)   Business Continuity Plan

C)   Incident Response Plan

D)   Risk Management Plan

Correct Answer: C) Incident Response Plan

Question 26: Which type of risk is described as the potential for loss due to a system's vulnerability being exploited?

A)   Inherent risk

B)   Residual risk

C)   Transfer risk

D)   Business risk

Correct Answer: A) Inherent risk

CHAPTER 10   FINAL REVIEW AND EXAM PREPARATION

Domain 6: Identity and Access Management (IAM)

Question 27: Which access control model grants permissions based on the user's role in an organization?

   A) Discretionary Access Control (DAC)

   B) Mandatory Access Control (MAC)

   C) Role-Based Access Control (RBAC)

   D) Attribute-Based Access Control (ABAC)

   Correct Answer: C) Role-Based Access Control (RBAC)

Question 28: What is the purpose of Single Sign-On (SSO)?

   A) To enhance password complexity

   B) To allow multiple users to share accounts

   C) To enable users to access multiple systems with one login

   D) To enforce multi-factor authentication

   Correct Answer: C) To enable users to access multiple systems with one login

Question 29: Which authentication protocol is used to provide secure, encrypted login sessions over a network?

   A) RADIUS

   B) LDAP

   C) Kerberos

   D) PAP

   Correct Answer: C) Kerberos

CHAPTER 10   FINAL REVIEW AND EXAM PREPARATION

Question 30: What is a common method to implement least privilege in an organization?

A) Assigning administrative rights to all users

B) Using access control lists (ACLs)

C) Allowing users to choose their access level

D) Disabling user access logs

Correct Answer: B) Using access control lists (ACLs)

Question 31: Which of the following is an example of two-factor authentication?

A) Username and password

B) Password and PIN

C) Smart card and fingerprint

D) Security question and email verification

Correct Answer: C) Smart card and fingerprint

Domain 7: Cryptography and PKI

Question 32: Which encryption algorithm is considered the strongest for securing sensitive data?

A) DES

B) 3DES

C) AES

D) MD5

Correct Answer: C) AES

425

CHAPTER 10   FINAL REVIEW AND EXAM PREPARATION

Question 33: What does the process of hashing accomplish?

A) Encrypts data using a public key

B) Converts plaintext into ciphertext

C) Generates a fixed-size string from input data

D) Compresses files to save space

Correct Answer: C) Generates a fixed-size string from input data

Question 34: Which cryptographic method uses two keys: a public key for encryption and a private key for decryption?

A) Symmetric encryption

B) Hashing

C) Asymmetric encryption

D) Steganography

Correct Answer: C) Asymmetric encryption

Question 35: What is the main purpose of a digital signature?

A) To encrypt a message

B) To verify the authenticity and integrity of a message

C) To hide data within an image

D) To create a secure password

Correct Answer: B) To verify the authenticity and integrity of a message

CHAPTER 10   FINAL REVIEW AND EXAM PREPARATION

Question 36: Which protocol is used to encrypt email messages?

    A) HTTPS

    B) S/MIME

    C) SSH

    D) DNSSEC

Correct Answer: B) S/MIME

Domain 8: Secure Network Design

Question 37: What is the primary function of a Virtual Private Network (VPN)?

    A) To detect malware

    B) To provide secure remote access

    C) To prevent phishing attacks

    D) To encrypt stored data

Correct Answer: B) To provide secure remote access

Question 38: What is a common feature of an intrusion detection system (IDS)?

    A) Encrypts network traffic

    B) Monitors network traffic for suspicious activity

    C) Manages network configurations

    D) Blocks incoming email spam

Correct Answer: B) Monitors network traffic for suspicious activity

CHAPTER 10   FINAL REVIEW AND EXAM PREPARATION

Question 39: What technology isolates network segments to enhance security and reduce the risk of unauthorized access?

A) VLAN

B) DHCP

C) DNS

D) VPN

Correct Answer: A) VLAN

Question 40: Which protocol secures the transfer of files over the internet?

A) FTP

B) TFTP

C) SFTP

D) HTTP

Correct Answer: C) SFTP

Question 41: Which of the following is a method used to verify the identity of a user during the authentication process?

A) Encryption

B) Password cracking

C) Multi-factor authentication

D) Data backup

Correct Answer: C) Multi-factor authentication

CHAPTER 10   FINAL REVIEW AND EXAM PREPARATION

Question 42: What is the primary purpose of a firewall in a network?

  A) To block access to malicious websites

  B) To encrypt network traffic

  C) To monitor user activity

  D) To control incoming and outgoing network traffic based on security rules

Correct Answer: D) To control incoming and outgoing network traffic based on security rules

Question 43: Which of the following is NOT a component of the CIA triad?

  A) Confidentiality

  B) Integrity

  C) Availability

  D) Authentication

Correct Answer: D) Authentication

Question 44: What type of attack attempts to overwhelm a network or server with excessive traffic to make it unavailable?

  A) Phishing

  B) DoS (Denial of Service)

  C) SQL Injection

  D) Cross-Site Scripting (XSS)

Correct Answer: B) DoS (Denial of Service)

CHAPTER 10   FINAL REVIEW AND EXAM PREPARATION

Question 45: Which of the following is an example of a physical security control?

A) Firewall

B) Biometric scanner

C) Encryption

D) Anti-virus software

Correct Answer: B) Biometric scanner

Question 46: What is the main difference between a vulnerability assessment and a penetration test?

A) Vulnerability assessments identify weaknesses, while penetration tests exploit them.

B) Vulnerability assessments are performed manually, while penetration tests use automated tools.

C) Penetration tests identify weaknesses, while vulnerability assessments exploit them.

D) There is no difference between the two.

Correct Answer: A) Vulnerability assessments identify weaknesses, while penetration tests exploit them.

Question 47: Which type of encryption key is used in asymmetric encryption for encrypting data?

A) Private key

B) Public key

C) Secret key

D) Symmetric key

Correct Answer: B) Public key

CHAPTER 10   FINAL REVIEW AND EXAM PREPARATION

Question 48: What type of backup captures only the changes made since the last full or incremental backup?

A) Differential backup

B) Full backup

C) Incremental backup

D) Snapshot backup

Correct Answer: C) Incremental backup

Question 49: What is the purpose of a sandbox in cybersecurity?

A) To isolate potentially harmful programs and prevent them from damaging the system

B) To allow attackers to bypass security measures

C) To detect email phishing attempts

D) To encrypt sensitive files

Correct Answer: A) To isolate potentially harmful programs and prevent them from damaging the system

Question 50: Which security measure prevents unauthorized access to a system based on user roles?

A) Biometric authentication

B) Role-Based Access Control (RBAC)

C) CAPTCHA

D) Single Sign-On (SSO)

Correct Answer: B) Role-Based Access Control (RBAC)

CHAPTER 10   FINAL REVIEW AND EXAM PREPARATION

Domain 9: Security Operations and Incident Response

Question 51: What is the purpose of a Security Information and Event Management (SIEM) system?

    A) To manage network traffic

    B) To monitor and analyze security events in real time

    C) To backup critical data

    D) To configure firewalls

Correct Answer: B) To monitor and analyze security events in real time

Question 52: Which of the following is a characteristic of a distributed denial-of-service (DDoS) attack?

    A) It uses multiple compromised systems to flood a target with traffic.

    B) It targets individual users' devices with malware.

    C) It attempts to steal confidential information from a network.

    D) It exploits software vulnerabilities.

Correct Answer: A) It uses multiple compromised systems to flood a target with traffic.

CHAPTER 10   FINAL REVIEW AND EXAM PREPARATION

Question 53: Which action should be taken FIRST during the containment phase of an incident response?

A) Eradicate the threat.

B) Restore services.

C) Identify the scope of the incident.

D) Notify external stakeholders.

Correct Answer: C) Identify the scope of the incident.

Question 54: Which of the following is a type of social engineering attack?

A) SQL Injection

B) Phishing

C) Buffer Overflow

D) Cross-Site Scripting (XSS)

Correct Answer: B) Phishing

Question 55: What is the purpose of a business continuity plan (BCP)?

A) To manage financial transactions securely

B) To ensure that critical business functions can continue during and after a disaster

C) To monitor network traffic for threats

D) To ensure that systems remain unpatched to avoid vulnerabilities

Correct Answer: B) To ensure that critical business functions can continue during and after a disaster

CHAPTER 10   FINAL REVIEW AND EXAM PREPARATION

Question 56: Which of the following is a critical component of an effective incident response plan?

A) Determining the cause of the incident

B) Identifying key stakeholders

C) Estimating the potential financial loss

D) Conducting a root cause analysis

Correct Answer: B) Identifying key stakeholders

Question 57: In which phase of the incident response process are compromised systems completely removed from the network for analysis?

A) Containment

B) Recovery

C) Eradication

D) Preparation

Correct Answer: A) Containment

Question 58: Which process involves identifying, preventing, and mitigating potential cybersecurity risks in an organization?

A) Incident Response

B) Risk Management

C) Disaster Recovery

D) Business Continuity Planning

Correct Answer: B) Risk Management

Question 59: What type of attack exploits a vulnerability in an application that allows the attacker to execute arbitrary code?

A) Man-in-the-Middle

B) Cross-Site Scripting (XSS)

C) Remote Code Execution (RCE)

D) SQL Injection

Correct Answer: C) Remote Code Execution (RCE)

Question 60: What is the purpose of an incident response team's post-incident report?

A) To blame the responsible individuals

B) To identify and resolve vulnerabilities exploited during the incident

C) To restore business operations

D) To provide legal counsel

Correct Answer: B) To identify and resolve vulnerabilities exploited during the incident

Domain 10: Disaster Recovery and Business Continuity

Question 61: Which of the following is a goal of a disaster recovery plan (DRP)?

A) To secure physical access to the server room

B) To restore data and applications as quickly as possible after an incident

CHAPTER 10   FINAL REVIEW AND EXAM PREPARATION

    C) To conduct regular penetration tests

    D) To perform an ongoing security audit

Correct Answer: B) To restore data and applications as quickly as possible after an incident

Question 62: What is the primary objective of a business continuity plan (BCP)?

    A) To eliminate all security threats

    B) To ensure the availability of critical business operations during and after a disaster

    C) To prevent unauthorized access to confidential data

    D) To monitor network traffic for anomalies

Correct Answer: B) To ensure the availability of critical business operations during and after a disaster

Question 63: What does the Recovery Time Objective (RTO) measure in disaster recovery planning?

    A) The time it takes to restore operations to full capacity

    B) The time it takes to conduct a vulnerability assessment

    C) The maximum acceptable downtime before operations must resume

    D) The amount of time required for a business continuity test

Correct Answer: C) The maximum acceptable downtime before operations must resume

CHAPTER 10   FINAL REVIEW AND EXAM PREPARATION

Question 64: What is the function of a cold site in disaster recovery?

A) A fully equipped site that is ready to take over operations immediately after a disaster

B) A site that is prepared with only basic infrastructure for recovery

C) A temporary site used for business operations until the primary site is restored

D) A site with real-time replication of data from the primary site

Correct Answer: B) A site that is prepared with only basic infrastructure for recovery

Question 65: Which of the following is a key factor in determining the effectiveness of a disaster recovery plan?

A) The number of security tools implemented

B) The ability to restore critical systems and data

C) The level of network segmentation

D) The presence of an antivirus program

Correct Answer: B) The ability to restore critical systems and data

CHAPTER 10   FINAL REVIEW AND EXAM PREPARATION

Exam Strategies for Success in the Security+ Exam

Approach to Multiple-Choice Questions

- **Read Questions Thoroughly**: Ensure you understand what the question is asking before selecting an answer. Watch for qualifiers like *"most," "best,"* or *"least"* as they often indicate subtle differences between options. For example, when a question asks for the *"most secure"* option, think about the strongest security measure among the choices.

- **Use Process of Elimination**: If you're unsure about a particular answer, eliminate the obviously wrong answers first. Narrowing down your choices increases the likelihood of selecting the correct one, especially when you have no clear answer in mind. For example, if two options are clearly less relevant to the question, you're left with a higher chance of choosing the right one between the remaining options.

- **Answer Confidently**: Once you've gone through the options and narrowed down your choices, make your selection confidently. Don't second-guess yourself too much; it's better to make an educated guess than to leave a question unanswered.

Approach to Scenario-Based Questions

- **Break Down Scenarios into Smaller Components**: Many questions will present a scenario that might seem complex at first. Take a moment to break it down into manageable parts. Identify the key details and consider what actions need to be taken in the given context. For example, if the question describes a network security incident, isolate the components such as the type of attack, the affected system, and the response required.

- **Identify the Most Critical Elements**: Focus on the core elements of the scenario that directly influence the decision. In security contexts, this might include factors such as the immediate impact on confidentiality, integrity, or availability. For example, if a data breach is described in the scenario, the best course of action will often focus on mitigating damage to the affected systems and protecting sensitive information.

General Tips

- **Time Management**: Be mindful of your time during the exam. Aim to spend an average of 1 minute per question. If you're stuck on a question, make an educated guess and move on. You can always come back to it later.

- **Read All Answer Choices**: Never rush to select an answer without considering all the options. Sometimes, the correct answer may not be the first one you think of, so it's important to review each possible choice.

- **Stay Calm Under Pressure**: It's easy to get stressed during an exam but staying calm and focused will help you think more clearly. Take a deep breath if you start feeling overwhelmed and stay positive.

These strategies, when applied, will help improve your performance on multiple-choice and scenario-based questions on the exam. By carefully considering the phrasing of the questions and using elimination tactics, you'll be better equipped to make the right decisions.

Time Management

Effective time management is a crucial skill that helps you balance the need to complete each question with the necessity of reviewing and handling challenging problems. By carefully managing your time, you can reduce anxiety, avoid rushing, and ensure that you're able to answer as many questions as possible within the exam's time constraints.

- **Allocate Time Based on the Number of Questions**: The first step in effective time management is to plan how much time you will spend on each question. Begin by dividing the total time available by the number of questions in the exam. For example, if you have 90 minutes to answer 100 questions, the calculation would be approximately 54 seconds per question. Of course, some questions will be easier than others, but this is a good baseline. If a question feels too complicated or time-consuming, move on, and return to it later if you still have time. By keeping track of the time, you ensure that you're pacing yourself properly and don't run out of time before completing the exam.

- **Move On from Questions That Are Too Time-Consuming**: It's easy to get bogged down in difficult questions, but spending too much time on a single problem can prevent you from completing the rest of the exam. If you come across a question that you can't answer after a reasonable amount of time, mark it and move on to the next one. This keeps your momentum going and ensures you tackle easier questions first, which can help boost your confidence. Once you've answered all the other questions, return to the difficult ones. Sometimes, a fresh perspective after tackling other questions can make it easier to find the correct answer.

- **Practice with Timed Exams to Build Pace and Endurance**: One of the best ways to prepare for time management challenges during the exam is to practice with timed mock exams. Use practice exams that simulate the real test environment to get a feel for the pacing. Time yourself strictly according to the limits of the actual exam and try to answer as many questions as possible within the allotted time. Practicing under these conditions builds endurance and allows you to identify areas where you may need to adjust your time. Over time, you'll become more adept at managing your time effectively, ensuring that you can work through the exam with confidence and without feeling rushed.

CHAPTER 10   FINAL REVIEW AND EXAM PREPARATION

Mindfulness and Relaxation Techniques

Mindfulness and relaxation techniques are essential tools for managing the mental and emotional stress that often comes with exams. By integrating these practices into your exam preparation, you can improve your ability to stay calm, focused, and present during the test. Reducing stress not only helps you think more clearly but also allows you to perform at your best.

- **Before the Exam**
    - **Practice Deep-Breathing Exercises**: Anxiety often rises before an exam, and practicing deep-breathing exercises is a simple but effective way to calm your mind and reduce physical stress. Try the **4-7-8 breathing technique**: inhale deeply through your nose for four seconds, hold your breath for seven seconds, and exhale slowly through your mouth for eight seconds. This technique slows your heart rate, reduces blood pressure, and activates the parasympathetic nervous system, which helps you relax. By practicing deep breathing in the days leading up to the exam, you can make it a habitual response when stress arises.
    - **Engage in Light Physical Activity**: A quick walk, some light stretching, or even a few yoga poses before your exam can help release physical tension and improve circulation. This light activity stimulates your body and mind, increasing blood flow and focus. Physical activity releases endorphins, the body's natural stress relievers, which can help alleviate feelings of anxiety and nervousness. Engaging in physical exercise before

an exam also helps you transition into a calm, focused state, preparing you mentally for the task ahead.

- **During the Exam**
  - **Use the "4-7-8" Breathing Technique**: During the exam itself, if you begin to feel anxious or overwhelmed, use the **4-7-8 breathing technique** to quickly reset your mental state. By focusing on slow, controlled breathing, you calm your nervous system and can return to your work with a clearer mind. As you breathe deeply and slowly, you divert your focus away from stressors and back to the task at hand. This short pause helps you refocus and approach each question with a fresh perspective.
  - **Take Short, Strategic Breaks**: If the exam allows for short breaks, use this opportunity to step away for a moment and reset. Close your eyes and take a few deep breaths. Even just a 30-second break can help you regain focus and reduce stress. If breaks are not allowed, simply taking a brief moment to relax and refocus between questions can still be beneficial. If you're feeling mentally fatigued, closing your eyes for a moment or shifting your attention to something relaxing can refresh your focus.
  - **Visualization Techniques**: Visualization is a powerful tool for reducing anxiety and building confidence. Before the exam and during breaks, take a moment to **visualize success**. Imagine yourself calmly moving through the questions, answering each one confidently and effectively. Picture yourself staying calm and

collected, no matter how difficult the questions may seem. By visualizing a successful experience, you can help reframe your mindset, reinforcing positive beliefs about your ability to succeed. Visualization can also reduce the impact of negative thoughts and fears, boosting your overall confidence.

- **Post-Exam Relaxation:** Once the exam is over, it's important to give yourself time to relax and decompress. Engaging in an enjoyable or relaxing activity after the exam helps you transition from "exam mode" back to a normal, balanced state of mind. This could include anything from taking a walk, listening to music, practicing meditation, or reading a book. By taking time to unwind, you allow your body and mind to recover from the stress of the exam, which can help you feel rejuvenated and prevent burnout.

By combining **time management** techniques with **mindfulness and relaxation practices**, you can improve your focus, reduce stress, and increase your chances of success. These strategies help you manage both the mental and emotional aspects of the exam, allowing you to remain composed, confident, and clear-headed throughout the testing process.

Resources for Continued Learning in Cybersecurity

Cybersecurity is a fast-evolving field, and continuous learning is essential to staying up-to-date with the latest trends, technologies, and best practices. Whether you're advancing your career or seeking to deepen your expertise in specialized areas, a range of certifications, online resources, and communities can help you enhance your knowledge and skills.

Advanced Certifications

CompTIA Advanced Security Practitioner (CASP+)

CASP+ is a certification for professionals looking to go beyond the foundational concepts of cybersecurity and demonstrate hands-on skills in advanced security solutions. It covers complex security environments, risk management, enterprise security, and incident response. CASP+ is ideal for those who are in or aspiring to roles like Security Architect, Security Engineer, or Chief Information Security Officer (CISO).

Certified Information Systems Security Professional (CISSP)

CISSP is one of the most prestigious certifications in the cybersecurity industry. It is designed for professionals responsible for developing and managing security programs. This certification demonstrates knowledge in key areas such as security governance, risk management, asset security, and software development security. CISSP is widely recognized and often required for senior security roles in large organizations.

Certified Ethical Hacker (CEH)

CEH focuses on offensive security and ethical hacking. It is designed for professionals who want to specialize in penetration testing and vulnerability assessments. CEH covers a wide array of hacking techniques, tools, and strategies used by cybercriminals, enabling professionals to think like attackers and protect systems by identifying weaknesses before malicious hackers can exploit them.

Certified Information Security Manager (CISM)

CISM is aimed at professionals who are responsible for managing and governing an enterprise's information security program. The certification focuses on risk management, governance, incident response, and security program development. CISM is valuable for individuals in managerial or leadership roles, such as Information Security Manager or IT Governance Officer, who need to oversee security policy implementation and ensure alignment with business objectives.

Certified Cloud Security Professional (CCSP)

With the increasing adoption of cloud services, CCSP is designed for cybersecurity professionals who want to focus on securing cloud computing environments. The certification addresses challenges unique to the cloud, such as securing data in multi-tenant environments, cloud governance, and compliance. CCSP is ideal for those working in cloud security or overseeing cloud infrastructure.

Websites and Forums

Engaging with online communities can be a great way to stay informed, seek advice, and discuss new developments in cybersecurity. A few notable communities include

- **Reddit's r/Cybersecurity**

    A vibrant community where professionals discuss the latest news, trends, and challenges in the cybersecurity field. It's a good place to get advice, share resources, or learn from others' experiences.

- **TechExams**

    A forum where individuals pursuing certifications and cybersecurity careers can interact. The site hosts discussions on various certifications, study materials, exam preparation tips, and general cybersecurity topics. It's particularly useful for those looking to exchange experiences and recommendations for exam preparation.

Online Courses

Taking advanced courses in specialized areas is one of the most effective ways to deepen your expertise in cybersecurity. Some prominent online platforms offering relevant courses include

- **Cybrary**

  Cybrary offers a range of courses in cybersecurity, from beginner to advanced levels. It also provides specialized certifications and skills training in areas like ethical hacking, threat analysis, and cloud security.

- **Udemy**

  Udemy features a broad selection of courses covering a variety of cybersecurity topics, including penetration testing, network security, cloud security, and security auditing. These courses cater to both beginners and seasoned professionals and are often taught by industry experts.

- **Pluralsight**

  Known for its high-quality, expert-led content, Pluralsight offers comprehensive training in cybersecurity disciplines such as cloud security, ethical hacking, cryptography, and threat intelligence. Their courses are structured in learning paths that cater to professionals looking to acquire specialized skills.

CHAPTER 10   FINAL REVIEW AND EXAM PREPARATION

Books and Journals

Staying updated with the latest industry trends and methodologies is crucial for continued learning. A few ways to stay informed include

- **Cybersecurity Journals**

  Journals like the *Journal of Cybersecurity* and *IEEE Security & Privacy* feature articles on cutting-edge research, industry case studies, and technological advancements in cybersecurity.

- **Books**

  Reading books by respected cybersecurity authors can provide deeper insights into specific topics. Popular books include

  - *The Web Application Hacker's Handbook* by Dafydd Stuttard and Marcus Pinto, for penetration testers and security researchers.

  - *Hacking: The Art of Exploitation* by Jon Erickson, which delves into computer security and ethical hacking techniques.

  - *Cybersecurity and Cyberwar: What Everyone Needs to Know* by P.W. Singer and Allan Friedman, for a broad understanding of the field.

- **Whitepapers and Research Papers**

  Many leading cybersecurity companies and organizations publish whitepapers and research reports on the latest vulnerabilities, threat landscapes, and security solutions. Subscribing to these resources can help you stay ahead of emerging threats and best practices.

By continuously seeking advanced certifications and engaging with online communities, courses, books, and journals, you can stay current with the ever-changing landscape of cybersecurity. These resources will not only expand your knowledge but also help you network with other professionals, gain practical experience, and stay competitive in the field. Continuous learning is key to thriving in the fast-paced and dynamic cybersecurity industry. Top of FormBottom of Form

Preparing for the Day of the Exam

Preparation for the exam day is as important as your study process. Ensuring you have everything you need, understanding the testing environment, and knowing what to expect can significantly reduce anxiety and help you perform at your best. Here's what you should know.

What to Bring

Two Forms of Valid ID

- **Government-Issued ID (with photo):** Most testing centers require at least one government-issued photo ID, such as a driver's license or passport.

- **Secondary ID:** The second ID could be something simpler like a student ID, credit card, or another form of identification that shows your name.

Exam Appointment Confirmation

- Bring a printout or digital copy of your appointment confirmation email. This serves as proof of your registration and may be required for entry.

CHAPTER 10   FINAL REVIEW AND EXAM PREPARATION

Basic Supplies

- **Pens/Pencils:** While most exams are computer-based, having a pen or pencil can be handy for any rough work or note-taking if permitted.

- **Water and Light Snack:** If the testing center allows, bring a bottle of water and a small, non-messy snack. Staying hydrated and maintaining your energy levels can help keep you focused.

What to Expect

Security Checks

- Be prepared for a thorough identity verification process, which may include photo matching and signature checks. Some centers also employ biometric scans, like fingerprints, to confirm your identity.

- You'll likely have to store personal belongings, including electronic devices, in a locker or designated area, as these are not permitted in the exam room.

Exam Environment

- Expect a quiet and controlled setting. Most exams are proctored either by an in-person proctor or remotely via video monitoring to ensure test integrity.

- The testing center may provide earplugs or noise-canceling headphones if allowed. This can help minimize distractions during the exam.

Time Management

- Most certification exams, including those for Security+, are between 90 to 120 minutes long. Plan your time accordingly and monitor it throughout the exam. Remember, the clock does not stop, even if you take a short break.

Common Pitfalls to Avoid

Understanding and avoiding common mistakes can save you from losing valuable points. Here's a look at some pitfalls and strategies to tackle them.

Misreading Questions

Strategy

- Carefully read each question in full, paying close attention to every word. Keywords like "**except**," "**not**," or "**only**" often change the entire meaning of the question.
- Avoid rushing through the options. Read all the choices before selecting your answer, even if you think you've spotted the correct one early.

Common Traps

- Watch for **distractors**—options that seem correct but do not fully satisfy the question.
- Ensure you understand any technical terms or acronyms. If unsure, try to recall their definitions or the context from your studies.

CHAPTER 10   FINAL REVIEW AND EXAM PREPARATION

Overthinking Answers

Strategy

- Trust your initial instinct. If you've prepared well, your first choice is often the correct one. Second-guessing typically stems from anxiety rather than logic.

- Change an answer only if you realize you made an error in your initial reading or if a later question clarifies your understanding.

Exam Day Mentality

- Stay composed and remind yourself of your preparation efforts. Confidence can help reduce the urge to overanalyze and self-doubt.

- Focus on each question as it comes without worrying about the previous ones or what might be next.

Additional Preparation Tips

Regular Practice

- Taking full-length practice exams is one of the best ways to prepare. This not only helps you get used to the format and question types but also builds endurance for the exam duration.

- Analyze your performance after each practice exam. Identify weak areas and review those topics thoroughly before attempting the next mock test.

CHAPTER 10   FINAL REVIEW AND EXAM PREPARATION

Performance Review

- Pay close attention to the questions you get wrong. Is it due to a lack of knowledge, misreading, or a time constraint? Understanding why you missed a question is crucial to improving your performance.

Simulate Actual Conditions

- Create a quiet, distraction-free space at home to mimic the testing environment. This helps you practice focusing on a similar setting to what you'll experience on the exam day.

- If possible, use practice tests that replicate the actual exam interface. This will familiarize you with the layout, including how to navigate between questions, mark items for review, and use any on-screen tools like calculators.

Time Constraints

- Set a timer during your practice tests to simulate the actual exam time limits. This helps you learn how to pace yourself, ensuring you have enough time to answer all questions without rushing.

Preparing well for the exam day involves not just studying the material but also getting familiar with the testing environment, refining your time management, and developing strategies to minimize common errors. Taking a proactive approach to these aspects can greatly improve your confidence and performance during the actual exam.

CHAPTER 10   FINAL REVIEW AND EXAM PREPARATION

Conclusion and Final Thoughts

Congratulations! You've reached the final chapter of your Security+ journey, and that alone is a significant achievement. It's been a road filled with countless hours of studying, reviewing, and practicing, and now it's time to bring everything together. Let's wrap up with some parting thoughts, practical advice, and a few words of encouragement as you head into the final stretch.

Closing Advice: Setting the Stage for Success

Think of This As the Beginning, Not the End

- The Security+ exam is an important milestone, but remember, it's just the start of your journey in cybersecurity. Think of it as laying a strong foundation for what's to come. This certification shows that you have a solid understanding of core security principles, but the field is vast and continuously evolving. New threats emerge every day, new technologies are developed, and with that comes the need for constant learning and adaptation.

- Use this certification as a steppingstone. You've built a solid base; now it's time to start stacking additional knowledge and skills on top of it. Consider this as your entry ticket into a world that offers endless opportunities to learn and grow. Dive deep into areas that interest you, be it cloud security, penetration testing, or compliance, and build on what you've learned.

Beyond the Textbooks: Practical Experience Is Key

- While you've spent a great deal of time hitting the books, don't forget that real-world experience is where the magic happens. The theories, concepts, and definitions are crucial, but applying them in practice is what will truly solidify your understanding.

- Get hands-on whenever possible. This could mean setting up your own lab environment at home, participating in Capture the Flag (CTF) competitions, volunteering for cybersecurity tasks at your workplace, or even joining local cybersecurity groups. The more you immerse yourself in practical scenarios, the better prepared you'll be for challenges beyond the exam room. Remember, employers value candidates who not only understand the theory but can also demonstrate their skills in real-world settings.

Keep Up with the Latest Trends and News

- Cybersecurity is one of the fastest-evolving fields out there. What you studied today might look slightly different in a year due to advancements in technology and emerging threats. Make it a habit to read industry news, subscribe to cybersecurity newsletters, and follow thought leaders on social media. Staying updated will not only help you in your career but also keep you sharp for any recertifications or advanced exams you might want to pursue in the future.

CHAPTER 10   FINAL REVIEW AND EXAM PREPARATION

Encouragement: You've Got This

Acknowledge Your Hard Work and Dedication

- Preparing for an exam like Security+ is no small feat. The sheer volume of information you've had to absorb is impressive. Take a moment to reflect on how far you've come—from learning the basics of networking to understanding complex security protocols, encryption standards, and risk management strategies. You've put in the hours, made sacrifices, and pushed through challenging topics. That dedication speaks volumes about your commitment and passion for this field.

- It's easy to get caught up in the stress of the final exam but remember to give yourself credit for all the effort you've already invested. You're not just walking into that exam room as someone who studied; you're walking in as someone who is ready to take on the challenge with confidence.

Trust Yourself and Your Preparation

- Confidence is key when it comes to taking any exam, and Security+ is no different. You've prepared extensively, and you've seen the types of questions that might come up. Trust your instincts. Often, your first answer is the correct one because it's based on all the knowledge and practice you've done. Resist the urge to second-guess yourself unless you have a clear reason to change an answer.

- On the day of the exam, try to stay calm and composed. Use relaxation techniques like deep breathing if you feel overwhelmed. Remind yourself that you've done everything possible to prepare for this moment. You're ready.

Keep the Big Picture in Mind

- It's natural to feel anxious or even doubt your abilities as the exam day approaches. But remember, passing this exam is just one part of your larger career journey. Regardless of the outcome, you've gained a tremendous amount of knowledge that will be invaluable in your professional life. Don't be discouraged if you don't pass on the first attempt—many successful cybersecurity professionals have been in that position. The key is to learn from any mistakes, fill in the knowledge gaps, and come back stronger.

Celebrate Your Achievements, Big and Small

- Don't forget to celebrate the small wins. Whether it's mastering a particularly difficult concept, scoring well on a practice test, or even making it through a tough study session, these are all steps forward. When you finally pass your exam, take the time to celebrate properly. It's a big deal, and you've earned it. Share the news with friends, family, or colleagues who've been supporting you. Enjoy that moment because it's a testament to your hard work and dedication.

CHAPTER 10   FINAL REVIEW AND EXAM PREPARATION

The Road Ahead: Your Future in Cybersecurity

Plan Your Next Steps

- Once you've passed your Security+ exam, think about where you want to go next. Are there specific areas of cybersecurity that interest you? Maybe you want to dive deeper into ethical hacking, pursue cloud security, or specialize in compliance and risk management. Consider looking into advanced certifications like CISSP, CEH, or CISM, depending on your interests. Each of these can open new doors and provide more specialized knowledge that can further your career.

- Additionally, networking is a powerful tool in cybersecurity. Attend conferences, join online forums, and connect with other professionals in the field. Learning from others' experiences and insights can be incredibly valuable as you navigate your career.

Stay Curious and Keep Learning

- Cybersecurity is a field where lifelong learning is not just encouraged—it's essential. The landscape is always changing, and new challenges are always on the horizon. Keep feeding your curiosity. Whether it's through reading books, taking courses, attending webinars, or participating in hands-on projects, continue to build your skill set. The more you learn, the more valuable you'll become as a cybersecurity professional.

CHAPTER 10   FINAL REVIEW AND EXAM PREPARATION

Final Words of Wisdom

- Your journey doesn't end with the exam—it's just getting started. You now have the foundational knowledge to tackle real-world cybersecurity challenges, and this is something to be proud of. The skills you've acquired will be instrumental in protecting organizations, securing data, and making the digital world a safer place.

- Believe in yourself, keep pushing forward, and never lose that drive to learn and improve. Cybersecurity is a challenging but rewarding field, and with your passion and determination, you have the potential to make a significant impact.

Good luck on your exam, and here's to your success in the exciting world of cybersecurity! You've got this—now go show them what you're made of!

Glossary of Key Terms

1. **Access Control**

   Mechanisms and policies used to regulate who can view or use resources in a computing environment.

2. **Access Control List (ACL)**

   A list of permissions attached to an object specifying who can access it and what actions they can perform.

3. **AES (Advanced Encryption Standard)**

   A symmetric encryption algorithm used to secure data, often regarded as a standard for modern encryption.

4. **Agent-Based Monitoring**

   A security system where software agents are installed on systems to monitor and report activities.

5. **Application Layer**

   The top layer in the OSI model that facilitates communication between software applications and underlying network services.

6. **Asset Management**

   The practice of managing an organization's assets, ensuring proper control, usage, and disposal.

7. **Attack Surface**

   The sum of all potential entry points where an attacker could gain unauthorized access to a system.

8. **Auditing**

   The process of tracking and recording activities in an information system to ensure compliance and monitor potential security risks.

9. **Authentication**

   The process of verifying the identity of a user, device, or system.

10. **Authorization**

    The process of granting or denying access to resources based on the identity of the authenticated entity.

11. **Backup**

    A copy of data made to prevent loss in the event of data corruption or disaster.

12. **Bloatware**

    Software that is pre-installed by a manufacturer, carrier, or vendor that is non-beneficial to the user. Such as, free-trials, utility applications, or remote monitoring tools.

13. **Buffer Overflow**

    A form of attack that occurs when the amount of data in the buffer exceeds storage capacity and in return the overflowing data dumps into adjacent memory locations.

GLOSSARY OF KEY TERMS

14. **BCP (Business Continuity Planning)**

    The process of ensuring that essential business functions continue during and after a disaster or disruption.

15. **BIA (Business Impact Analysis)**

    The process of evaluating the impact of disruptions on critical business functions and identifying recovery strategies.

16. **Biometrics**

    Physical or behavioral characteristics used for authentication, such as fingerprints, retina scans, or voice recognition.

17. **Block Cipher**

    A method of encryption where data is processed in fixed-size blocks, as opposed to stream ciphers which encrypt data one bit at a time.

18. **Brute Force**

    This is a form of password cracking that will attempt every possible combination with the parameters given to uncover a password. Theoretically, this is possible to crack any password, if given enough time and computing resources; however, this could take seconds, minutes, or decades.

19. **Bug Bounty**

    A program where organizations reward ethical hackers and cybersecurity researchers for identifying and responsibly disclosing security vulnerabilities in their systems or applications. These programs help organizations proactively address weaknesses, reducing the risk of exploitation by malicious actors.

20. **BYOD (Bring Your Own Device)**

    A policy that allows employees to use their personal devices (smartphones, laptops, etc.) for work-related activities.

21. **CIA Triad (Confidentiality, Integrity, Availability)**

    A model designed to guide security policies: confidentiality ensures privacy, integrity ensures data accuracy, and availability ensures **resources are accessible.**

22. **Cloud Security**

    Measures and policies to protect data, applications, and services stored and processed in cloud environments.

23. **Common Vulnerabilities and Exposures (CVE)**

    A publicly available list of standardized identifiers for known cybersecurity vulnerabilities in software and hardware. It enables organizations and researchers to communicate and address security flaws consistently and efficiently across systems.

24. **Common Vulnerability Scoring System (CVSS)**

    A standardized framework used to assess the severity and risk of security vulnerabilities. It provides a numerical score and qualitative rating to help organizations prioritize vulnerability management and remediation efforts.

GLOSSARY OF KEY TERMS

25. **Compartmentalization**

    Dividing a network or system into smaller, isolated segments to limit the impact of a potential breach.

26. **Compliance**

    Adhering to laws, regulations, and industry standards to ensure security practices meet legal requirements.

27. **Confidentiality**

    Ensuring that information is accessible only to those who are authorized to view it.

28. **Cross Site Request Forgery (CSRF)**

    An attack that forces authenticated users to submit a request to a web app to which they are currently authenticated.

29. **Cross-Site Scripting (XSS)**

    A type of injection that inserts malicious code into an otherwise benign and trusted webpage.

30. **Cryptoanalysis**

    The study of breaking or analyzing cryptographic systems to uncover vulnerabilities.

31. **Cryptographic Key**

    A secret value used in encryption and decryption processes, such as in symmetric and asymmetric encryption algorithms.

GLOSSARY OF KEY TERMS

32. **Cultural Risk**

    The risk posed by organizational culture or individual behavior that may contribute to security vulnerabilities.

33. **Data Loss Prevention (DLP)**

    Tools and techniques used to prevent the unauthorized loss or transfer of sensitive data.

34. **Defense in Depth**

    A layered security strategy where multiple protective measures are implemented across different levels of the network or system.

35. **Denial of Service (DoS)**

    An attack that aims to overwhelm a network or system, making it unavailable to legitimate users.

36. **Directory Traversal**

    A form of pivoting where the attacker swaps between directories in order to gain root access or alternatively access to a more important directory.

37. **Disaster Recovery**

    The process of recovering IT systems and data after a disaster or disruption.

38. **DMZ (Demilitarized Zone)**

    A network segment that acts as a buffer between an internal network and external networks (like the internet), used to host public-facing services securely.

GLOSSARY OF KEY TERMS

39. **DNS (Domain Name System)**

    A system that translates domain names into IP addresses, allowing users to access websites and services using human-readable names.

40. **DMZ (Demilitarized Zone)**

    A physical or logical subnetwork used to isolate and protect an organization's internal network from untrusted external networks like the internet.

41. **Endpoint**

    Any device that connects to a network, including computers, smartphones, and servers.

42. **Encryption**

    The process of converting data into a coded format that is unreadable without a decryption key.

43. **FIPS (Federal Information Processing Standards)**

    Standards for computer systems used by US government agencies and contractors to ensure consistency and security.

44. **Firewall**

    A network security device that monitors and filters incoming and outgoing network traffic based on predetermined security rules.

45. **Forensics**

    The process of investigating and analyzing data after a security incident to understand its cause, impact, and scope.

GLOSSARY OF KEY TERMS

46. **Forgery**

    This is the act of altering or digitally manipulating data or media to deceive individuals into believing it is of a legitimate source.

47. **Hacking**

    The act of exploiting vulnerabilities in computer systems or networks to gain unauthorized access.

48. **Hacktivisit (Threat Actor)**

    These are individuals that are acting based on a personal belief in order to achieve a common goal. It is common to see this in human rights, animal abuse, or climate groups, as these individuals are not doing it for profit but for the belief that it is the right course of action.

49. **Hashing**

    A one-way function that converts data into a fixed-length string for the purpose of verifying integrity.

50. **HIPAA (Health Insurance Portability and Accountability Act)**

    A US regulation that mandates the protection of sensitive patient information and healthcare data.

51. **Honeyfile**

    This is a single file or folder that is intentionally "sensitively" named and left vulnerable to attract attackers. The goal of this deployment is to monitor the attacker's behavior in order to gain intelligence on their tactics without fear of exposing sensitive data.

GLOSSARY OF KEY TERMS

52. **Honeynet**

    This is a broader network that is designed and left vulnerable to attract cyber attackers. The goal of this deployment is to monitor the attacker's behavior in order to gain intelligence on their tactics without fear of exposing sensitive data.

53. **Honeypot**

    This is a decoy system that is intentionally left vulnerable to attract cyber attackers. The goal of this deployment is to monitor the attacker's behavior in order to gain intelligence on their tactics without fear of exposing sensitive data.

54. **Honeytoken**

    This is a false digital resource that is used to detect and monitor unauthorized access or malicious activity in a controlled environment. The goal of this deployment is to monitor the attacker's behavior in order to gain intelligence on their tactics without fear of exposing sensitive data.

55. **HTTPS (Hypertext Transfer Protocol Secure)**

    A secure version of HTTP that uses SSL/TLS to encrypt web traffic.

56. **Identity and Access Management (IAM)**

    The processes and technologies used to manage and secure user identities and access to resources.

57. **IDS (Intrusion Detection System)**

    A system that monitors network traffic for suspicious activity and generates alerts when potential threats are detected.

GLOSSARY OF KEY TERMS

58. **IPS (Intrusion Prevention System)**

    A system that monitors and actively blocks malicious activities in real-time.

59. **Incident Response Plan (IRP)**

    A documented strategy for responding to and recovering from security incidents, including detection, containment, eradication, and recovery.

60. **Injection Attack**

    This occurs when an attacker exploits a vulnerability in order to send a malicious code or program into a target environment.

61. **IPsec (Internet Protocol Security)**

    A suite of protocols that encrypts and authenticates IP communications to secure data transmitted over a network.

62. **ISO/IEC 27001**

    An international standard for managing information security within an organization.

63. **Key Management**

    The process of securely generating, storing, and distributing cryptographic keys used for encryption.

64. **Keylogger**

    A form of malware that will monitor the keystrokes a user inputs to their peripheral keyboard and relays it to a remote listener.

GLOSSARY OF KEY TERMS

65. **Least Privilege**

    A security principle that ensures users or systems are given the minimum level of access necessary to perform their job functions.

66. **LDAP (Lightweight Directory Access Protocol)**

    A protocol used for accessing and managing directory services, often used for user authentication and management.

67. **Logic Bomb**

    This is a form of malware that is designed to go off under very specific conditions in order to cause a negative effect in an environment. It acts similarly to "If User A does not log-in daily, then the file server will delete itself" and is meant to cause harm in the event of the conditions being met.

68. **Malware**

    Malicious software designed to disrupt or damage systems, steal data, or gain unauthorized access.

69. **Memory Injection**

    This is an attack that occurs when an attacker injects code into a program or query to inject malware onto a computer in order to execute remote commands.

70. **MD5 (Message Digest Algorithm 5)**

    A widely used hashing algorithm that produces a 128-bit hash value, often used for integrity checks (although considered insecure for cryptographic purposes).

GLOSSARY OF KEY TERMS

71. **MFA (Multi-Factor Authentication)**

    An authentication method that requires two or more verification methods (e.g., something you know, something you have, something you are).

72. **Mitigation**

    Efforts to reduce the impact or likelihood of a risk occurring.

73. **Nation State (Threat Actor)**

    These are often seen as advanced persistent threats and pose the greatest challenge. Nation state actors are highly funded and skilled, quite often militarized or government endorsed acting on the benefit of a nation at large.

74. **Next Generation Firewall (NGFW)**

    A firewall that is designed to protect against modern cyber threats and offers advanced features such as application-level inspection, intrusion prevention, and deep packet inspection. These firewalls go well above that of a traditional firewall and offer more granular control and protection of an environment.

75. **NIST (National Institute of Standards and Technology)**

    A US government agency that develops standards and guidelines for various areas of information technology, including cybersecurity.

76. **NTP (Network Time Protocol)**

    A protocol used to synchronize the clocks of computers over a network to ensure accurate timestamps.

GLOSSARY OF KEY TERMS

77. **OAuth**

    An open standard for access delegation commonly used for token-based authentication.

78. **Organized Criminal Organization (Threat Actor)**

    A criminal organization that utilizes cyberattacks to further their criminal activities.

79. **Open Source Intelligence (OSINT)**

    This refers to the practice of collecting and analyzing publicly available data from a multitude of sources, such as social media, public record, and articles in order to gather information on specific topics.

80. **Password Spraying**

    A tactic in which an attacker uses a single password to attempt to break into multiple target accounts. This is a version of a brute-force attack.

81. **Penetration Testing**

    Simulating an attack on a system or network to identify vulnerabilities before an attacker can exploit them.

82. **PKI (Public Key Infrastructure)**

    A framework for managing digital keys and certificates to secure communications and transactions.

83. **Privilege Escalation**

    This is a step that an attacker will take in order to gain privileged or administrative access within an environment by exploiting vulnerabilities.

84. **Proxy Server**

    A server that acts as an intermediary between a client and a server, often used for content filtering and privacy protection.

85. **Race Conditions**

    This is a software bug that occurs when a computing system's control doesn't properly enforce the order in which multiple operations should execute. In addition, please review Time of Check to Time of Use.

86. **Ransomware**

    An attack that encrypts or similar locks down a target environment and requests monetary compensation to return to a normal state.

87. **Responsible Disclosure**

    A process where security researchers report vulnerabilities to organizations in a private and ethical manner, allowing them time to fix the issues before they are publicly disclosed. This approach helps mitigate security risks while promoting collaboration between researchers and organizations to improve overall cybersecurity.

88. **RTO (Recovery Time Objective)**

    The maximum acceptable time a system can be down before it causes significant disruption to business operations.

GLOSSARY OF KEY TERMS

89. **RPO (Recovery Point Objective)**

    The maximum acceptable amount of data loss, measured in time, after a disaster.

90. **Rootkit**

    A form of malware that is composed of various computer software or code that is meant to gain access to a system at the root level, without being detected, and create points of compromise for access.

91. **RSA**

    An asymmetric encryption algorithm widely used for secure data transmission.

92. **Script Kiddies (Threat Actor)**

    These are a form of threat actor with limited technical knowledge who readily utilize available hacking tools and scripts to carry out cyberattacks, most commonly without understanding the underlying technology or malicious impact it will have.

93. **Shadow IT (Threat Actor)**

    An individual or department within an organization that uses unauthorized software, hardware, or cloud deployment without the knowledge or approval of the IT department and/or Security teams.

GLOSSARY OF KEY TERMS

94. **SIEM (Security Information and Event Management)**

    A security system that collects, analyzes, and correlates data from various sources to identify security threats in real time.

95. **SLA (Service Level Agreement)**

    A contract between a service provider and a customer that outlines the expected level of service.

96. **Smart Card**

    A physical device used for authentication, typically requiring a PIN or other form of verification.

97. **Spyware**

    This acts similar to a worm in that it is designed to stealthily live in a target environment while exfiltrating data from within.

98. **SQL Injection**

    A common attack vector that utilizes malicious SQL code in order to manipulate the backend of a database and access information that was not intended for access.

99. **SSL/TLS (Secure Sockets Layer/Transport Layer Security)**

    Cryptographic protocols used to secure data transmitted over networks, ensuring confidentiality and integrity.

100. **SSO (Single Sign-On)**

    A method of authentication that allows a user to access multiple applications with a single login.

GLOSSARY OF KEY TERMS

101. **Symmetric Encryption**

    An encryption method that uses the same key for both encryption and decryption.

102. **Threat Actors**

    There are various forms of threat actors such as, hacktivists, nation-states, script kiddies, shadow IT, and organized criminals. These each represent a wide array of individuals with similar goals and means to meet their desired outcome.

103. **Time of Check to Time of Use (TOC/TOU)**

    This refers to a condition that the system checks a file's permissions and then orders the commands in a sequential order. This is meant to ensure that the file is not altered between the time of check and the time of use.

104. **Trojan**

    In similar style to the Trojan Horse of old, this pretends to be a "Known Good" entity, whether an application, media, or similar item; while in reality, it is malicious in nature and meant to harm the downloader.

105. **Virus**

    Code that is capable of duplicating itself while having a negative effect on the targeted environment, whether destroying data or causing corruption.

GLOSSARY OF KEY TERMS

106. **Vulnerability Scanning**

    The use of automated tools to scan networks and systems for known vulnerabilities.

107. **VPN (Virtual Private Network)**

    A technology that creates a secure, encrypted connection between a device and a network over a public network, like the internet.

108. **Web Application Firewall (WAF)**

    A security tool that monitors and filters HTTP traffic to and from a website or web application; it is specifically designed to protect against SQL injection and XSS or similar attacks.

109. **WPA (Wi-Fi Protected Access)**

    A security protocol for wireless networks designed to secure Wi-Fi communications.

110. **Worm**

    A self-replicating form of malware that is intended to infiltrate an environment and spread across the domain. It is capable of installing backdoors, corrupt files, and steal sensitive data.

111. **Zero Trust**

    A security model that assumes no user or device is trustworthy, even if it is inside the network perimeter, requiring continuous authentication and authorization.

Index

A

AAA, *see* Authentication, authorization and accounting (AAA)
ABAC, *see* Attribute-Based Access Control (ABAC)
Acceptable Use Policy (AUP), 32, 348
Access control lists (ACLs), 146, 187, 425
Access control models, 186, 386, 391
Access control policy, 348
Access controls, 21, 36–37, 65, 214, 258
    authentication, 243
    DAC, 389
    and least privilege, 79–80
    physical controls, 38–40
    RBAC, 389
    security architecture, 70
Access management, 80
Account lockout mechanisms, 387
ACLs, *see* Access control lists (ACLs)
Active Directory (AD), 206–207
Advanced Encryption Standard (AES), 14, 268, 399
Advanced persistent threats (APTs), 74, 86
Adware, 96, 370
AES, *see* Advanced Encryption Standard (AES)
AH, *see* Authentication Header (AH)
AlienVault Open Threat Exchange (OTX), 57
Anomalies, 149, 324, 407
Antimalware solutions, 215–216
Antivirus (AV) software, 63, 215–216
APIs, *see* Application programming interfaces (APIs)
Application hardening, 221–222
Application programming interfaces (APIs), 70, 85–86, 208
Application security
    static application security testing (SAST), 250–253
Application whitelisting, 221–223
APTs, *see* Advanced persistent threats (APTs)

INDEX

Architecture and design
   questionaries, 417-418
   security, 381
   security professionals, 381
Artificial intelligence (AI), 5
Asset identification, 328
Asymmetric encryption, 269-271, 399-400, 404
Attacks, 367-368
   methods, 374
   questionaries, 415-416
Attack vectors, 368, 375
   Email, 373
   networks and wireless networks, 374
   social engineering, 374
   phishing, 373
   web applications, 373
Attribute-Based Access Control (ABAC), 192-194
Attributes, 193
Auditing, 65
   log management, 407
   and monitoring, 409
Audit trails, 19, 22
AUP, *see* Acceptable Use Policy (AUP)
Authentication, 121, 296, 386
   biometrics, 387
   certificate-based, 178-179
   mechanisms, 391
   password, 178
   Password-based, 387
Authentication, authorization and accounting (AAA), 153

Authentication Header (AH), 288
Authenticity, 403
Authorization, 183-186
Automated key rotation, 295
Automated patching systems, 232-234
Automated validation, 22
Availability, 16, 20, 22, 384, 413

B

Backup strategies, 317, 413
   differential backup, 319-320
   full backup, 317-318
   incremental backup, 318-319
   log analysis, 321
Backup systems, 61
Bandwidth-constrained environments, 278
BCP, *see* Business continuity plan (BCP)
Behavioral analysis, 309, 310, 314
Bell-LaPadula model, 23-24, 28, 68
BIA, *see* Business impact analysis (BIA)
Biba Integrity model, 24-25, 29
Biometrics, 174-175, 387, 391
Bitcoin, 296
BitLocker, 300
Black-box testing method, 253
Blockchain technology, 296
   applications, 276-277
4-7-8 breathing technique, 442, 443
Brewer-Nash model, 26, 29, 30

INDEX

Bring Your Own Device (BYOD) Policies
   access control, 258–259
   data protection, 258
   device security, 257–258
Brute force attacks, 158, 302, 387
Business continuity, 410
Business continuity plan (BCP), 16, 412–414, 436
Business impact analysis (BIA), 356, 392, 395–396, 398
   questionaries, 422–423
   steps, 356–358
BYOD practices, 257–259

C

CAB, *see* Change advisory board (CAB)
Capture the Flag (CTF), 455
CBC, *see* Cipher Block Chaining (CBC)
CCSP, *see* Certified Cloud Security Professional (CCSP)
CDNs, *see* Content Delivery Networks (CDNs)
CEH, *see* Certified Ethical Hacker (CEH)
Center for Internet Security (CIS), 138, 224
Central authority, 188
Certificate authority (CA), 203, 273, 401

Certificate-based authentication, 178–179
Certificate Revocation List (CRL), 203, 273
Certificates, 284
   types, 285–286
   X.509 certificates, 285
Certified Cloud Security Professional (CCSP), 446
Certified Ethical Hacker (CEH), 445
Certified Information Security Manager (CISM), 445
Certified Information Systems Security Professional (CISSP), 445
Chain of custody, 316–318, 412
Change advisory board (CAB), 45
Change management
   benefits, 47
   components, 45–46
   in cybersecurity, 44–45
   process, 46
Checksums, 15
CIA triad, *see* Confidentiality, integrity and availability (CIA) triad)
CI/CD, *see* Continuous integration/continuous deployment (CI/CD)
Cipher Block Chaining (CBC), 269
CIS, *see* Center for Internet Security (CIS)

INDEX

CISA, *see* Cybersecurity and Infrastructure Security Agency (CISA)
CISM, *see* Certified Information Security Manager (CISM)
CISSP, *see* Certified Information Systems Security Professional (CISSP)
Clark-Wilson model, 25, 28, 68
Classification levels, 188, 390
Cloud-based identity management, 195
Cloud-based threats
 account hijacking, 84
 advanced persistent threats (APTs), 86
 application programming interfaces (APIs), 85-86
 compliance violations, 87
 data breaches, 82-83
 denial of service (DoS) attacks, 85
 insider threats, 84
 loss of data, 86-87
 misconfigurations, 83-84
 security practices, 87-88
Cloud computing, 6, 280
Cloud security, 382-385
Cloud security models
 infrastructure as a Service (IaaS), 240-241
 platform as a Service (PaaS), 241-242

software as a Service (SaaS), 242-243
Cluster security, 244
Code review, 228
Code signing certificates, 201-202
Coding practices, 382
Cohesive assessment strategy, 139
Command-and-control (C2) servers, 114
Common Vulnerabilities and Exposures (CVE), 406
Common Vulnerability Scoring System (CVSS)
 base metrics, 126
 communication, 131
 patch management, 130
 prioritization, 128-129
 risk assessment, 129-130
 temporal metrics, 126-127
Communication, 46, 131, 304
Communication channels, 166
Complete snapshot, 317
Compliance, 18, 422
 global, 341-342
 regional, 342
 standards, 385
Compromised insiders, 77-78
CompTIA Advanced Security Practitioner (CASP+), 9
CompTIA (Computing Technology Industry Association), 2-3, 73, 445
 accessibility, 7
 affordability, 7

INDEX

career benefits, 8–9
certifications, 6
exam structure and
    objectives, 9–10
industry recognition, 8
retake policy, 10
security+ certification, 7
updates and changes, 11
vendor-neutral approach, 7
CompTIA Cybersecurity Analyst
    (CySA+), 9
Confidentiality, integrity and
    availability (CIA) triad
availability, 16
confidentiality, 14–15
financial services
    industry, 20–23
in healthcare industry, 18–20
health sector, 15
integrity, 15–16
interconnectedness, 17
security models and
    frameworks, 23–27
Configuration baselines, 223–225
Configuration management
    tools, 135
Consistency, 224, 232
Containerization, 258
Container security
    cluster security, 244
    description, 243
    image hardening, 248–250
    image scanning, 248
    isolation, 244

role-based access control
    (RBAC), 245
Containment, 116, 311–312
Content Delivery Networks
    (CDNs), 98
Continuous integration/continuous
    deployment (CI/CD), 64
Continuous monitoring, 79
Contractual agreements, 359
CRL, *see* Certificate Revocation
    List (CRL)
Cross-Site Request Forgery (CSRF/
    XSRF), 100
Cross-site scripting (XSS), 99, 227,
    229, 250, 371, 384
Cryptocurrencies, 296
Cryptographic signatures, 15
Cryptography
    algorithms, 399–401
    asymmetric
        encryption, 269–271
    decryption key, 398
    digital signatures, 272
    hashing, 271–272
    life cycle
        key destruction, 294
        key distribution, 291–292
        key generation, 290–291
        key rotation, 293
        online transactions, 296
    protocols and applications, 274
    questionaries, 425–427
    Security+ Exam, 274–275
    symmetric encryption, 268–269

INDEX

CRYSTALS-Kyber, 303
CSF, see Cybersecurity
    Framework (CSF)
CTA, see Cyber Threat
    Alliance (CTA)
CTF, see Capture the Flag (CTF)
Customization, 141
CVE, see Common Vulnerabilities
    and Exposures (CVE)
CVSS, see Common Vulnerability
    Scoring System (CVSS)
Cyberattacks, 1, 16, 20
    Denial of Service (DoS), 97–98
    malicious software
        (Malware), 95–97
    Man-in-the-Middle (MITM), 98
    Rootkits, 101
    social engineering, 102–103
    supply chain attack, 103
    zero-day attack, 104
Cybercriminals, 211, 373
Cybersecurity, 1, 3–4, 171, 364–368,
    375, 381, 392, 446, 455,
    458, 459
    books and journals, 448–449
    certifications, 444–445
    change management, 46–49
    defense in depth (DiD), 59–67
    emerging trends, 5–6
    layered security, 41–45
    online courses, 447
    organizations and individuals, 4
    professionals, 4
    risk management, 13, 47–52

threat identification, 52–57
threat intelligence, 57–58
time passes and
    technology, 2
websites and forums, 446
Cybersecurity and Infrastructure
    Security Agency (CISA), 58
Cybersecurity Framework
    (CSF), 138
Cyber Threat Alliance (CTA), 57
Cybrary, 447

D

DAC, see Discretionary access
    control (DAC)
DAST, see Dynamic Application
    Security Testing (DAST)
Data classification, 32, 354
Data confidentiality, 403
Data integrity, 282
Data Loss Prevention
    (DLP), 79, 214
    cloud-based, 353
    content inspection, 353
    contextual analysis, 353
    endpoint-based, 352–353
    policy enforcement, 354
    regular audits, 355
    types
        network-based, 352
    user training, 355
Data masking, 15
Data privacy, 242

484

INDEX

Data Protection Impact
    Assessments
    (DPIA), 363–364
Data security
    encryption, 65
Data sharing, 361
Data validation, 19
DDoS, *see* Distributed denial-
    of-service (DDoS)
Deauthentication attacks, 166–167
Decentralized identity, 276
Default configuration, 163
Defense in depth (DiD), 380, 382,
    385, 417
  implementation
    application security, 64
    data security, 65–66
    endpoint security, 63–64
    perimeter security, 61–62
  layered security
    administrative controls, 59
    physical controls, 60
    redundancy, 61
    technical controls, 60
  multi-layered security
    approach, 379
  pivotal role, 381
  strategies, 375, 380
Demilitarized zones (DMZs), 147,
    375, 379, 417
Denial-of-service (DoS), 22, 85,
    97–98, 120, 166, 329,
    370, 375
Dependency analysis, 358

DES (Data Encryption
    Standard), 269
Deserialization, 250
Device enrollment, 260
DevSecOps, 250
Dictionary attacks, 387
DiD, *see* Defense in depth (DiD)
Differential backup, 319–320
Digital certificates, 163, 404
Digital communication, 273–274
Digital signatures, 272, 282,
    296–297, 400, 401, 404
  email security, 283
  hashing, 283
  signing, 283
  software distribution, 284
  verification, 283
Disaster recovery, 410, 437
Disaster Recovery Planning (DRP),
    20, 412–415, 435–437
Discretionary access control
    (DAC), 186–188, 389, 391
Disk encryption, 300
Distractors, 451
Distributed denial-of-service
    (DDoS), 62, 97–98, 370, 432
Distributed ledger technology
    (DLT), 275
DKIM, *see* DomainKeys Identified
    Mail (DKIM)
DLP, *see* Data Loss
    Prevention (DLP)
DLT, *see* Distributed ledger
    technology (DLT)

INDEX

DMARC, *see* Domain-based Message Authentication, Reporting and Conformance (DMARC)
DMZs, *see* Demilitarized zones (DMZs)
Docker Swarm, 244
Domain-based Message Authentication, Reporting and Conformance (DMARC), 90
DomainKeys Identified Mail (DKIM), 90
Domain Validation (DV), 199–200
DoS, *see* Denial-of-service (DoS)
DPIA, *see* Data Protection Impact Assessments (DPIA)
DRP, *see* Disaster Recovery Planning (DRP)
DV, *see* Domain Validation (DV)
Dynamic Application Security Testing (DAST), 253–255

E

ECB, *see* Electronic Codebook (ECB)
ECC, *see* Elliptic Curve Cryptography (ECC)
ECDLP, *see* Elliptic Curve Discrete Logarithm Problem (ECDLP)
ECDSA, *see* Elliptic Curve Digital Signature Algorithm (ECDSA)
E-commerce, 16
EDR, *see* Endpoint detection and response (EDR)
EHRs, *see* Electronic health records (EHRs)
Electronic Codebook (ECB), 269
Electronic health records (EHRs), 15, 18, 29
Electronic protected health information (ePHI), 339
Elliptic Curve Cryptography (ECC), 270–271, 278–279, 302
Elliptic Curve Digital Signature Algorithm (ECDSA), 279
Elliptic Curve Discrete Logarithm Problem (ECDLP), 279
Email encryption, 283, 401
Email encryption certificates, 201–202
Email verification protocols, 93
Embedded systems, 278
Employee vetting, 81
Encapsulating Security Payload (ESP), 288
Encouragement, 456–457
Encryption, 14, 18, 21, 36, 65, 70, 88, 158, 214, 240, 257, 299, 354, 419
Endpoint detection and response (EDR), 63, 95, 213, 219–221

INDEX

Endpoint protection platforms (EPP), 106
Endpoint security
  best practices, 214–215
  components, 212
  cybersecurity, 212
  digital assets, 213
  patch management, 230–237
  system design (*see* Secure system design)
  technology, 213
End-to-end encryption, 297
Enforcement, 346–348
Entanglement, 303
Environmental conditions, 192
Environmental controls, 40–41
Environmental threats
  natural disasters, 56
  power outages, 56–57
ePHI, *see* Electronic protected health information (ePHI)
EPP, *see* Endpoint protection platforms (EPP)
Eradication, 312
Error handling, 227
Ethical hacking, 405
Event management, 408
Evil Twin attacks, 165
Exam environment, 450
Exam preparation
  government-Issued ID, 449
  pens/pencils, 450
  security checks, 450
  strategy, 451
  tips, 452–453
Extended validation (EV), 200
External threats, 53–54

F

Facial recognition, 387
Failover and redundancy, 381
Failover mechanisms, 61
Federated identity, 179–180, 185–186
Federated Identity Management (FIM), 197–199
File/Folder Encryption, 301
FIM, *see* Federated Identity Management (FIM)
Financial services industry
  availability, 22–23
  confidentiality, 21
  integrity, 21–22
Fingerprints, 387
Firewalls, 62, 111, 148–149, 375, 380
5G Networks, 169
Forensics, 411–414
Full backup, 317–318
Full Disk Encryption (FDE), 301

G

Galois/Counter Mode (GCM), 269
General Data Protection Regulation (GDPR), 243, 337–338, 342, 397, 423

INDEX

Global compliance, 341–342
   challenges, 344–345
   navigation, 345–346
   overlaps, 343–344
GNU Privacy Guard (GPG), 274
Google Authenticator (Authy), 388
Google identity platform, 197
Governance, 422–423
Gramm-Leach-Bliley Act (GLBA), 43

H

Hackers, 53, 78
Hacktivists, 372
Hardware security modules (HSMs), 402
Hardware tokens, 388
Hardware vulnerabilities, 119–120
Hash-based cryptography, 302
Hashing, 15, 19, 21, 271–272, 400–401
   applications, 282–283
   description, 280
   functions, 281
   properties of, 280–281
Healthcare industry, CIA triad
   availability, 20
   confidentiality, 18–19
   integrity, 19
Health Insurance Portability and Accountability Act (HIPAA), 15, 243, 338–339, 342, 396
High availability, 382, 385

Hijacking, 84
HIPAA, *see* Health Insurance Portability and Accountability Act (HIPAA)
HSMs, *see* Hardware security modules (HSMs)
HTTPS, *see* Hypertext Transfer Protocol Secure (HTTPS)
Human errors, 234
Human intelligence (HUMINT), 108
Human vulnerabilities, 121
HUMINT, *see* Human intelligence (HUMINT)
Hybrid approach, 144, 235
Hybrid cryptographic systems, 303
Hypertext Transfer Protocol Secure (HTTPS), 287, 378, 402
Hypervisor, 238, 239

I

IaaS, *see* Infrastructure as a Service (IaaS)
IAM, *see* Identity and Access Management (IAM)
Identify patterns, 321
Identity and Access Management (IAM), 88, 157, 171, 240, 242, 391, 424–426
   authentication factors, 172–174
   biometrics, 174–175
   federated identity, 179–180
   tools, 206–209

INDEX

Identity federation, 386, 390–392
Identity management, 279
    authentication and
        verification, 276–277
    cloud-based, 195
    decentralized, 276
Identity provider (IdP),
    179–182, 195
IDEs, *see* Integrated development
    environments (IDEs)
IdP, *see* Identity provider (IdP)
IDS, *see* Intrusion detection
    systems (IDS)
IDS/IPS, *see* Intrusion Detection
    and Prevention Systems
    (IDS/IPS)
Incident responders, 309
Incident response (IR)
    questionaries, 420–422
    teams, 107
Incident response plan (IRP), 414
    documented process, 410
Incident response process
    detection and analysis, 311
    preparation, 310–311
Incremental backup, 318–319
Indicators of compromise (IOCs),
    110, 113, 219, 314
    detection and monitoring, 116
    incident response, 116
    proactive defense, 117–118
    threat intelligence and
        sharing, 117
    types

        email-based IOCs, 115
        file-based IOCs, 114–115
        host-based IOCs, 115
        network IOCs, 113–114
Information Security Management
    System (ISMS), 71, 335
Information Sharing and Analysis
    Centers (ISACs), 57, 112
Infrastructure as a Service
    (IaaS), 240–241
Insider threats, 84, 121, 372
    mitigation, 78
    multifaceted approach, 75
    strategies
        detection, 78–80
        traditional security, 75
    types, 75–78
Integrated development
    environments (IDEs), 251
Integrity, 15–16, 19, 21–22, 201,
    202, 287, 403, 413
Internet of Things (IoT), 5, 157, 297
    default configuration, 163
    minimal processing
        capabilities, 163
    zero trust model, 164
Internet Protocol Security (IPsec),
    274, 288–289, 378, 380, 403
Intrusion Detection and
    Prevention Systems (IDS/
    IPS), 62, 149–150, 375
Intrusion detection systems (IDS),
    37–38, 60, 67, 106, 111, 149,
    226, 239, 376, 380, 427

489

INDEX

Intrusion prevention systems (IPS), 37–38, 42, 111, 149, 239, 376, 380
IOCs, *see* Indicators of compromise (IOCs)
IoT, *see* Internet of Things (IoT)
IPS, *see* Intrusion prevention systems (IPS)
IPsec, *see* Internet Protocol Security (IPsec)
IR, *see* Incident response (IR)
Iris scans, 387
IRP, *see* Incident response plan (IRP)
ISACs, *see* Information Sharing and Analysis Centers (ISACs)
ISMS, *see* Information Security Management System (ISMS)
ISO/IEC 27001, 335–337

J

Jamming attacks, 165–166

K

Kerberos platforms, 186
Key destruction, 294
Key distribution, 291–292
Key generation, 290–291, 402
Key management, 295, 402
Key rotation, 293
Key storage, 402

Kubernetes platforms, 244, 245, 247–248

L

Lattice-based cryptography, 302
Lattice-based model, 26–27
Layered security
  compliance and regulatory requirements, 43–44
  coverage and threats, 41–42
  defense, 41
  detection and response capabilitiesr, 42
  redundancy and reliability, 41
Least privilege, 156, 249, 350, 381, 383, 385
Legal requirements, 412
Load balancing, 16, 20
Locks and barriers, 38–39
Log analysis, 321
Log management, 407

M

MACs, *see* Message authentication codes (MACs)
Machine learning, 5
Malicious activity, 407
Malicious insiders, 75–76
Malicious software (Malware), 95–97, 374
  Ransomware, 369
  Trojans, 369

viruses, 368
worms, 369
Malware, 53–54
Mandatory Access Control (MAC), 188–190, 390, 391
Man-in-the-middle (MITM) attack, 98, 120, 292, 371
Manual patching, 233–235
Manual penetration testing, 139–143
MDM, *see* Mobile device management (MDM)
Message authentication codes (MACs), 400
Message Digest Algorithm 5 (MD5), 271, 281
MFA, *see* Multi-factor authentication (MFA)
Microsegmentation, 147
Mindfulness, 442–444
Misconfigurations, 83–84, 118, 241
Mitigation, 83
   measures, 362
   strategies, 54, 229
MITM attack, *see* Man-in-the-middle (MITM) attack)
Mobile device management (MDM), 260–262
Mobile devices, 278
Multi-factor authentication (MFA), 36, 60, 65, 67, 80, 83, 93, 125, 171–174, 205, 207, 215, 386, 388–389, 391, 418
Multiple-choice questions, 438–439

Mutual authentication, 297

N

NAT, *see* Network Address Translation (NAT)
National Institute of Standards and Technology (NIST), 71, 138, 302
Nation-state actors, 372
Negligent insiders, 76–77
NetFlow, 167
Network Address Translation (NAT), 155–156
Network design
   defense in depth, 379
Network protocols, 375
Network security
   demilitarized zone (DMZ), 147
   devices, 376
      Firewalls, 148–149
      Intrusion Detection and Prevention Systems (IDS/IPS), 149–150
      proxies, 150–151
   IoT Devices, 162–164
   microsegmentation, 147
   network monitoring and management, 167–168
   redundancy and fault tolerance, 168
   segmentation and segregation, 146
   threats, 169–170

INDEX

Network segmentation, 62, 161, 163, 375, 380, 381, 384
Network traffic analysis, 322–323
Network vulnerabilities, 120
Next-generation antivirus (NGAV), 216–218
Next-generation firewalls (NGFW), 148, 376
NGAV, *see* Next-generation antivirus (NGAV)
NGFW, *see* Next-generation firewalls (NGFW)
NIST Risk Management Framework (RMF), 333–335

O

OAuth, 179–180, 183–186, 390, 391
OCR, *see* Office for Civil Rights (OCR)
OCSP, *see* Online Certificate Status Protocol (OCSP)
Office for Civil Rights (OCR), 339
OIDC, *see* OpenID Connect (OIDC)
Okta, 207
One-time passwords (OTPs), 176
One-to-one mapping, 155
One-way function, 400
Online Certificate Status Protocol (OCSP), 204–205
Online transactions, 296
OpenID Connect (OIDC), 185, 391
Open Web Application Security Project (OWASP), 228–230
Operational threat intelligence, 107–108
Operational vulnerabilities, 121–122
Organization validation (OV), 200
Organized cybercrime, 373
OTPs, *see* One-time passwords (OTPs)
OV, *see* Organization validation (OV)
OWASP, *see* Open Web Application Security Project (OWASP)

P

PaaS, *see* Platform as a Service (PaaS)
Packet-filtering firewalls, 376
Password authentication, 177
Password-based authentication, 387
Password complexity, 387
Password policy, 349
PAT, *see* Port Address Translation (PAT)
Patch management, 63, 130, 214, 225, 382, 383, 385
    automated, 232–234
    documentation, 236
    life cycle, 230–231
    manual patching, 233–234
    review and update, 236
    staff training, 237
    strategy, 234–236

INDEX

Payment Card Industry Data Security Standard (PCI-DSS), 43, 339–341, 397
Payment Card Industry Security Standards Council (PCI SSC), 339
PCI-DSS, *see* Payment Card Industry Data Security Standard (PCI-DSS)
PCI SSC, *see* Payment Card Industry Security Standards Council (PCI SSC)
Penetration testing (pen testing) tools, 134, 405–406, 409
   customized testing, 134
   description, 133
   exploitability and real-world risks, 134
   reporting and documentation, 135
Personal health information (PHI), 18, 396
Personalized documentation, 234
Personally identifiable information (PII), 353
PGP, *see* Pretty Good Privacy (PGP)
PHI, *see* Personal health information (PHI)
Phishing, 93, 102, 370
   characteristics, 89
   description, 89
   detection, 94–95
   prevention, 90
   and social engineering, 121
Phishing attacks, 54
Photon transmitters, 304
Physical activity, 442
Physical destruction of hardware, 295
PIA, *see* Privacy Impact Analysis (PIA)
PII, *see* Personally identifiable information (PII)
PKI, *see* Public key infrastructure (PKI)
Platform as a Service (PaaS), 241–242
Pluralsight, 447
Policy enforcement, 260
POLP, *see* Principle of least privilege (POLP)
Port Address Translation (PAT), 155–156
Post-change review, 46
Post-quantum cryptography, 302
Pre-shared Keys (PSKs), 158, 292
Pretty Good Privacy (PGP), 274, 299
Principle of least privilege (POLP), 55
Privacy Impact Analysis (PIA), 361
Private key, 291, 399
Proxies, 150–151, 375, 380
PSKs, *see* Pre-shared Keys (PSKs)
Public key, 283, 291, 399
Public key encryption, 399

493

INDEX

Public key infrastructure (PKI), 199, 398, 401–402, 404
   applications, 273
   certificate
      revocation, 203–205
   code signing
      certificates, 201–202
   digital communication, 273–274
   email encryption
      certificates, 201–202
   SSL/TLS certificates, 199–200

Q

Quantum computing, 275, 279, 302, 305
Quantum cryptography, 301
   post-quantum, 302
   preparation, 302
   real-world
      applications, 304–306
Quantum Key Distribution (QKD), 303–305
Quantum-resistant cryptographic algorithms, 279

R

RA, *see* Registration authority (RA)
RADIUS, *see* Remote Authentication Dial-In User Service (RADIUS)
Rainbow table attacks, 282
Ransomware, 369

RBAC, *see* Role-based access control (RBAC)
Real-time monitoring, 136
Recovery Point Objective (RPO), 396, 413
Recovery time objectives (RTOs), 320, 357, 395, 398, 413, 436
Reddit's r, 446
Reduce recovery time, 411
Redundancy, 20, 382, 384
Regional compliance, 342
   challenges, 344–345
   overlaps, 343–344
Registration authority (RA), 273
Regular audits, 355
Regular vulnerability
   assessments, 64
Relaxation techniques, 442–444
Remote access VPNs, 298
Remote Authentication Dial-In User Service (RADIUS), 154, 156
Remote management, 260
Research papers, 448
Resource attributes, 192
Resource owner, 186
Responding to threats, 314
Risk assessment, 48–49, 129–130, 359
   components, 328–331
   matrix, 393
   qualitative *vs.* quantitative methods, 393–395
Risk-based approach, 235

INDEX

Risk likelihood, 331
Risk management, 392
    assessment, 48–49, 393–396
    business impact analysis (BIA), 395–396
    and compliance, 136, 385
    compliance and regulatory standards, 396–397
    mitigation, 49–50
    monitoring, 51–52
    qualitative and quantitative methods, 392
Risk Management Framework (RMF), 333
Risk matrix, 393
Risk mitigation, 49–50, 332–333
Risk monitoring, 51–52
Risk rating, 331
Risk treatment, 392, 394–395
Rivest-Shamir-Adleman (RSA) encryption, 270, 399
RMF, see Risk Management Framework (RMF)
Robust incident response plan, 81
Rogue access points (APs), 99–100
Role-based access control (RBAC), 14, 18, 37, 65, 88, 190–192, 243, 245, 389–391
Rootkits, 101
RPO, see Recovery Point Objective (RPO)
RTOs, see Recovery time objectives (RTOs)

S

SaaS, see Software as a Service (SaaS)
Sabotage, 329
SAE, see Simultaneous Authentication of Equals (SAE)
Salting, 282
SAML, see Security Assertion Markup Language (SAML)
Scalability, 305, 389
SCCM, see System Center Configuration Manager (SCCM)
Scenario-based questions, 439
SD-WAN, see Software-defined WAN (SD-WAN)
Secure coding practices, 385
Secure communication protocols, 151
Secure Development Lifecycle (SDLC), 64
Secure email technologies, 299
    encryption methods, 301
    encryption protocol, 299
    encryption tools, 300
Secure firmware updates, 164
Secure Hash Algorithm (SHA), 271, 400
    SHA-3, 400
    SHA-256, 281, 284, 400
Secure identity verification, 276
Secure key exchange protocols, 295

INDEX

Secure/Multipurpose Internet Mail Extensions (S/MIME), 300
Secure network design, 375
Secure Sockets Layer (SSL), 152, 153, 156, 199–200, 274, 286–287, 377, 378, 380, 401–404
Secure software development life cycle (SDLC), 384
Secure system design, 223
   configuration baselines, 223–225
   hardening, 225–227
   OWASP Top Ten, 228–230
Securing applications, 227–228
Security
   static application security testing (SAST), 250–253
Security+ certification, 2
Security+ exam, 274–275, 454
Security architecture
   access controls, 70
   controls, 67–68
   frameworks, 71–72
   models, 68–69
   network architecture, 70–71
   policies, 66–67
Security Assertion Markup Language (SAML), 180–182, 197, 390, 391
Security assessment tools, 132
Security awareness training programs, 80
Security-conscious culture, 81–82
Security controls, 13
   administrative controls, 32–35
   technical controls, 35–38
Security information, 408
Security Information and Event Management (SIEM), 42, 116, 136, 168, 408–410, 432–435
   compliance and forensics, 137
   reporting and alerting, 137
   security assessment frameworks, 138–139
   threat detection, 137
   tools, 322–324
Security labels, 188
Security models, 23
   Biba Integrity Model, 24–25
   Brewer-Nash model, 26
   Clark-Wilson model, 25
   consulting and legal firms, 30–31
   financial institutions, 28
   government agencies, 28–29
   healthcare providers, 29
   Lattice-Based model, 26
   military and defense contractors, 30–31
Security Operations Centers (SOCs), 106, 219, 307
   containment, 311–312
   eradication, 312

INDEX

forensics and evidence
    handling, 315–317
incident responders, 309
post-incident review, 313
recovery phase, 312–313
Tier 1 analysts, 308
Tier 2 analysts, 308
Tier 3 analysts, 308–309
Security Orchestration and
    Automated Response
    (SOAR) Tools, 324–326
Security policies
    key security policies, 348–350
    policy development, 346–348
    procedures and
        practices, 350–351
Security testing, 256, 405–406
Self-Sovereign Identity, 276–277
Sender Policy Framework
    (SPF), 90
Service chain attacks, 101–102
Service-level agreements
    (SLAs), 130
Service Provider (SP), 180
SHA, *see* Secure Hash
    Algorithm (SHA)
Shared responsibility model, 87,
    240, 385
Side-channel attacks, 119
SIEM, *see* Security Information and
    Event Management (SIEM)
Simple Network Management
    Protocol (SNMP), 167

Simulated attack, 405
Simultaneous Authentication of
    Equals (SAE), 158, 167
Single Sign-On (SSO), 171, 172,
    196–198, 205, 207, 386, 391,
    392, 424
Site-to-Site VPNs, 298
SLAs, *see* Service-level
    agreements (SLAs)
Smaller key size, 278
Smart cards, 175–176, 388
Smart contracts, 277
S/MIME, *see* Secure/Multipurpose
    Internet Mail Extensions
    (S/MIME)
SNMP, *see* Simple Network
    Management
    Protocol (SNMP)
SOAR Tools, *see* Security
    Orchestration and
    Automated Response
    (SOAR) Tools)
Social engineering, 102–103
Social media
    integration, 183
SOCs, *see* Security Operations
    Centers (SOCs)
Software as a Service (SaaS),
    242–243, 353
Software-defined WAN
    (SD-WAN), 169
Software development life cycle
    (SDLC), 382

INDEX

Software vulnerabilities, 118–119
SP, *see* Service Provider (SP)
Spear phishing, 93, 102, 370
    characteristics, 90–91
    definition, 90
    detection, 94–95
    prevention, 91
Spectrum analyzers, 166
SPF, *see* Sender Policy Framework (SPF)
Spyware, 370
SQL injection, 250, 371
SSL, *see* Secure Sockets Layer (SSL)
SSO, *see* Single Sign-On (SSO)
Stakeholders, 362
Stateful inspection firewalls, 376
Strategic threat intelligence, 105–106
Subnet, 163
Subnetting, 146
Superposition, 303
Supply chain attacks, 103
Supply chain security, 279
    Smart contracts, 277
    transparency and traceability, 277
Symmetric encryption, 268–269, 399, 404
System Center Configuration Manager (SCCM), 135
System development life cycle, 385
System hardening, 225–227

T

Tactical threat intelligence, 106–107
Tactics, techniques and procedures (TTPs), 105, 110
TechExams, 446
Technical threat intelligence, 108–109
Technologies and tools
    domain, 375
    network security devices, 376–378
    secure protocols, 378–380
Terminal Access Controller Access-Control System Plus (TACACS+), 154
Testing, 414
Third-party auditing, 366
Third-party risk management, 358–360
Threat actors, 368, 374
    hacktivists, 372
    insider threats, 372
    Nation-state actors, 372
Threat assessment, 328–330
Threat hunters, 310–311
Threat hunting, 110, 313–315
Threat identification
    environmental threats, 56–57
    external threats, 53–54
    human error, 55
    insider threats, 55
    internal threats, 54–56

INDEX

privilege abuse, 55
Threat intelligence, 57–58
  security strategy
    collaboration and
      information sharing, 112
    controls, 111
    decision-making, 111–112
    operations, 110–111
  and sharing, 117
  types of, 105–109
Threat modeling, 58–59
Threats, 367–368
  questionaries, 415–416
Time-based One-Time Passwords (TOTP), 388
Time constraints, 453
Time-consuming, 441
Timeliness, 232
Time management, 439–441, 444, 451
TLS, *see* Transport Layer Security (TLS)
Token-based authentication, 176–177
Tokens, 176–177, 184, 388
Top Secret, 188
TOTP, *see* Time-based One-Time Passwords (TOTP)
TPMs, *see* Trusted Platform Modules (TPMs)
Traditional antivirus (AV) software, 216–217
Transport Layer Security (TLS), 152, 156, 199–200, 274, 286–287, 377, 378, 380, 401–404
Transport mode, 379
Trojans, 369
Trusted Platform Modules (TPMs), 300
TTPs, *see* Tactics, techniques and procedures (TTPs)
Tunnel mode, 379

U

UBA, *see* User behavior analytics (UBA)
Udemy, 447
User behavior analytics (UBA), 78, 91
User characteristics, 192
User privacy, 258
User productivity
  costs, 261
  user experience, 261
User training, 355

V

Vendors, 225, 226
VeraCrypt, 300
Virtualization and Cloud Security, 243
Virtual Local Area Network (VLAN), 146, 161, 163, 238
Virtual machine monitor (VMM), 238

INDEX

Virtual machines (VMs)
　isolation and
　　segmentation, 238–239
　software-based
　　representations, 238
Virtual private networks (VPNs),
　　152–153, 298, 375, 377,
　　403, 427–430
　encryption protocols, 299
　types, 298
Viruses, 368
Visualization techniques, 443–444
VLAN, see Virtual Local Area
　　Network (VLAN)
VMM, see Virtual machine
　　monitor (VMM)
VMs, see Virtual machines (VMs)
Voice patterns, 387
VPNs, see Virtual private
　　networks (VPNs)
Vulnerabilities, 44, 64, 111, 127,
　　140, 178, 211, 227, 330,
　　367–368, 415–416
　assessment, 124–125, 330
　attack surface, reduction, 123
　description, 118
　hardware, 119–120
　human, 121
　impacts of, 122–123
　limitations, 133
　management
　　strategies, 127–128
　mitigation, 125
　network, 120

　operational, 121–122
　real-time detection and
　　reporting, 133
　scanning, 406
　software, 118–119 (See also
　　Common Vulnerability
　　Scoring System (CVSS)
Vulnerability scanners,
　　132–133, 406

W

Web applications, 99, 132, 373
Web proxy, 377
Whaling, 93, 103
　characteristics, 92–93
　description, 92
　detection, 94–95
　prevention, 93
Whitepapers, 448
WIDS, see Wireless Intrusion
　　Detection Systems (WIDS)
Wi-Fi configurations, 120
Wireless Intrusion Detection
　　Systems (WIDS), 165
Wireless networks
　deauthentication
　　attacks, 166–167
　description, 157
　Evil Twin attack, 165
　IoT Devices, 162–164
　Jamming attacks, 165–166
　security settings, 160–162
Worms, 96, 369

INDEX

WPA3 (Wi-Fi Protected
Access 3), 157
enhancement, 157
transitioning, 159–160
WPA3/WPA2 mixed mode, 159

X, Y

802.1X, 154

X.509 certificates, 285
XSS, *see* Cross-site scripting (XSS)

Z

Zero-day attacks, 104
Zero Trust Architecture (ZTA), 86, 156–157, 164, 385
Zero trust model, 164, 385

GPSR Compliance

The European Union's (EU) General Product Safety Regulation (GPSR) is a set of rules that requires consumer products to be safe and our obligations to ensure this.

If you have any concerns about our products, you can contact us on

ProductSafety@springernature.com

In case Publisher is established outside the EU, the EU authorized representative is:

Springer Nature Customer Service Center GmbH
Europaplatz 3
69115 Heidelberg, Germany

www.ingramcontent.com/pod-product-compliance
Lightning Source LLC
LaVergne TN
LVHW010332260326
834688LV00036B/674